ARIZONA TRIPS

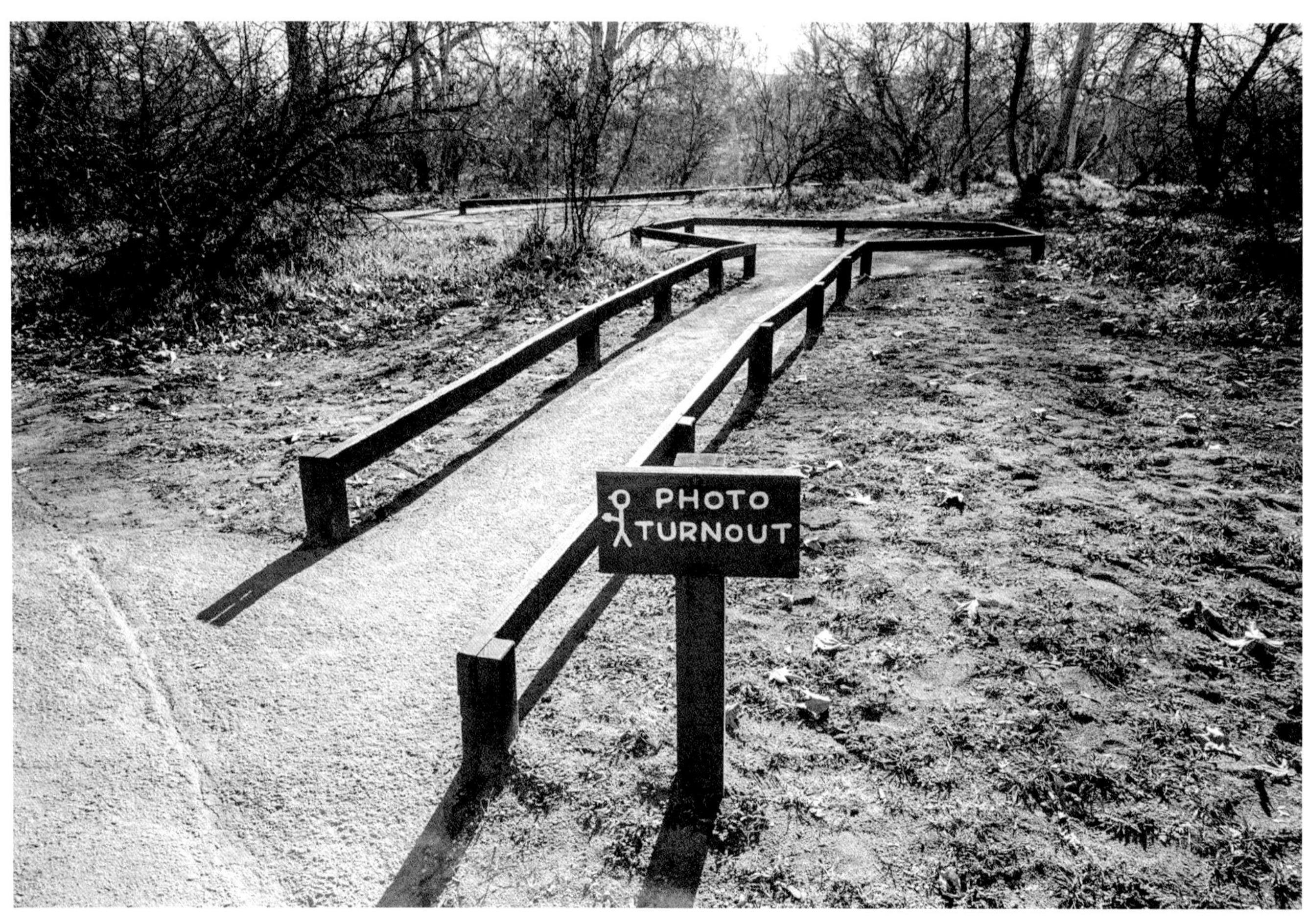
PHOTO
TURNOUT

ARIZONA TRIPS
David Hurn

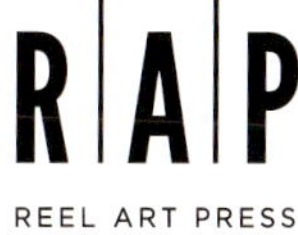

REEL ART PRESS

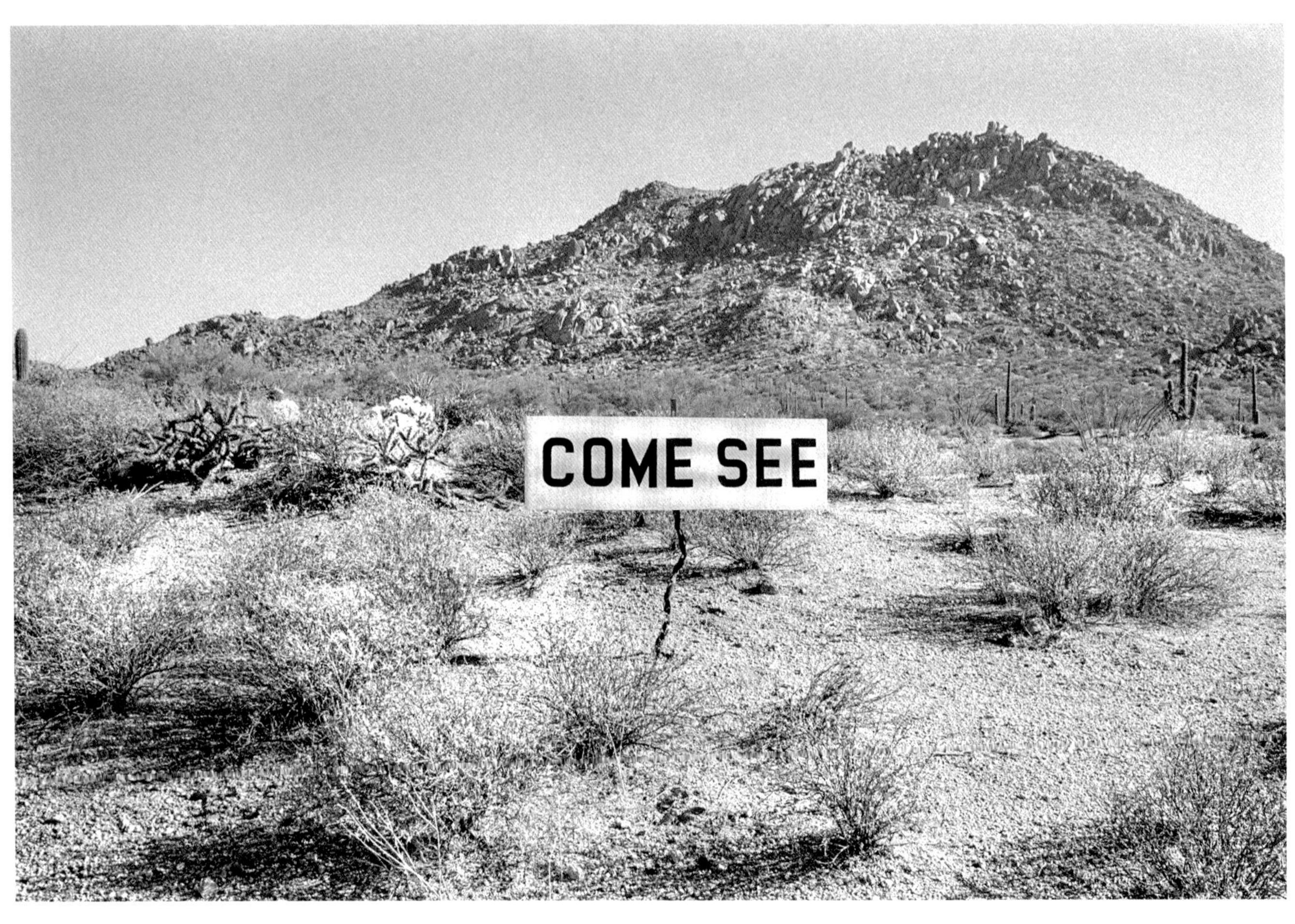
COME SEE

Contents

6
DAVID HURN IN CONVERSATION WITH CULTURAL
HISTORIAN SIR CHRISTOPHER FRAYLING

12
PHOTOGRAPHS

158
CAPTIONS

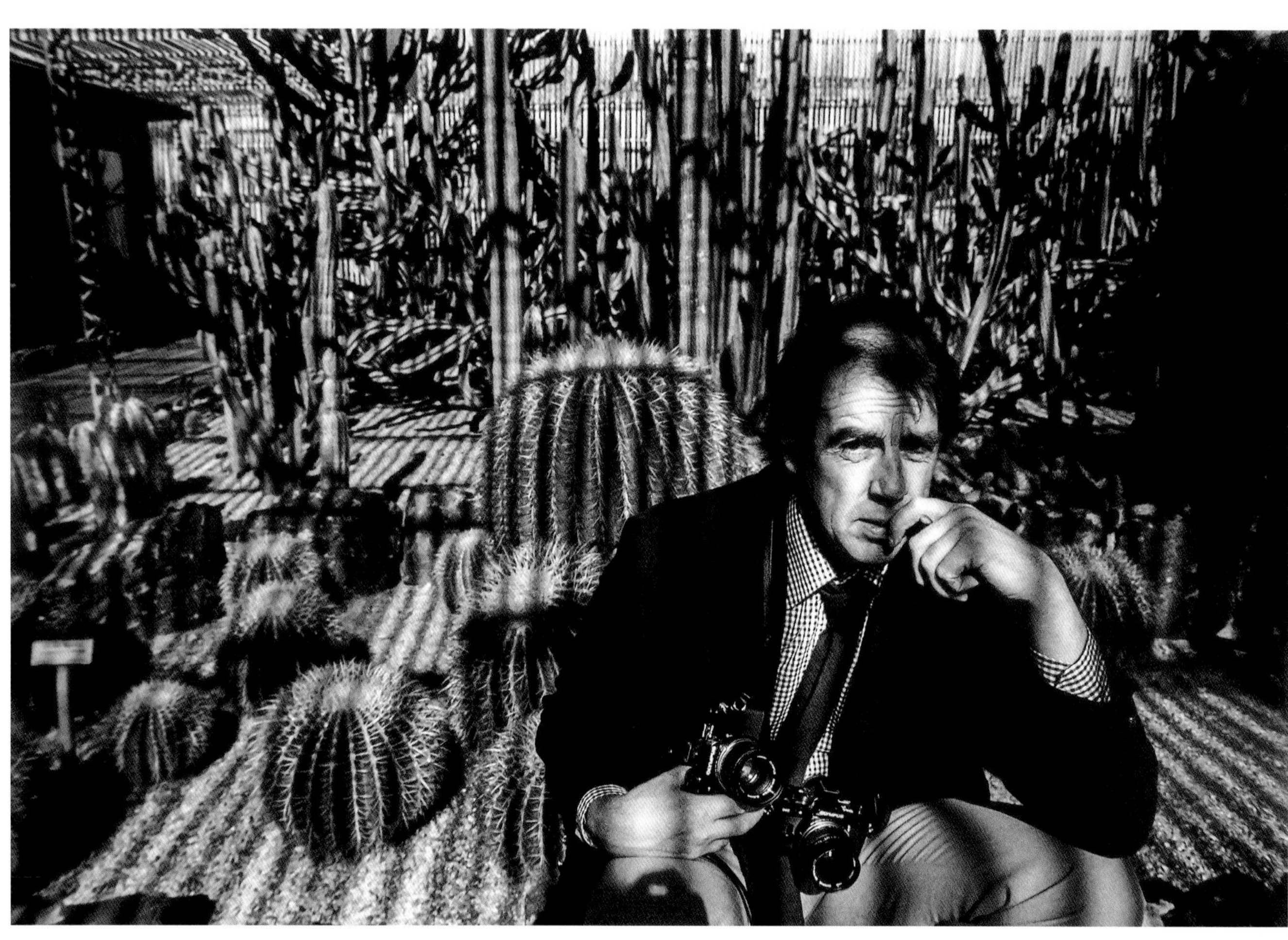

David Hurn in Conversation with Cultural Historian Sir Christopher Frayling

Christopher Frayling: In 1979-80 you are awarded a Bicentennial Fellowship, a UK-US fellowship, and the rubric is that you spend a year in America; you choose to photograph for one year in Arizona.

David Hurn: Yes, and I chose Arizona because, well a few reasons, in terms of going to the Embassy and discussing with them why I feel I should get in. It was the most right-wing state in America and Wales at that time was probably the most left-wing part of the UK. Also it's the driest state in America and Wales is the wettest. So it seemed to me it was such an extraordinary contrast . . . and if you have that kind of contrast you're starting off from an easy point. It happened that I knew a few people in Arizona as well.

Christopher: Had you been there before?

David: I'd been, in fact, the year before. I'd gone and done a workshop there. One of my closest ever friends was a guy called Bill Jay, who in many ways was the guy that raised photography of a journalistic type into a slightly more . . . whatever you'd like to call it. The first editor of *Creative Camera*. He was at Arizona State University there. So one of the things that I suggested to the Embassy was that I should be linked to a university and the reason for that was that I knew that they would give me a dark room.

Christopher: . . . get wired into their facilities.

David: Yes, and also Phoenix is very central.

Christopher: I always associate Arizona and photography with landscape—with that monthly pictorial magazine *Arizona Highways*, which has been going since 1925.

David: Very good magazine.

Christopher: . . . with Josef Muench and all those great landscape photographers. I interviewed Muench once about his photographs of the canyons. And with those Western movies where you get stage coaches hurtling through the Arizona desert.

David: John Ford made many of his movies there.

Christopher: Monument Valley. Or going way back to the photographer Edwin S. Curtis, with his romantic photos of *The*

North American Indian or *The Vanishing Race* in the Canyon de Chelly surrounded by the ecology of Arizona. And yet you are not a landscape man. The obvious thing would be to say at the Embassy, "I want to go to Arizona to photograph the canyons", but you are a people person . . .

David: Well you know Phoenix has probably got a few million people in it. Tucson a few million people in it. And I remember I loved that romantic idea of the rodeo. Rodeo is spectacular; it's like sheep dog trials on a high. If anybody comes to Wales, I say if you really want to understand Wales go and see a sheep dog trial. In America I say if you really want to know America go to a rodeo. So there was that there and I'd read about Wickenburg where all the great bluegrass musicians . . . they have a festival of bluegrass and I like the idea of people playing banjos and things.

Christopher: You're drawn to festivals and pageants and gatherings of people, aren't you? A lot of these photographs are of a rodeo or a dance class or keep-fit or a prom or a pageant or a state fair. You seem to like moments where there are gatherings of people; where there's a density to the social group.

David: I enjoy very much looking at things that I would not normally do because the more experience I get, the more I find that when masses of people do things they usually do them for a reason. They usually have fun, they're not watching telly, they're doing all these things and so photography to me is an entrée to these worlds. I'm a very shy person but if you have a camera and you go through the door and there are people doing whatever they're doing and they say "what are you doing?" and you say "I'm a photographer", if you can somehow say that with a respect for them and an interest in them, virtually every time they invite you in. As long as you show respect and as long as you show interest people enjoy you being there because by and large people quite like being photographed. It makes them feel as though you're interested in them.

Christopher: Did you get to know them at all before you photographed them?

David: Very rarely.

Christopher: Because they seem to trust you. Looking at these pictures they trust you not to make fun of them.

David: I think you do that by the way you talk, the way you react, and also the real interest you take in what they're doing. So if you go to, say, ballroom dancing and you start asking them about the dresses, how they make them etc, they pick up on the fact that you're genuinely interested. So I don't think those are ever problems. Before I start even on the smallest projects, stories, whatever—you have to be careful now with words—every time you say a 'story' somebody's going to pick you up and say "oh it's a narrative, that's what he does" and so you start inventing words like it's an 'essay'. Essay is good, essay is looser. But whatever I'm doing I tend to lay down a spider's web first. If I go to Arizona I would say obviously the desert is important so that's the centre and then I would think of offshoots. Education I need to deal with, and if I need to deal with education I need to deal with university, I need to deal with a small school. Sport. Arizona is all to do with university football, that's the major thing in the University. The highest paid guy in Arizona State University is the coach of the football team! And then I'd ask myself what other things do they do. Bizarrely, Arizona being the driest state in America it has more boats per head of population than anywhere else. Now instantly I love that, the idea of that. So I have to do something on boats. So I'll make a sort of map almost. It's a very loose map but what it does is it means that I'm working out the time I'm going to be there, it means that over the course of that year I am actually going to do a coverage and it'll be a coverage of the things that I'm interested in . . . Therefore, it seems to be a legitimate point of view. People might not like the pictures but if they look at the whole I hope they can at least say this is serious. Someone is seriously looking at this, not making propaganda. I'm not very interested in propaganda but I think you're bound to make some kind of political statement if you're genuinely trying to be you.

Christopher: With a little p.

David: Yes, with a little p.

Christopher: You mention the desert but most of the photographs in this collection of the desert are of human interventions in the desert. Whereas the *Arizona Highways* approach is to present it as the wilderness. You've got cactuses with paper or plastic cups protecting them or signs and banners erected in the desert. Different kinds of human intervention. Or a cave painting, a painting on the rock. So it's not the wilderness approach, it's what human beings have done to the desert that seems to be your interest.

David: Yes that's always my interest . . .

Christopher: Which is unusual I think. Most people are in awe of this lunar landscape and they have to figure out how to present it in majestic ways.

David: Maybe if I could do it as well as some people do it . . .

Christopher: No, no, that's not what I'm saying . . . [laughter]

Christopher: It's an interesting take: what have humans done to the environment? That seems to be your interest.

David: Yes it is a major thing for me and I'm doing a project on Wales at the moment which is exactly the same. What man does to the environment. When you go out into the landscape, frankly if you're saying I think this a wonderful landscape and you take a picture, why didn't you buy a postcard? The people that do postcards have spent more time, they know the light and they get it right. It just doesn't interest me that much. There's a great photographer there I met called Mark Klett who interests me a lot: he realised that the people who photographed the opening up of the view of the West were photographing things that in Arizona hadn't changed that much since those days. He went back and very accurately rephotographed their photographs. So accurately that the Geological Society could measure soil erosion from the accuracy of one of his photographs.

Christopher: The original photographs would be from the 1860s onwards?

David: Yes. They were either working for the railroad or the Geological Society or something called the Catastrophe Society, which I never quite understood what that was. Many of the men were with Mathew Brady in the Civil War. The end of the Civil War they were out of work and they became landscape photographers. I like all that and I like the Klett approach because it had a purpose, I understood what it was about. It was about him saying nothing has changed.

Christopher: It's not usual, as I say, to photograph these giant cactuses and avoid the temptation of the pretty picture postcard—and actually to have paper cups stuck all over them to protect the prickles.

David: It's because at night they get frostbite. So they put the paper cups over them to protect them, it's ingenious but it's so funny.

Christopher: Another theme is elderly people. You have a lot of photographs of gatherings of old folks in retirement communities and the like. What I hadn't realised until I saw your book is that clearly a lot of people retire to Arizona in the third age

David: Well there is a wonderful place there, which if I had the energy I would go back to. It's called Quartzsite or something like that.

Christopher: It's not Sun City is it?

David: No, but there was Sun City as well . . . This one is in the middle of the desert and it has a population of about 3,500. There's a date, let's say it's the 1st of November. It suddenly expands to half a million. It's all the people coming down from Canada and North America in their big off-road vehicles because they can park them there for virtually nothing for the whole of the winter. So they set up a whole city, retirement city. It is just extraordinary. I love that idea. At the time I was there I was in my mid 40s, I was just beginning to look at people who were a bit older . . . Sun City was another thing. I worked with Bill Jay to look at Sun City, I'll say naughtily with tongue in cheek to start with but we came away nearly buying property. I mean it was so impressive. Their argument, basically, was that we tend to stay within our age group all our life. We go to nursery school together. We go to primary school together. We go to secondary school together. We go to university together and then for some reason when it gets to the other end everybody sort of splits up a little bit. Well, at Sun City you have to be over 55, maybe over 60, to actually stay there and it's like a walled city of its own but it has all these people of the same age. The beauty about that is that none of them feel old because everybody's walking at the same pace. So there's a logic to it which I hadn't understood before I went there. They do incredible things and you get people like Nobel Prize winners giving classes in whatever they do. They are very serious about it. In Sun City West there's the Heart Bypass Club or something and they're there every morning in the swimming pool together.

Christopher: Did you know all this before you went? When you were doing your map did you think you must photograph old people?

David: No no no.

Christopher: You found out about Sun City when you were there?

David: The map is more like a crutch to fall back on if I get into trouble but most of the time what I do in a place is kind of word of mouth. Somebody will say something and that will lead to something else and lead to something else and lead to something else. Or if I'm thinking about my map I might say "do you know a particularly good small school?". One of the things about working in America is that the people are incredibly open to you coming and visiting them. I remember the school I went to which was a wonderful little school. I just made an

appointment with the headmaster at that time, went to see him, explained what I was doing and he just gave me the run of the school. I mean it was extraordinary. He had this faith that I think I manage usually to give to people, that I'm not going to abuse them or anything.

Christopher: Trust is so important.

David: It is enormously important.

Christopher: What sort of camera? Did you have a small camera?

David: Yes, I used Leicas then.

Christopher: So nothing intrusive looking?

David: No, nothing at all and no flash or anything like that. Just found light.

Christopher: That helps.

David: Yes, it helps a lot.

David: I would just go from thing to thing and I also had a base to come back to. When I first got there I read somewhere that Arizona was the worst state in America for infant mortality. The idea of reading that there's such a thing as a state where more babies die is bizarre. But I don't trust statistics so I wrote to Washington to the Department of Statistics and the Americans are very good, they are so open about all these things. Instantly a reply came back saying, "These figures are absolutely correct but they are 12 years out of date. Arizona is now the second best state in America for infant mortality." So I thought if it's gone from being the worst I'd better do a bit of nosing around because that's a major change. It came about because two doctors, William Daley and Jay Hayes, had realised there was this huge state with two major cities and hospitals clustered in the middle. So all around the outside if you had a premature baby you didn't have anybody to tell you how to look after it. The only people who knew were in the middle. And very often round the outside were the seven Indian tribes in Arizona. They were the Apaches or the Navajos or the Hopis . . I'm saying this because I remember the names.

Christopher: Yes, impressive.

David: Very impressive. They realised that if they set up a free air transport system by which if the doctors out there could say, "Look we've got a premature baby", they could fly a plane out with an isolette which is like a goldfish bowl they put the babies in. They fly them back to the center and they have more chance of saving them. The snag with that is that they couldn't say openly that it was a free system because that would be socialised medicine and Arizona was the most right-wing state of the Union. And *Life* magazine published the story. I spent a year there going with them when anything was happening.

Christopher: Was this during your scholarship year?

David: Yes this was during the year. And it gave me an entrée into the Native American tribes which was very useful because it's very difficult to get to them but if you went in with a doctor it was a different ball game. So that was the great entrée to do that. It's another example of that networking thing of how you get to know certain types of people. And that leads to something else.

Christopher: You're much more interested in groups than in individuals. People enjoying life together and there are a lot of photographs of that, particularly recreations of one kind or another. Beauty pageants, drum majorettes, rodeo people, lookalike contests. You like people bonding in your pictures. Not so much individual portraits of Western characters—like Richard Avedon's portfolio of individual Westerners for example.

David: Lewis Hine said a wonderful thing a long time ago, I used to have it on my wall when I was teaching. It said "We should be photographing two things. The things that should be put right and the things that should be appreciated". Now I'm in the appreciation field. I just love it all. I love people touching each other. I think it's a very nice thing to do. Togetherness. The second thing is that I don't really want to set up anything or stage things. Photography has all sorts of genres . . . but one of the things that I think it does better than anything else is to record life as it is.

Christopher: Capture a moment.

David: Capture a moment. Now how you analyse that afterwards is a whole debate of course. But I do think it's possible to capture and not only that but most people looking at a picture can get an enormous amount of detailed information that they can't normally get out of any of the other communication forms. I don't need to analyse what that information means.

Christopher: Roland Barthes wrote in *Camera Lucida* about the accidental things, the personally touching things—the things that make an emotional connection that even the photographer may not notice but they stand out in retrospect when you look at a frozen moment. He calls these details the 'punctum'.

David: Yes. Well the debate is does the photographer know it or notice it or not? Undoubtedly for me the greatest pictures are those that not only have that information but they have that information within a sort of pattern or geometry or whatever you'd like to call it which projects so that you see what is the point of the picture. That's the point to me: that it has projected what you want it to project. Photography can never be anything

other than a box with a hole in the front and light comes through that hole and records things on the back. It cannot do anything else but that. Therefore in theory we should all take the same bloody pictures. But the answer is that in the same way as there is Rembrandt and we don't muddle him up with Matisse. I'm sure Matisse didn't sit down and say, "Well I'm going to paint like this because I don't want to paint like Rembrandt". To me the extraordinary thing about photography is that great photographers are recognizable from their work. Why is it that if you pick, you can't do it with one picture, but if you get 10 Cartier-Bresson pictures . . .

Christopher: You can recognise the style.

David: Yes, you could say that's by Bresson, that's by Weegee, that's by Bill Brandt. I think that's extraordinary.

Christopher: That's by David Hurn.

David: Well that would be lovely if it was.

Christopher: It's true.

David: Well it would be lovely. The particular thing that I like is that I don't want to set things up. Now I'm a hypocrite in a certain way because every so often you do a portrait. It's likely that you might set up a portrait and if you do commercial work obviously that's a different genre, you're setting it up all the time. But I just want to go and look at the world and obviously I try to make a picture because to me photography is about pictures. I don't want nine pages of text telling me how I ought to look at that picture. I have a picture on my wall at home by Philip Jones Griffiths and it's of a Vietnamese person covered in bandages. It's on the way to the loo. People come down and they come back into the room and they're crying, I think that's extraordinary. Photography can have this extraordinary emotional thing and it can have an extraordinary ability to counteract propaganda.

Christopher: In your photographs, there's so much going on, you can see so many different things because it's groups of people in an unusual social situation, here's line dancing or whatever it is, and there's so much information in there to intrigue the viewer and look at details. And people will see different things obviously like any work of art, people bring things to it people take different things away from it. But the photographs are often quite busy, there are lots of things going on in them and there's lots to intrigue the eye. Did you ever say "Do it again for me"?

David: No. Never.

Christopher: They're all real moments?

David: They're all real moments. And as I get older I become more paranoid about that. I'm not making it into a religion or anything but it's just that that's what I like to do.

Christopher: Most of us, I would think, see Arizona through the movies. So our way of seeing is dominated by all those widescreen films and deserts and Ford's Monument Valley. And you have done a lot of work for the movies, famously James Bond, *Barbarella*, and *A Hard Day's Night* and so on. But I don't get that at all from your photographs, that they're inflected through the movies. Your way of seeing isn't dominated by movie images—you can have your own approach. Is that fair?

David: Yes I think that's fair. The people who are dominated by the movies are very often dominated by a style, a style or look. You'll see Fassbinder or you'll see John Ford and that has never particularly interested me. If I have a style it's very mundane. It's very ordinary.

Christopher: I think it's more feet on the ground. I mean it's not ordinary, it's grounded.

David: I shall quote you on that now.

Christopher: It's grounded. You're wearing a stout pair of shoes and it's very grounded. You're not being pushed around by any fashion.

David: It's not good or bad. It's just that it doesn't interest me. One hopes that the result will intrigue people. In other words it doesn't become wallpaper. And one hopes it has a big public. I'm not the least bit interested in prints under the bed and I'm not desperately interested, basically because of my background, I'm not interested in big prints for merchant bankers. It seems to be of all the forms of communication, art, whatever you'd like to call them, photography is perhaps the one which is most likely to get to a huge public. For the first time in history virtually everybody in the world loves photography. Nobody ever said, "Everyone's gone home with their notebook and pencil" but now everyone's got an iPhone. Photographs of themselves and each other. So if I was starting again in education my whole thing would be how do I move people from that just up a little tiny bit. For example, if within a museum you have a little exhibition of, say, six pictures, one by Brandt, one by Koudelka, one by whoever you like, Weegee, this that and the other. You then bring in the school and say we're going to have a competition now. Each of you has to pick a picture you like best, you're going to get a prize if you do it, and your job now is to go out on your iPhone, try to redo that picture. I reckon you'll get 10 percent of the class, at least, doing it. And if you can get 10 percent or 20 percent of them doing it you might have two of them that actually think, "Hang on. This is fun".

Christopher: Have you ever exhibited these photographs in Arizona?

David: Some of them were shown at Arizona State University. There are two universities there in Arizona—one is Arizona University, which is in Tucson, and Arizona State, which is in Phoenix. Whilst I was there I gave a couple of talks as well . . .

Christopher: I wonder what the reaction was of the people who were the subjects.

David: Well I suspect at that time politeness, they're nice people, open people. I suspect nowadays there'd be a lot of interest because they were taken a long time ago and the difference . . .

Christopher: Yes, they take on an historical significance.

David: One of the great things about photography is that whatever level it's done at, almost by definition it gets better because it takes on historical associations, sociological associations etc. Even a bad photograph is interesting if we can say people didn't wear socks at that time! In 50 years time that's of interest.

Christopher: I know you hate labels. You have a healthy suspicion of labels. And I know you don't like setting things up to photograph them. Would you see yourself as a documentary photographer? Reportage? Does it matter?

David: It just doesn't matter to me.

Christopher: But if you had a category of photographer?

David: You can quote other people . . . Bresson was once asked, "Are you a journalist?" He said, "I'm perfectly happy to be a journalist if that means the keeping of a journal". Which I thought was a very bright remark. So that's there in the back of my mind. An essayist?

Christopher: A Visual Essayist.

David: A Visual Essayist. I suppose what one is struggling to do is not only to make the essay which implies a group of pictures that somehow work as a group but within it there are individual pictures which . . .

Christopher: . . . are themselves.

David: . . . have merit standing by themselves.

Christopher: I think Visual Essayist is good. I like that.

David: Until somebody deconstructs that . . .

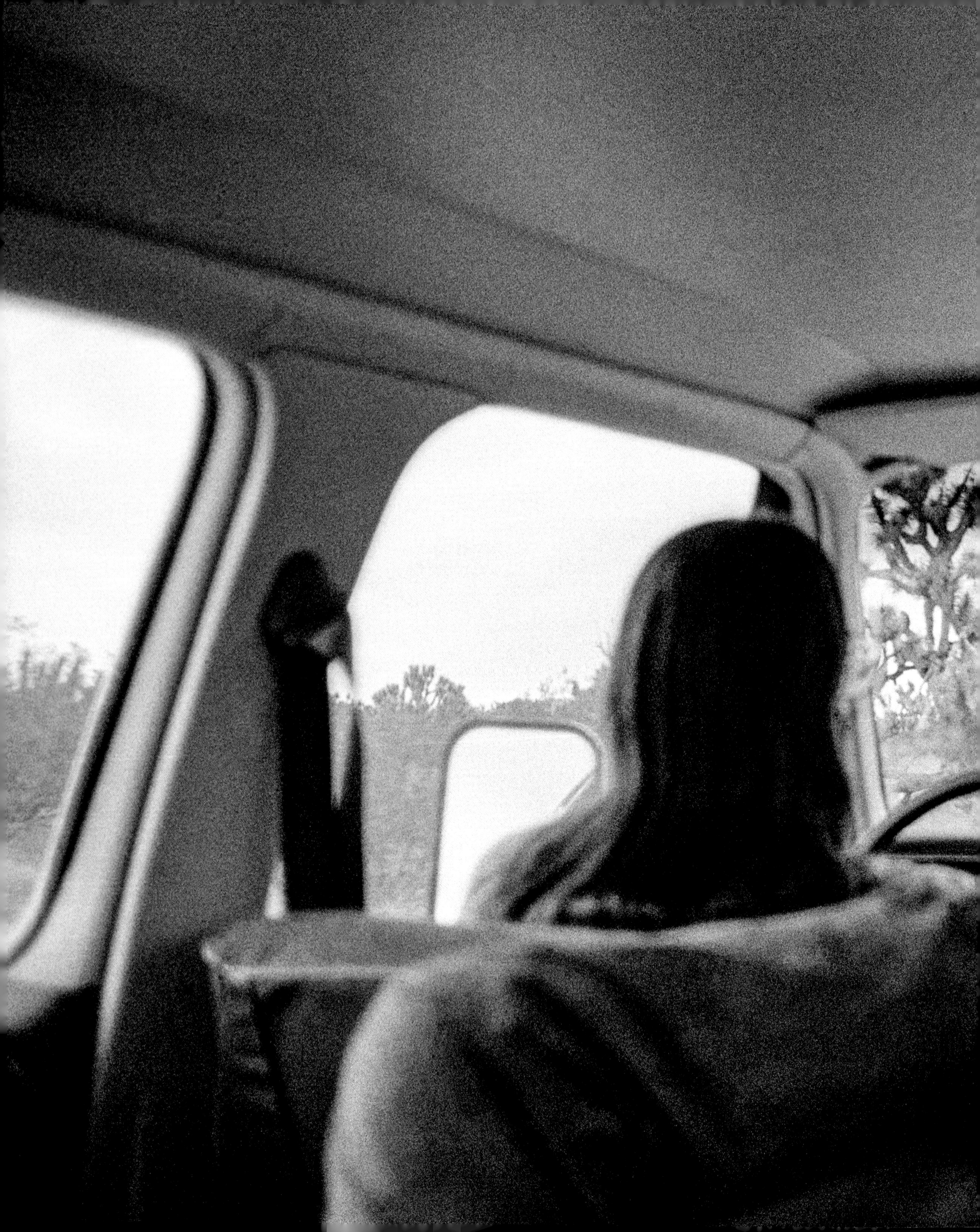

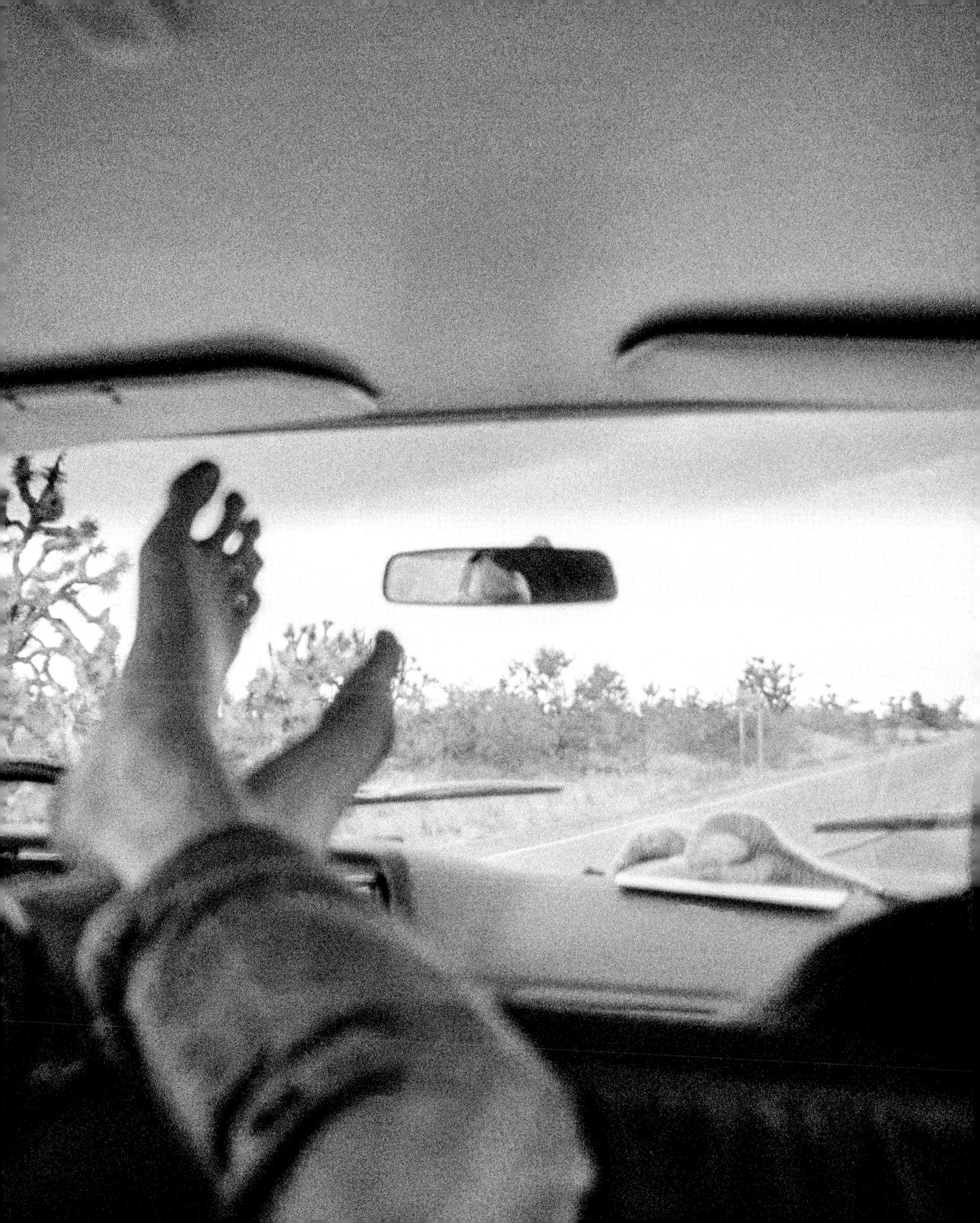

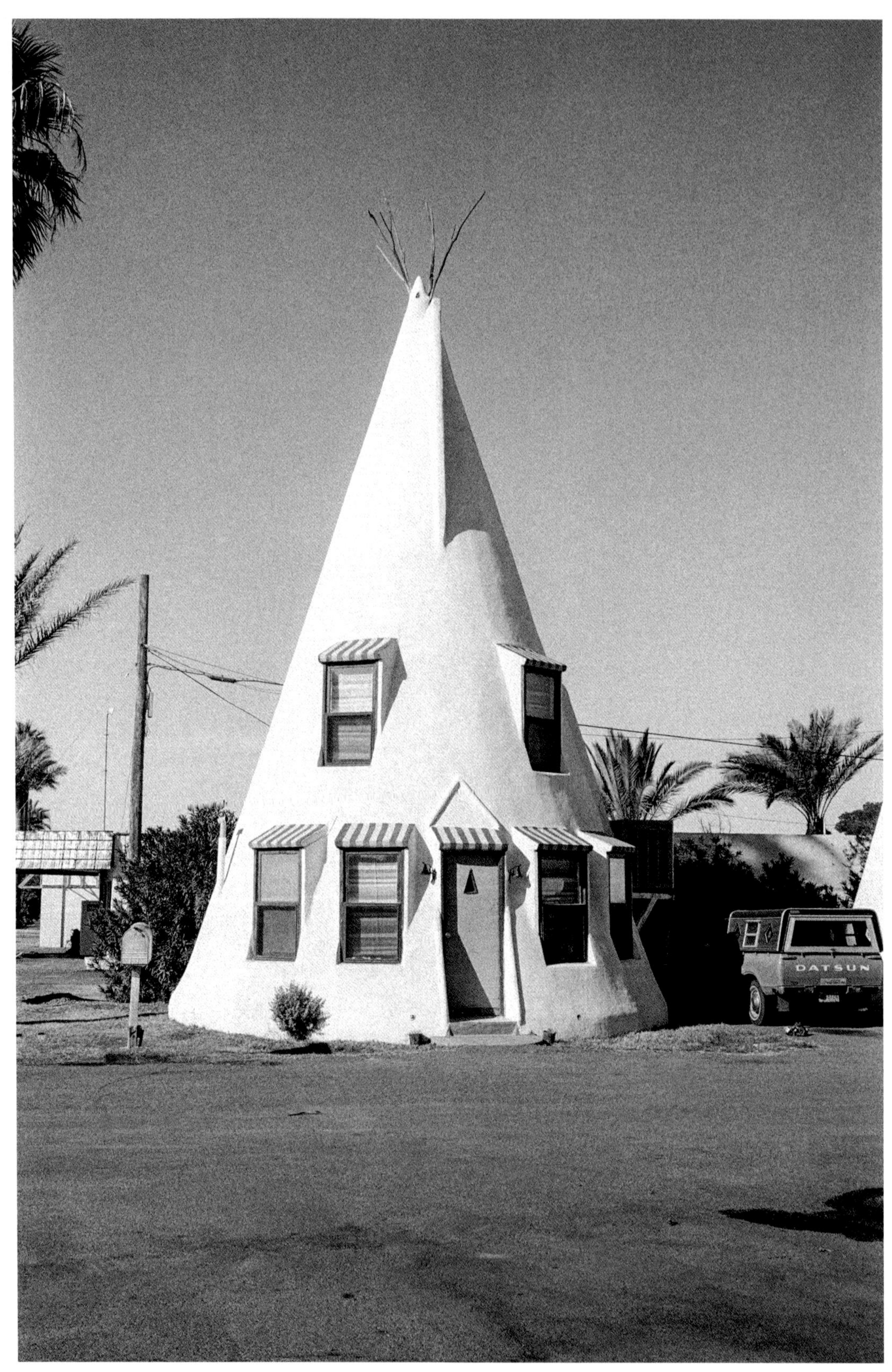

DATSUN

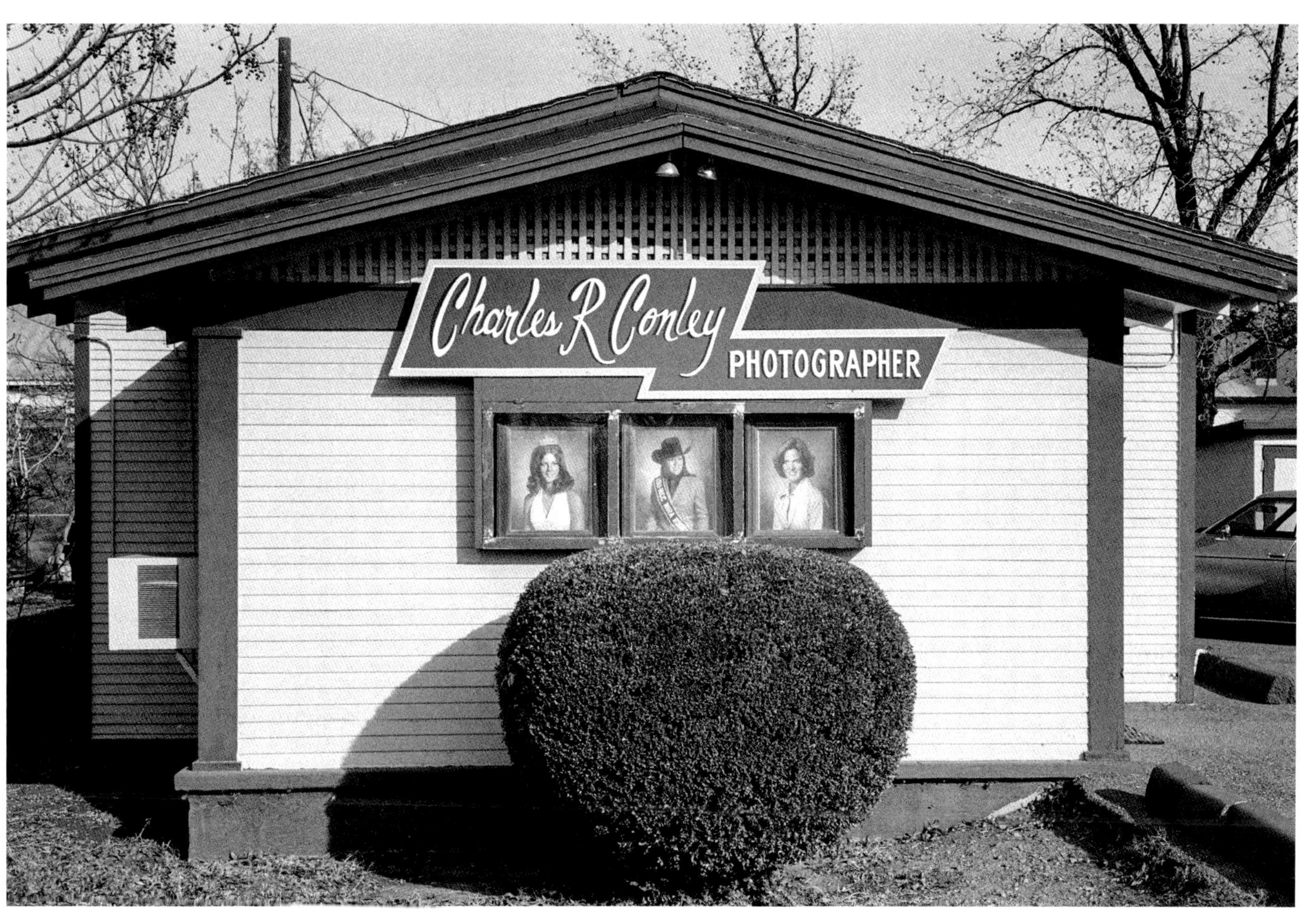

Charles R Conley
PHOTOGRAPHER

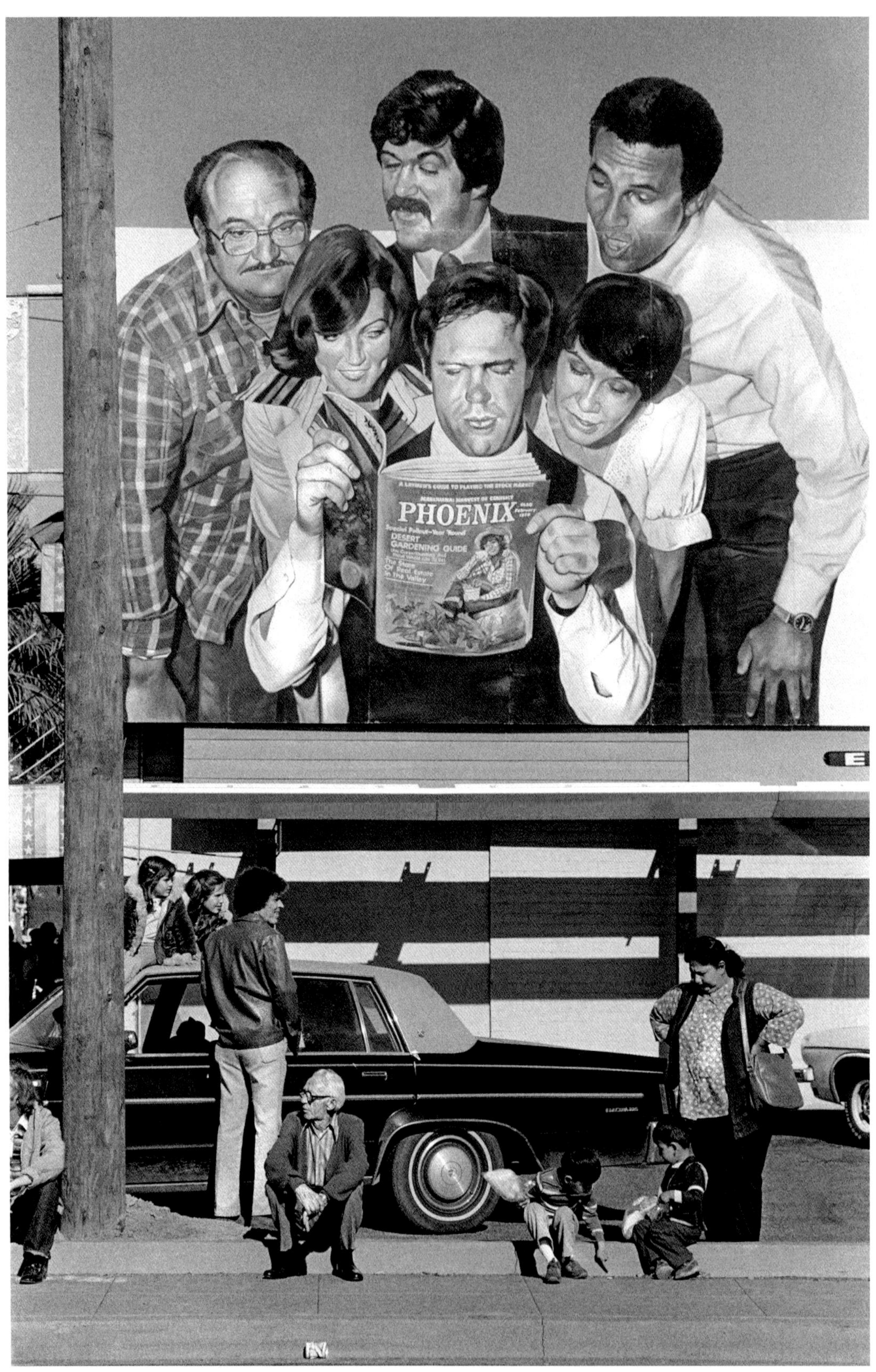
A LAYMAN'S GUIDE TO PLAYING THE STOCK MARKET
PHOENIX
Special Pullout—Year 'Round
DESERT
GARDENING GUIDE
The Best
Of Real Estate
In the Valley

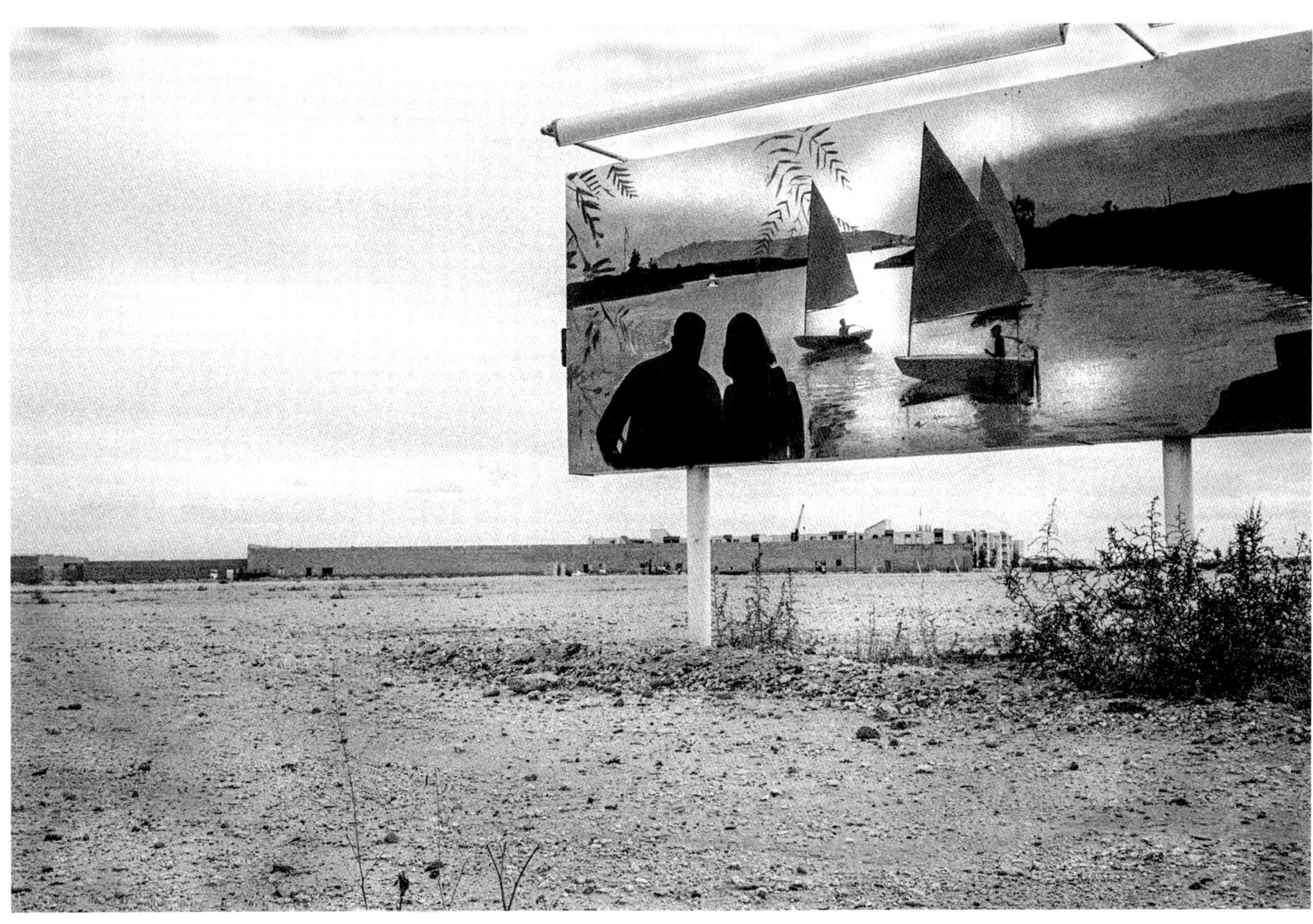

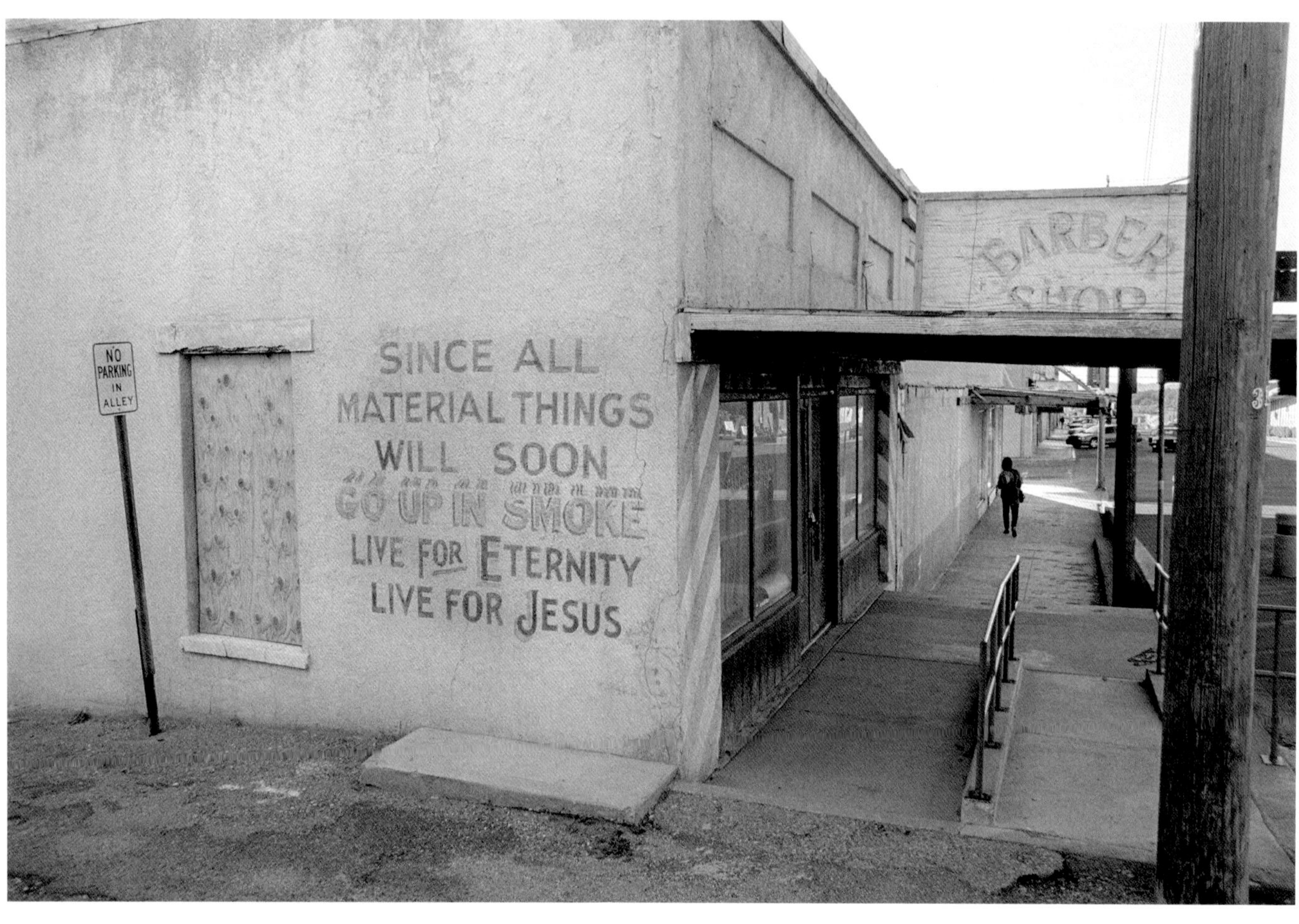

NO PARKING IN ALLEY
SINCE ALL
MATERIAL THINGS
WILL SOON
GO UP IN SMOKE
LIVE FOR ETERNITY
LIVE FOR JESUS
BARBER SHOP

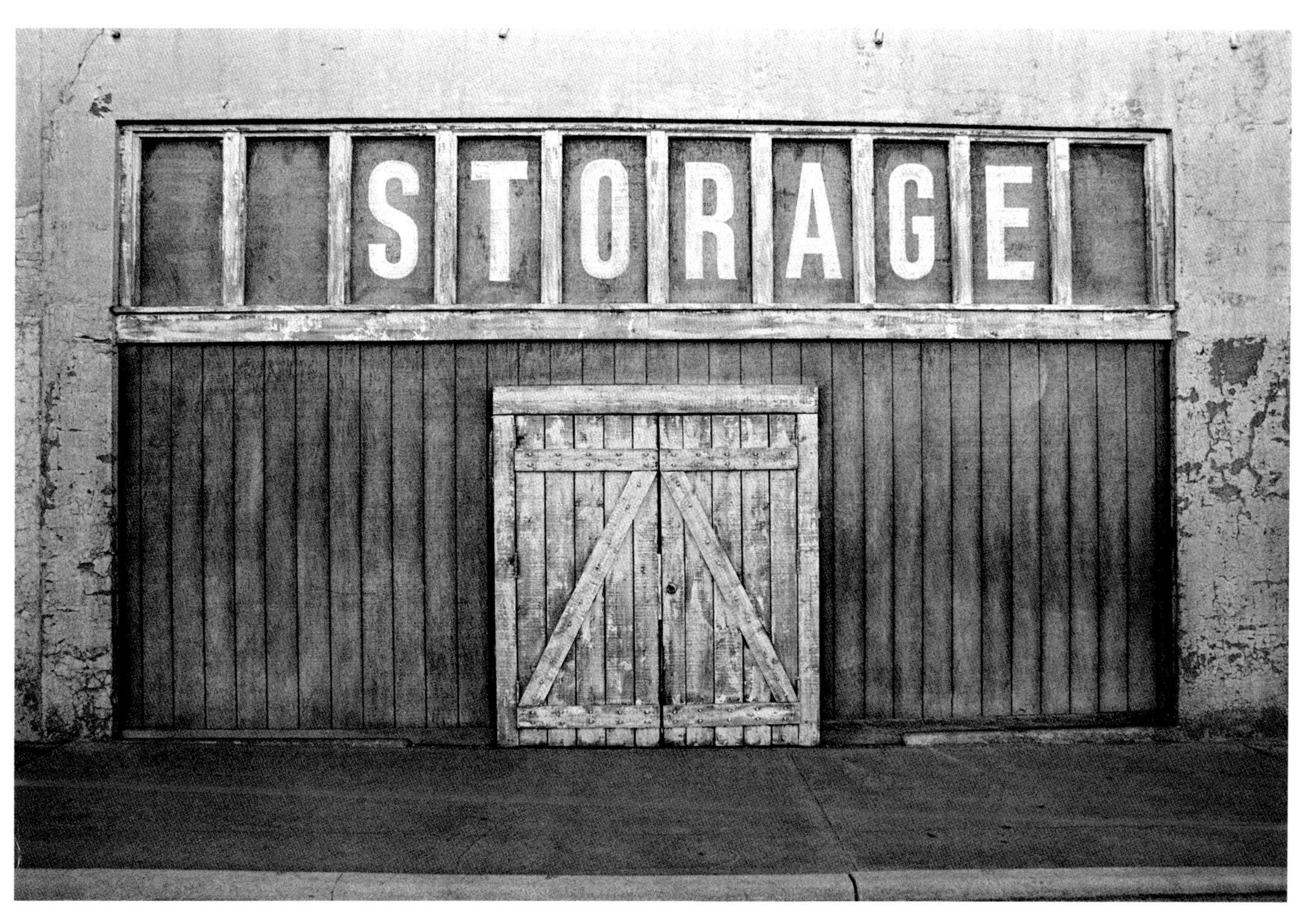

STORAGE

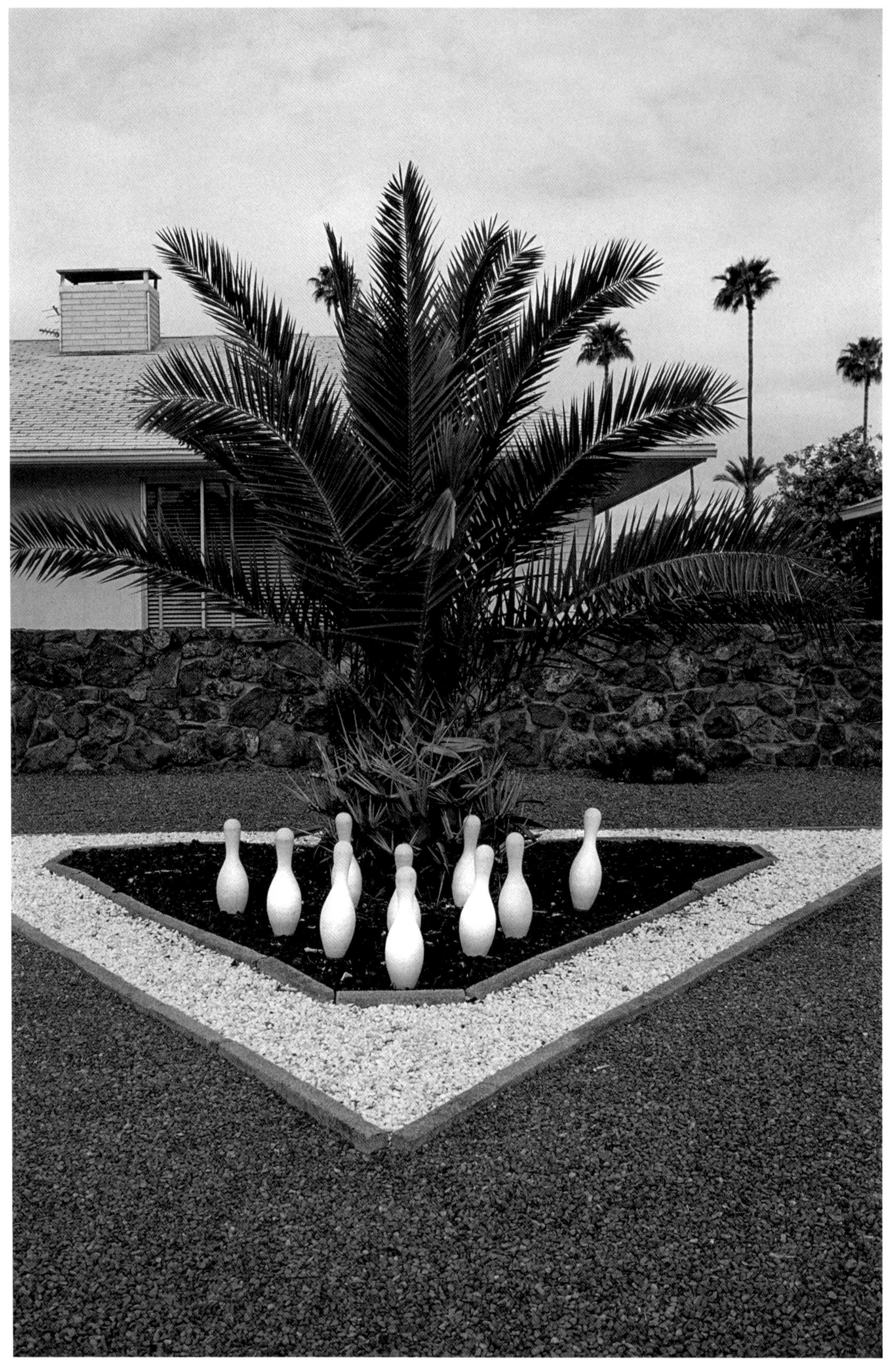

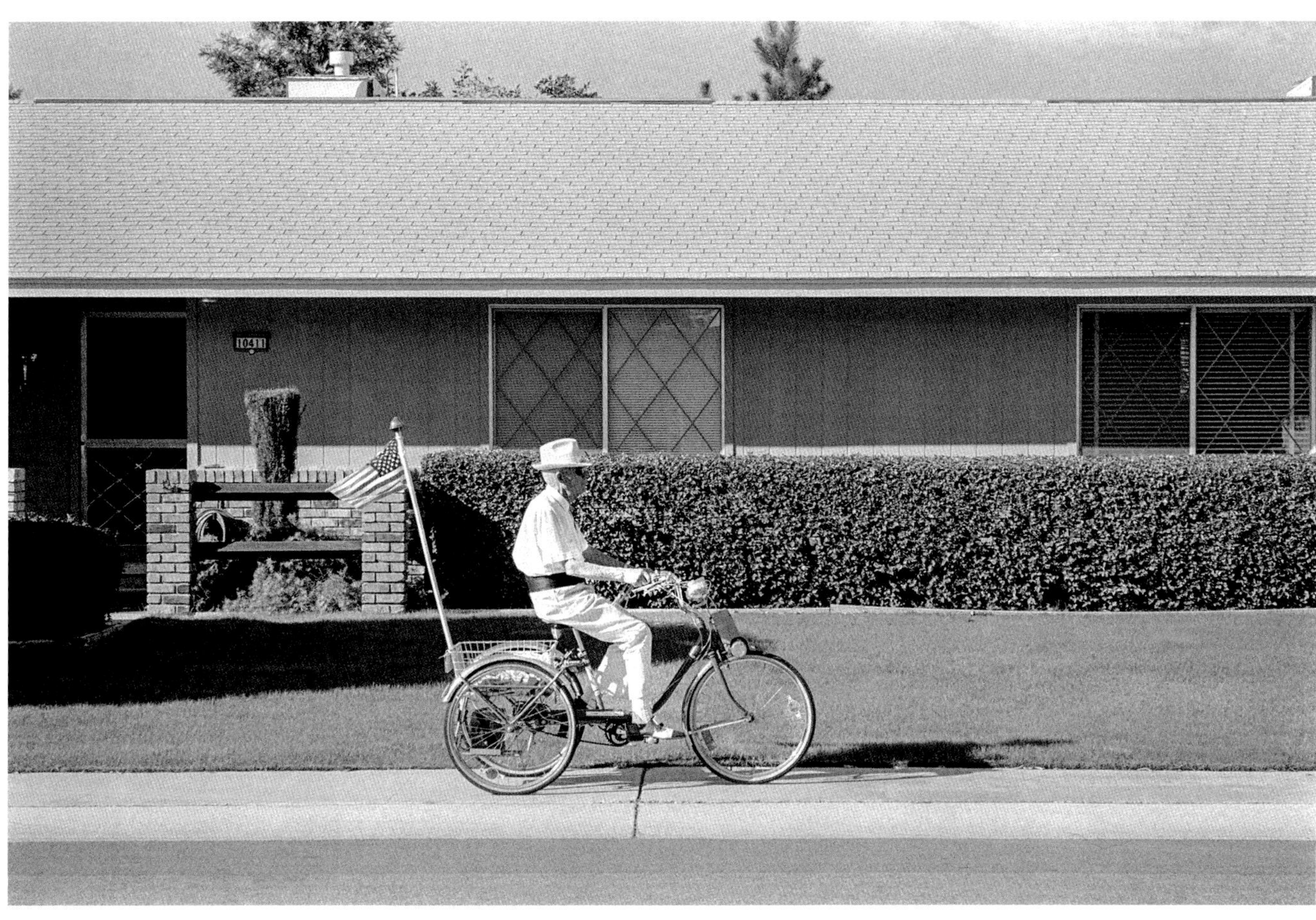

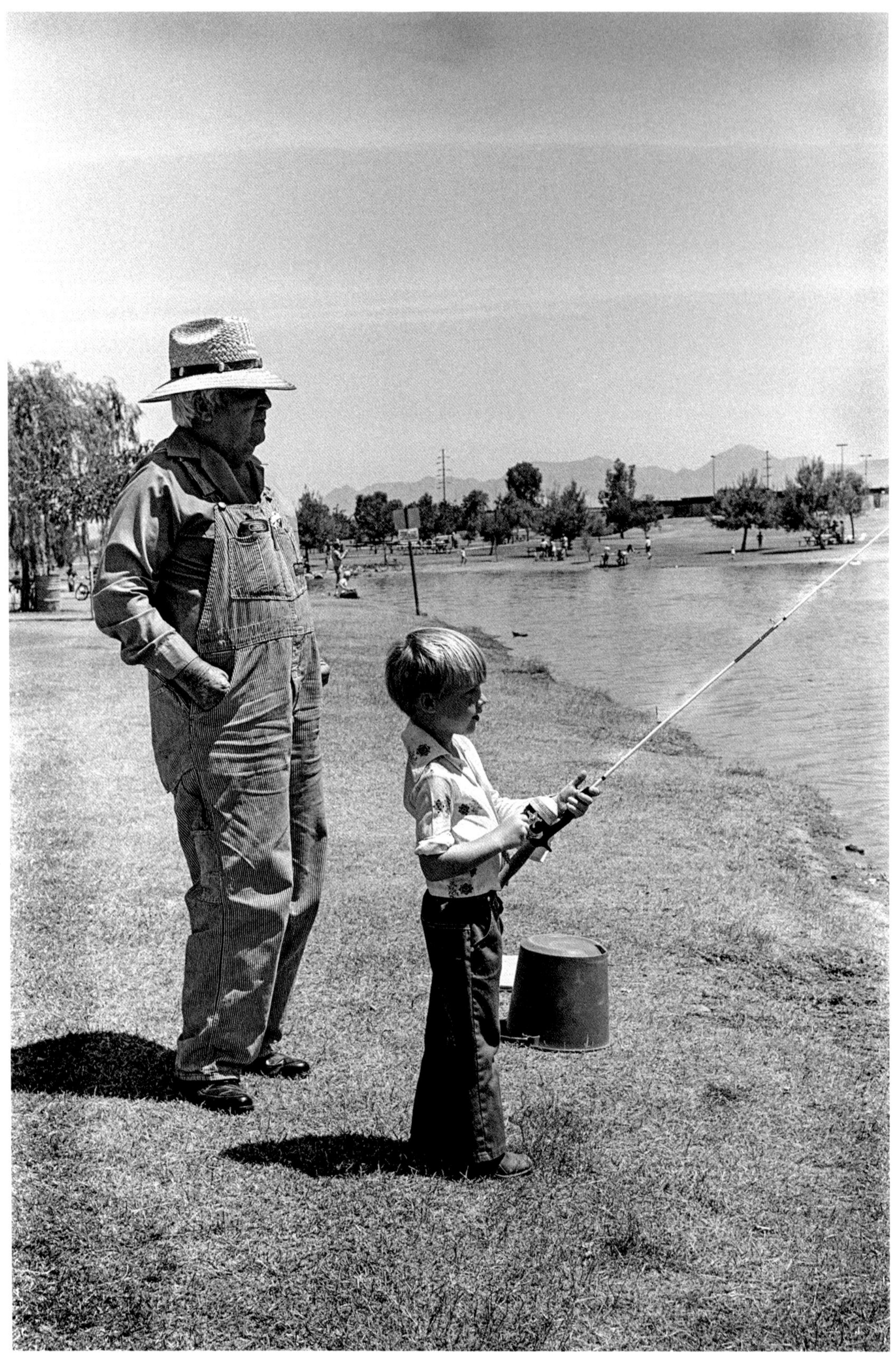

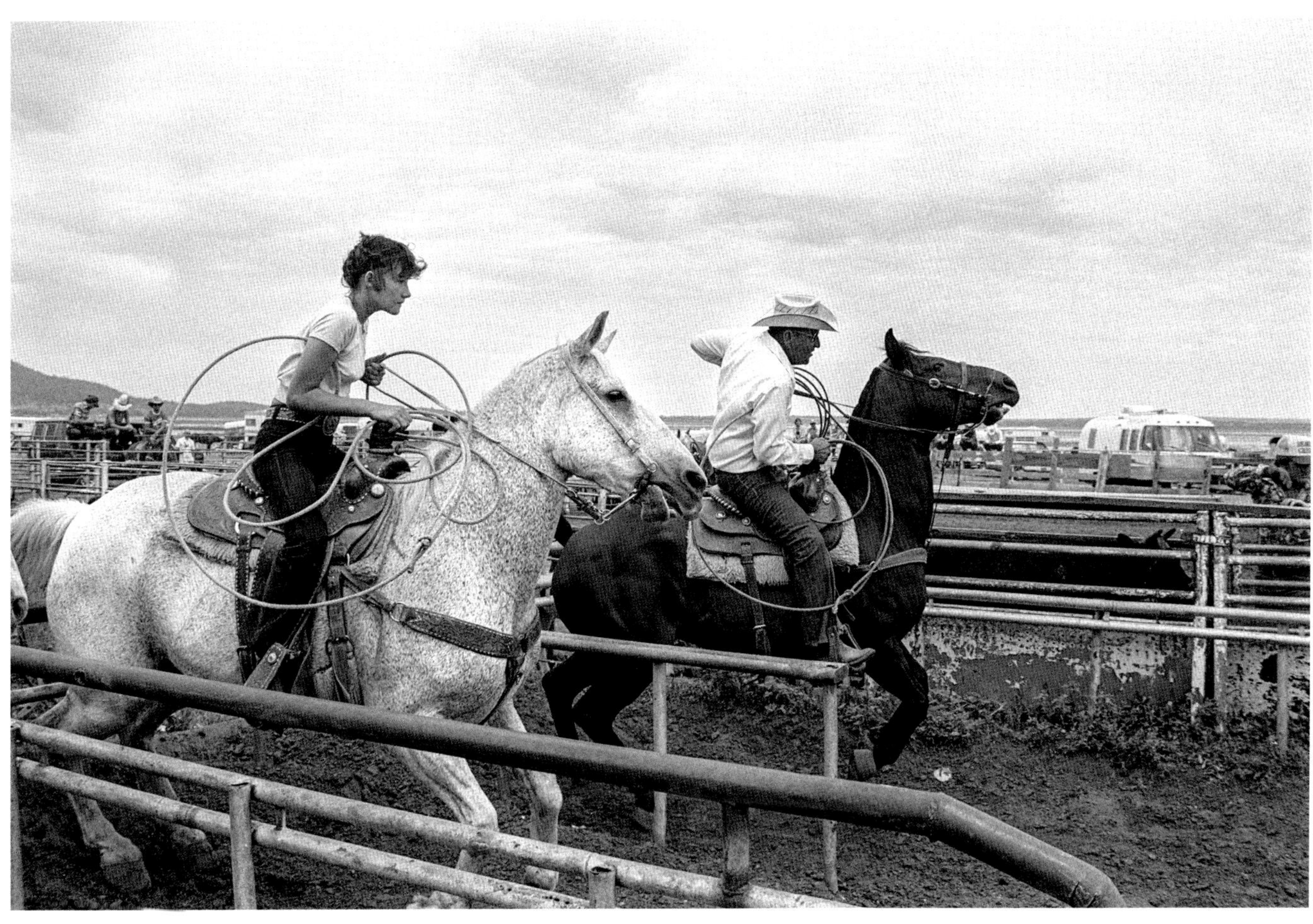

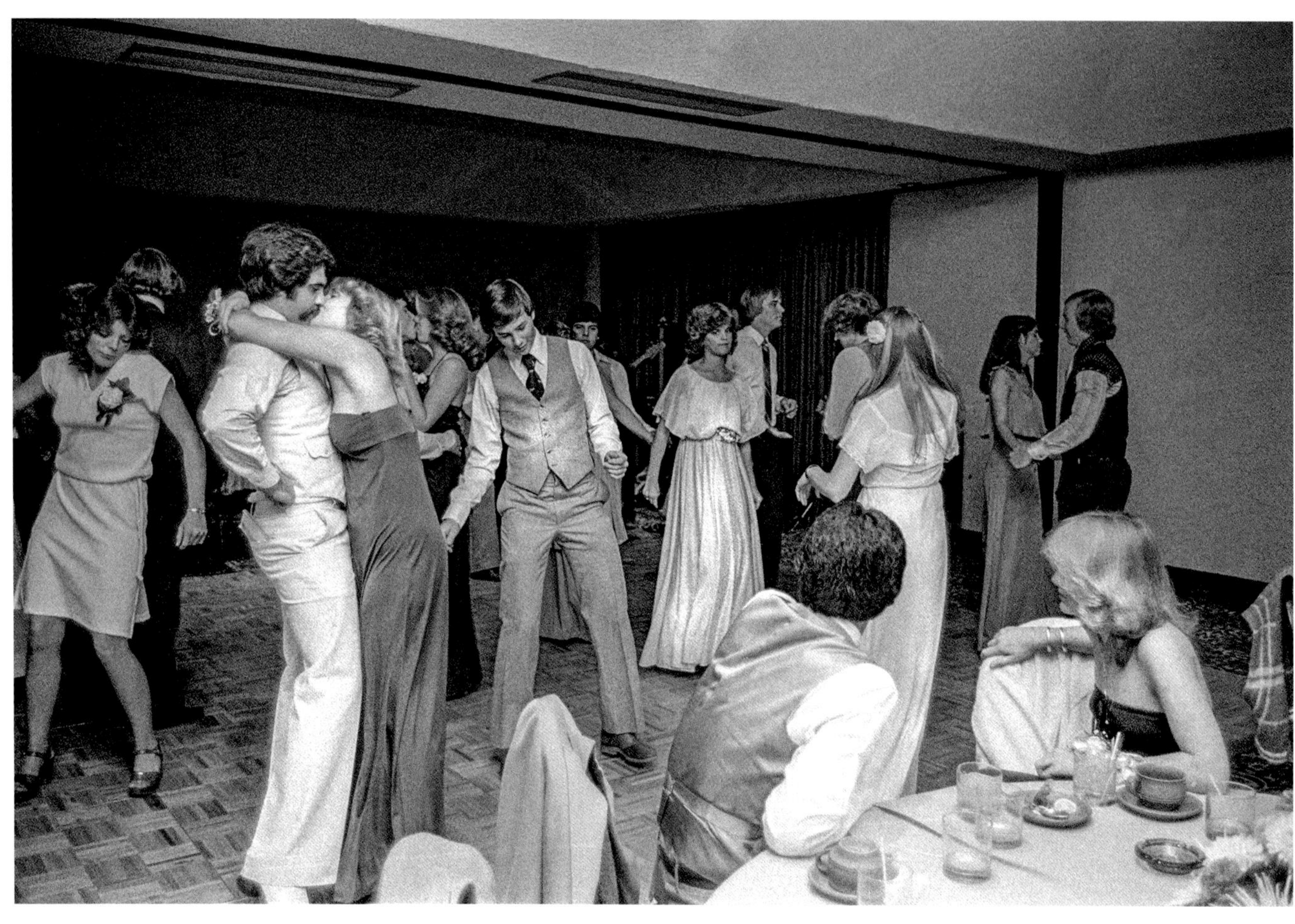

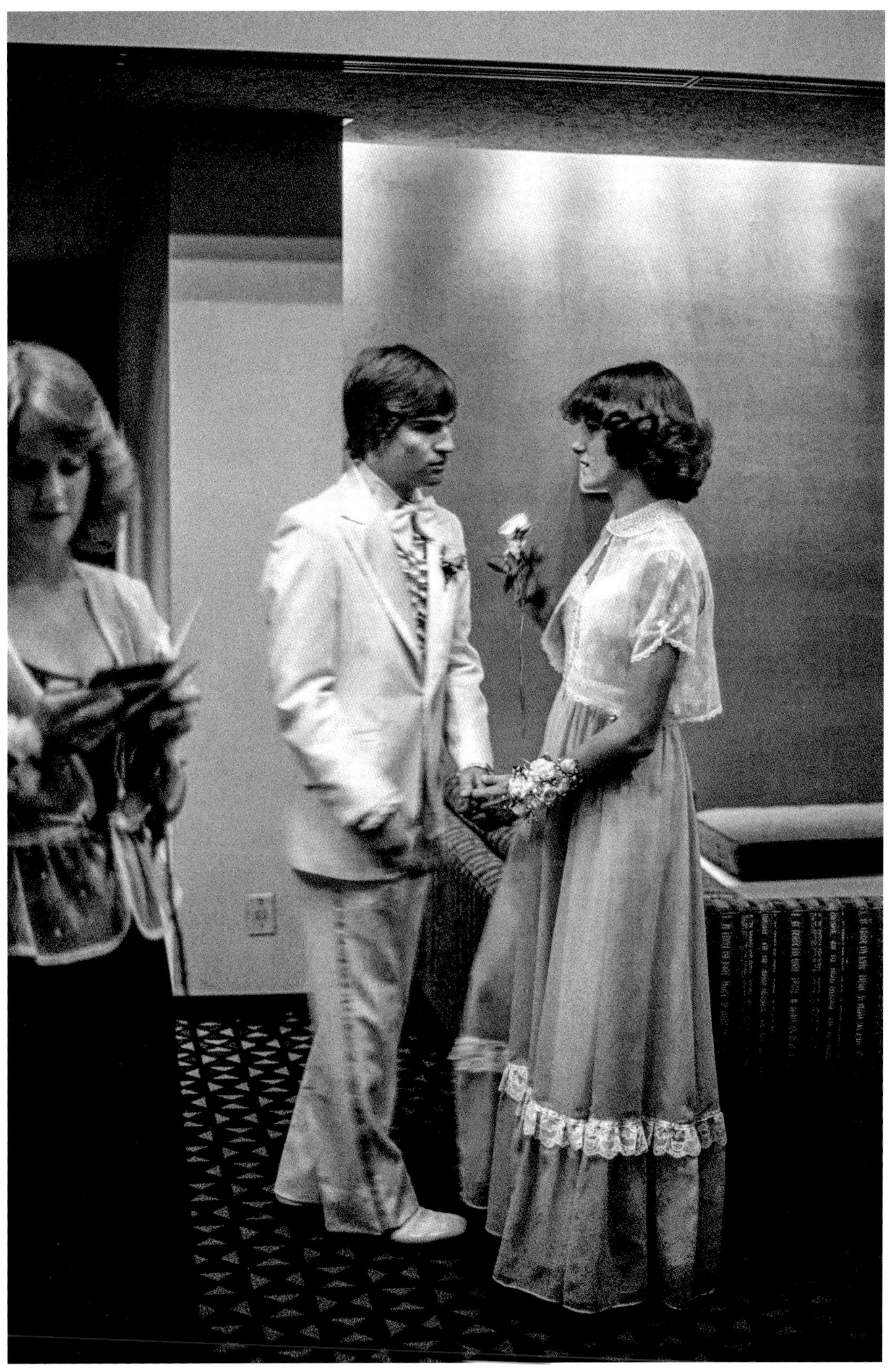

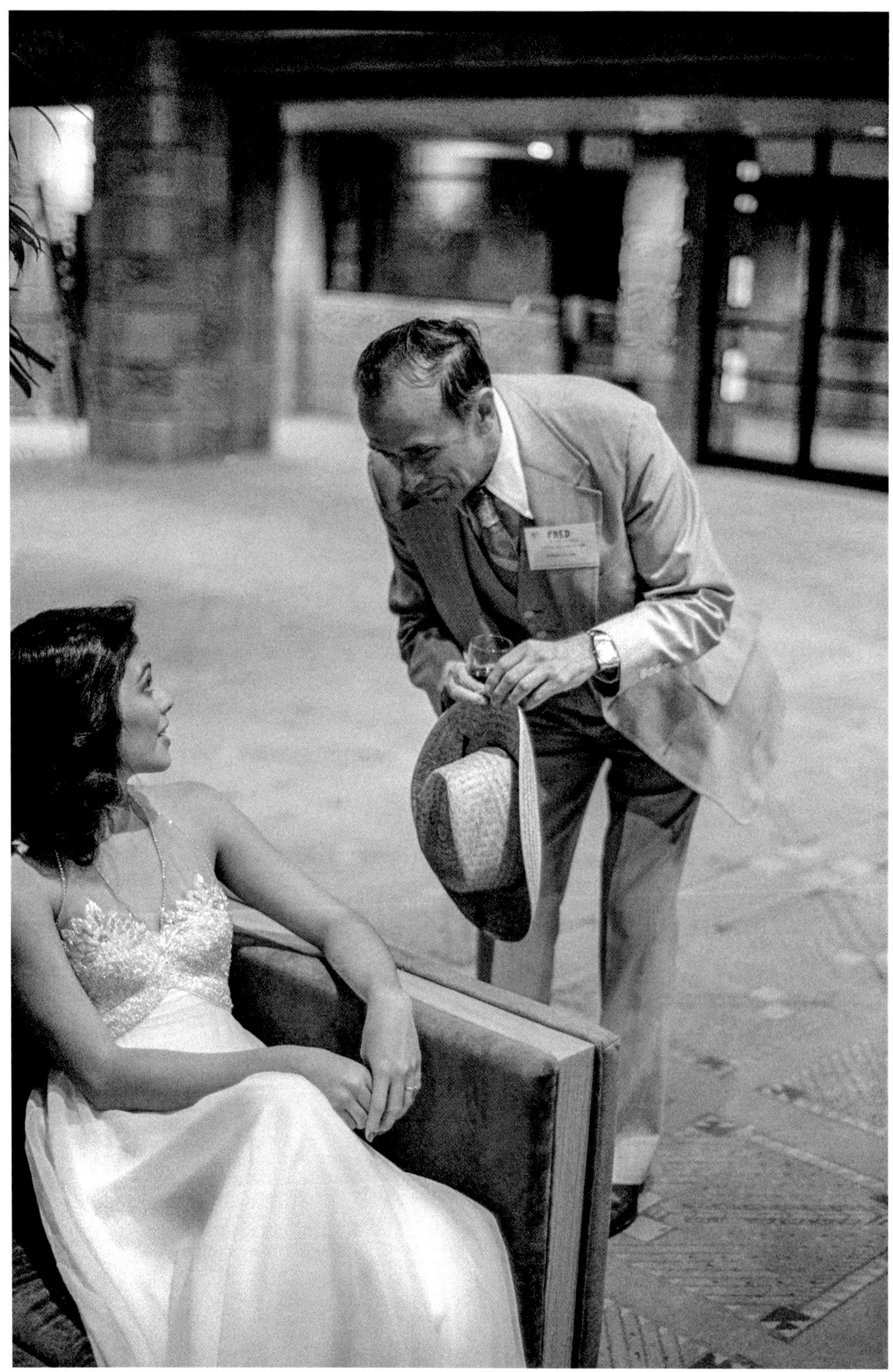

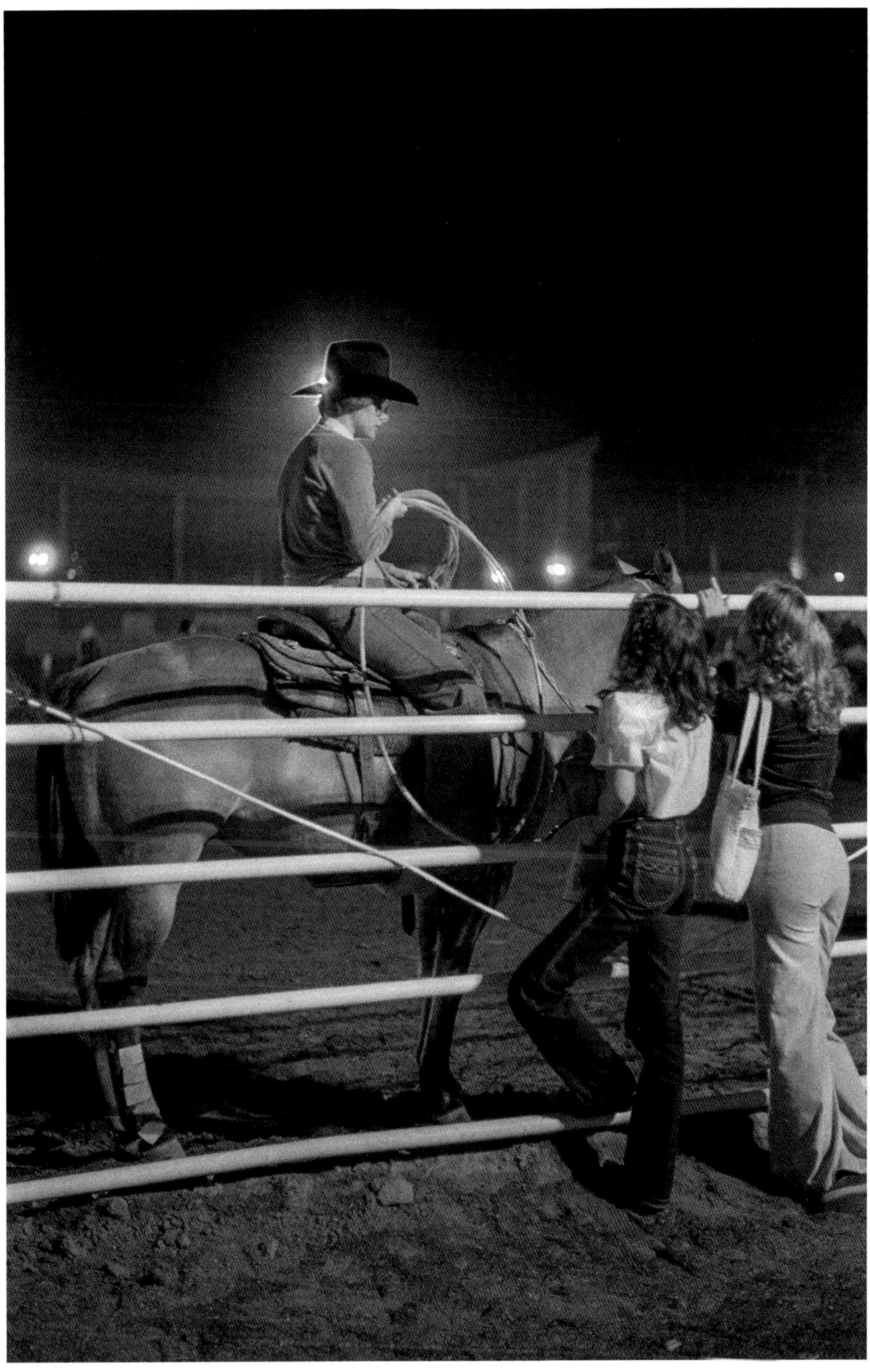

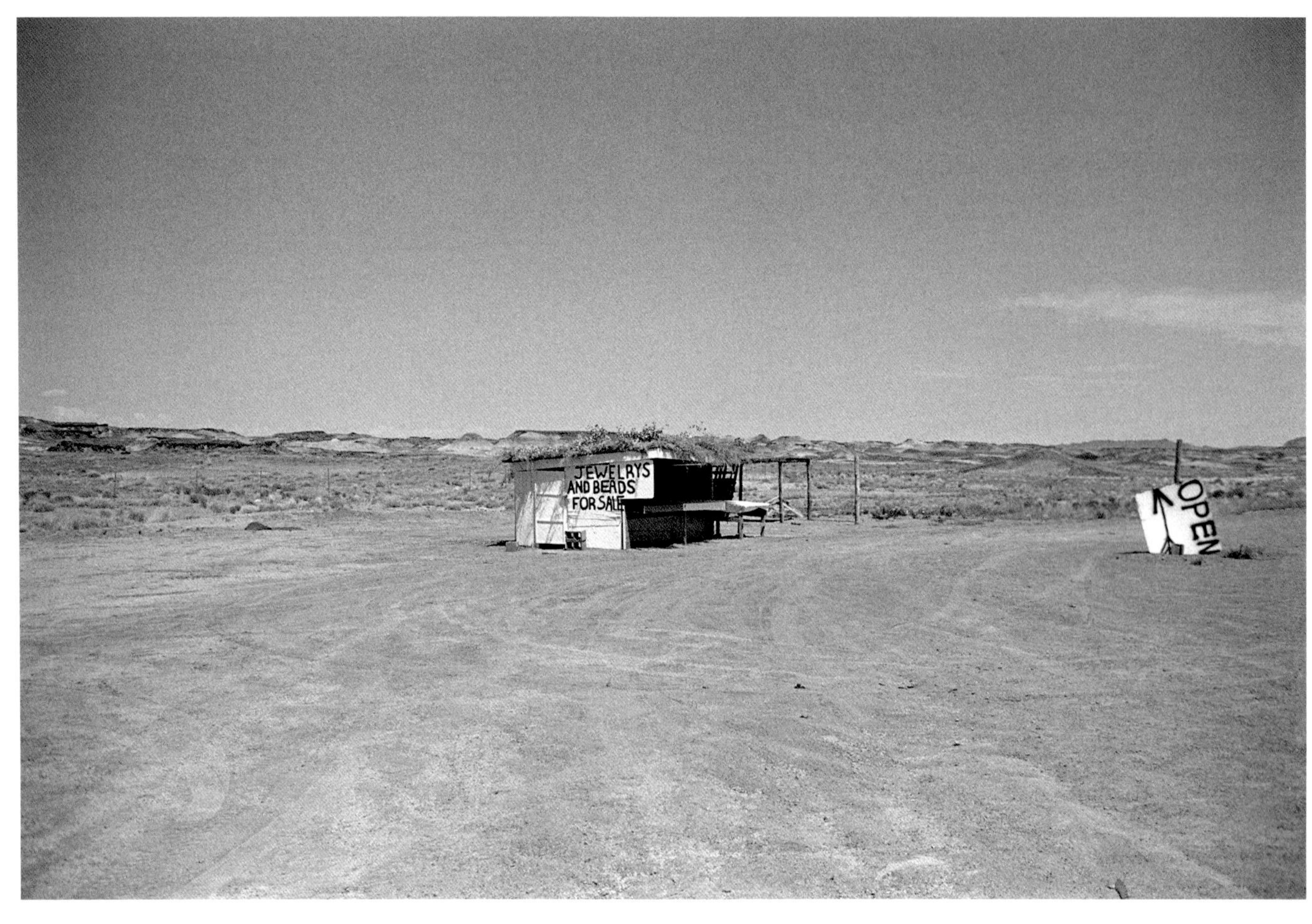

JEWELRYS
AND BEADS
FOR SALE
OPEN

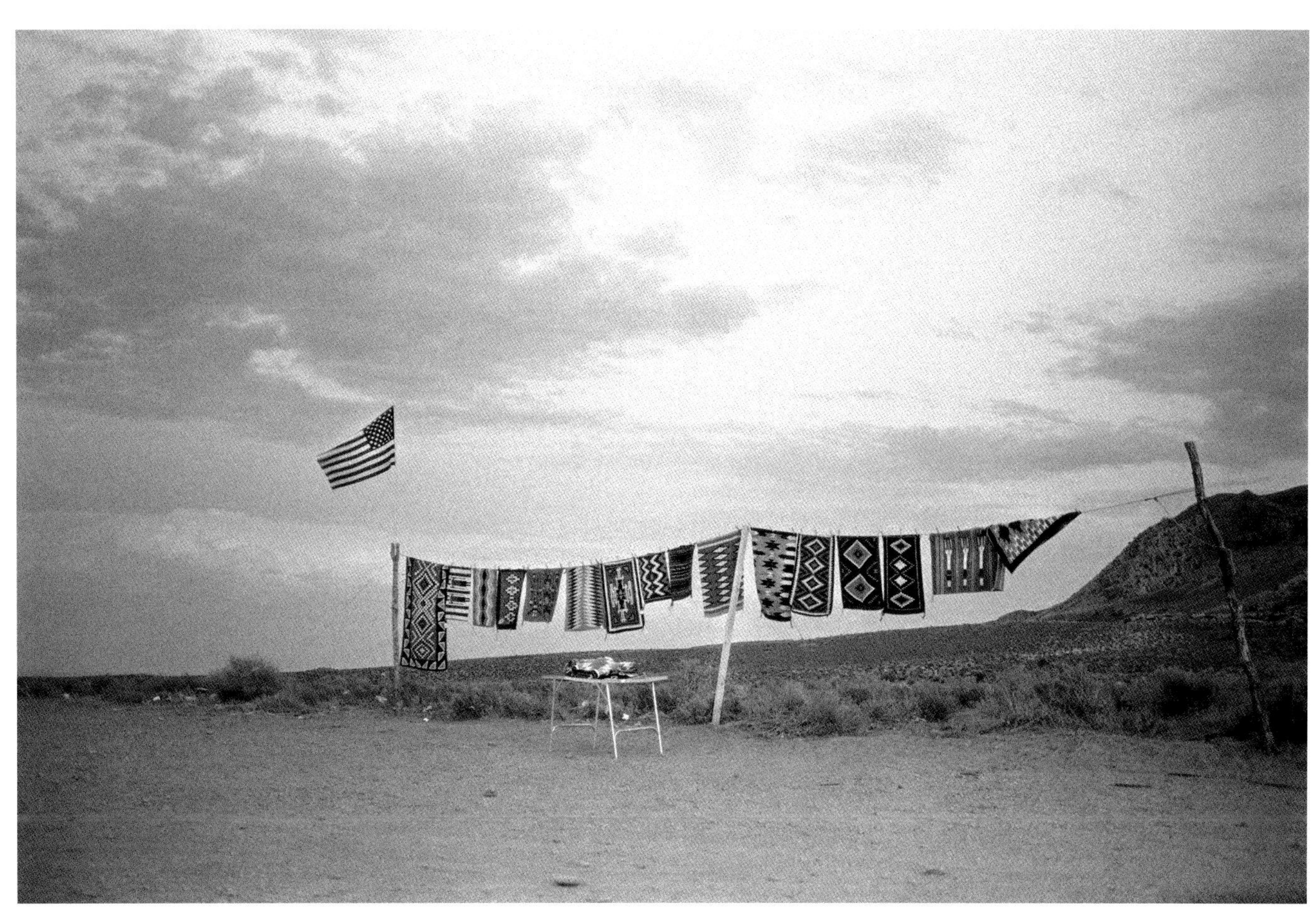

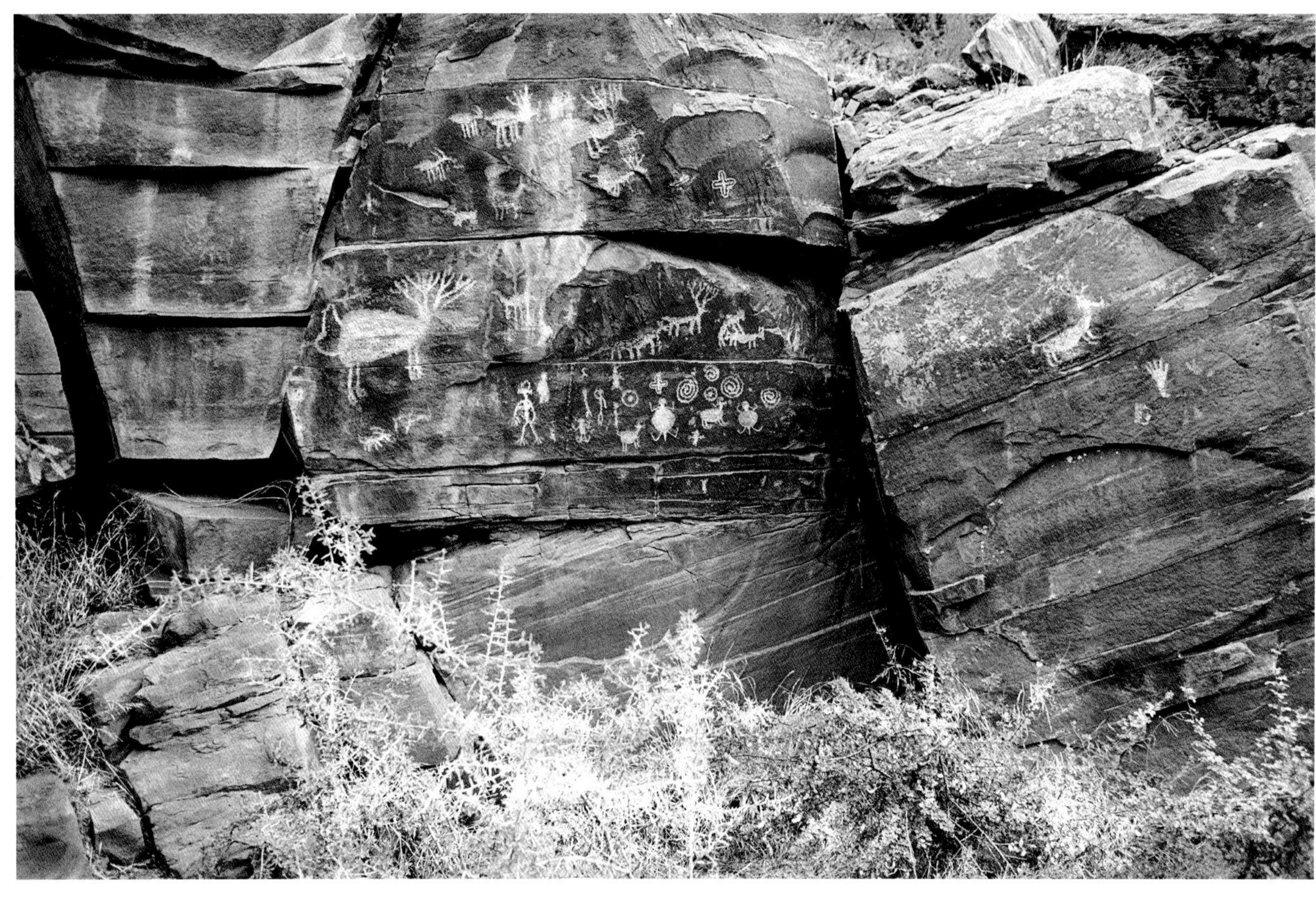

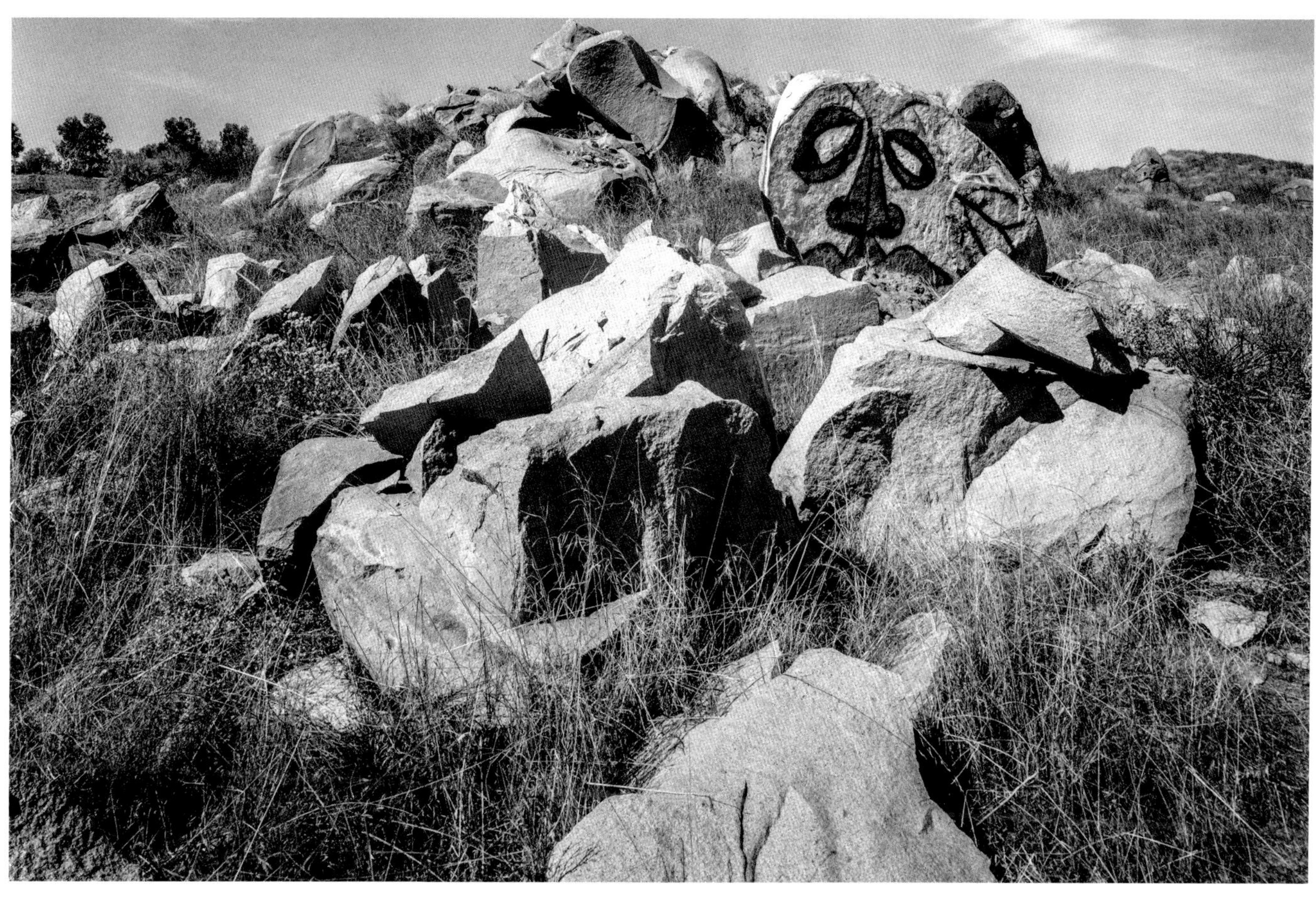

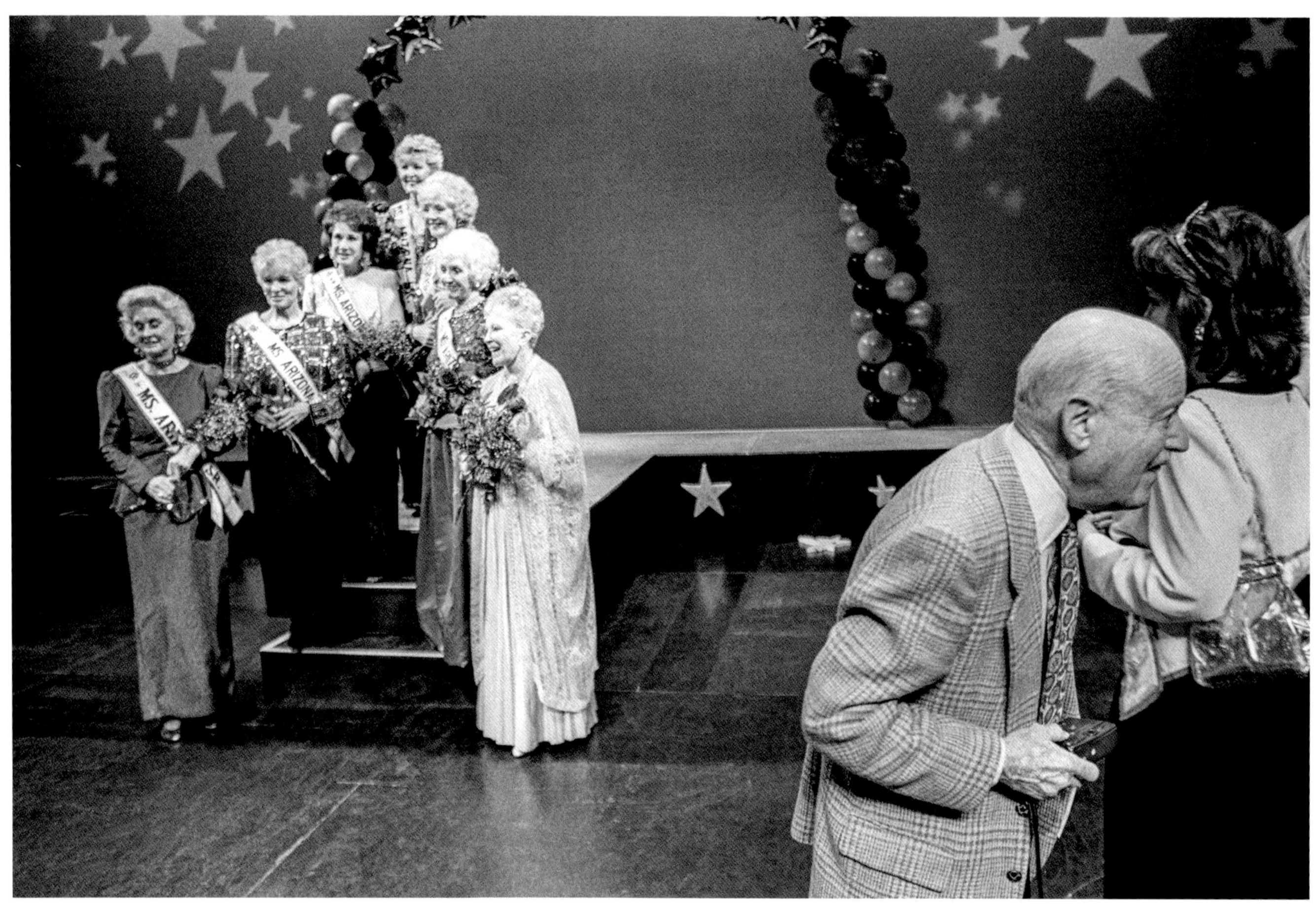

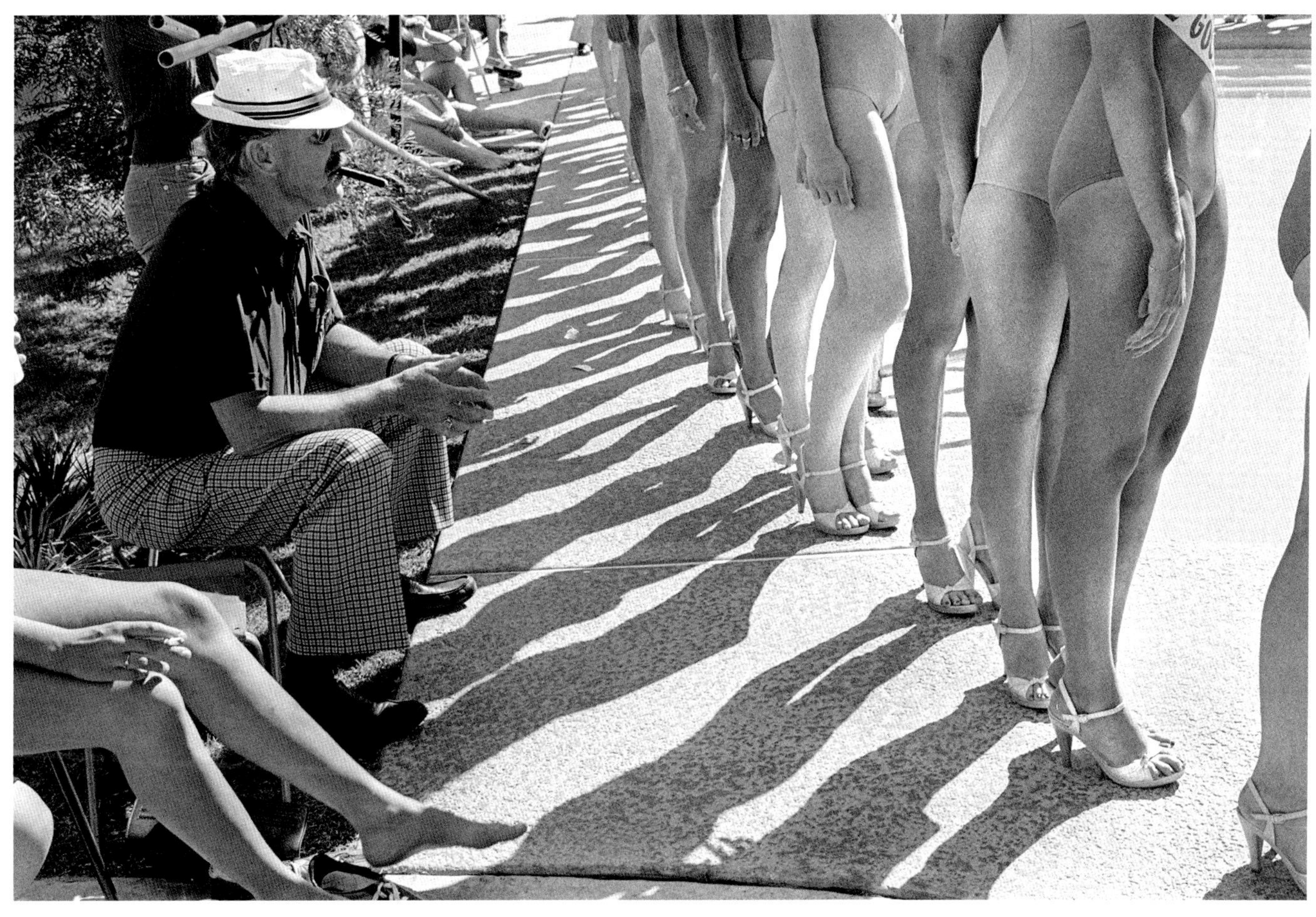

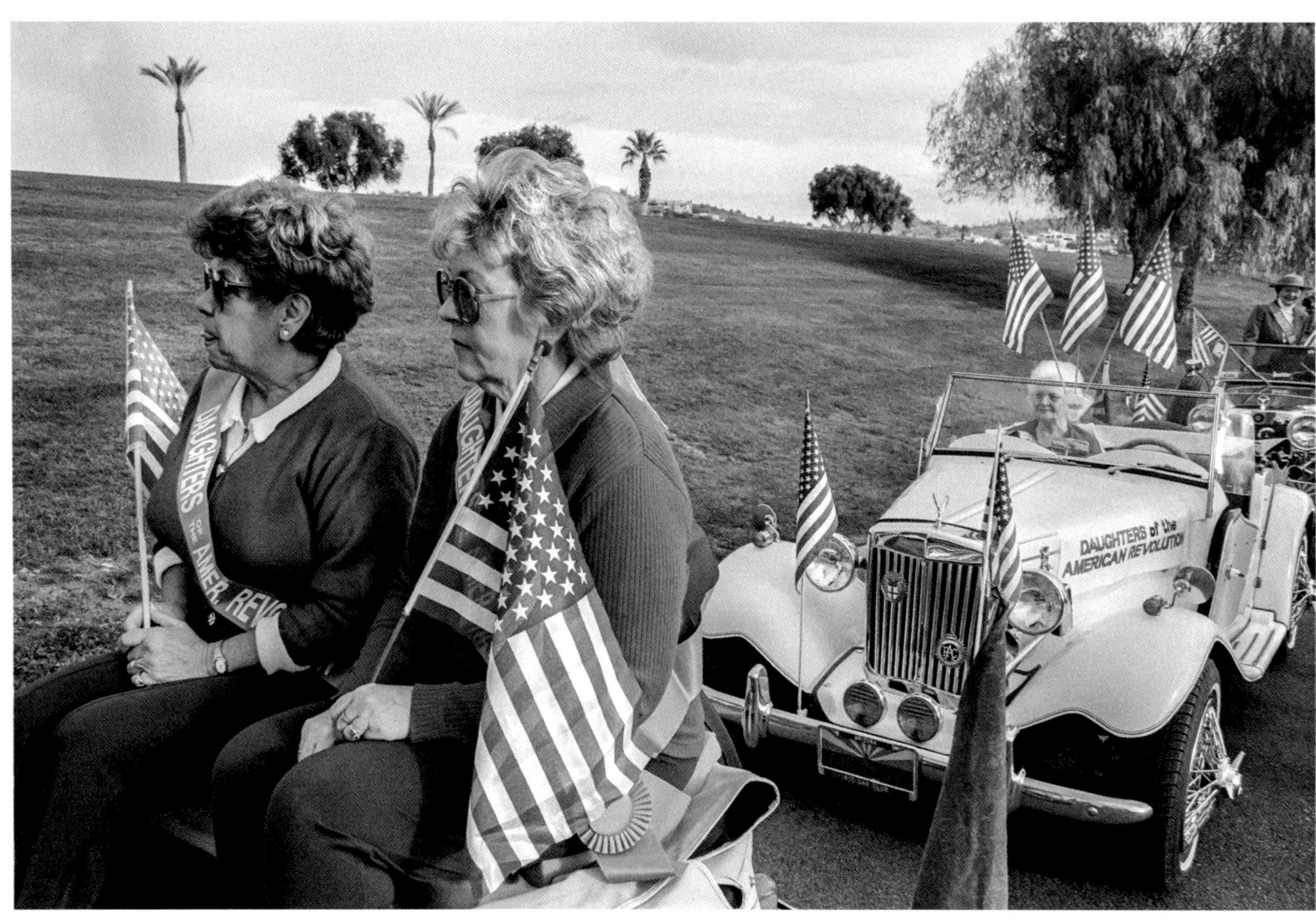

DAUGHTERS
OF THE
AMER. REVO
DAUGHTERS of the
AMERICAN REVOLUTION

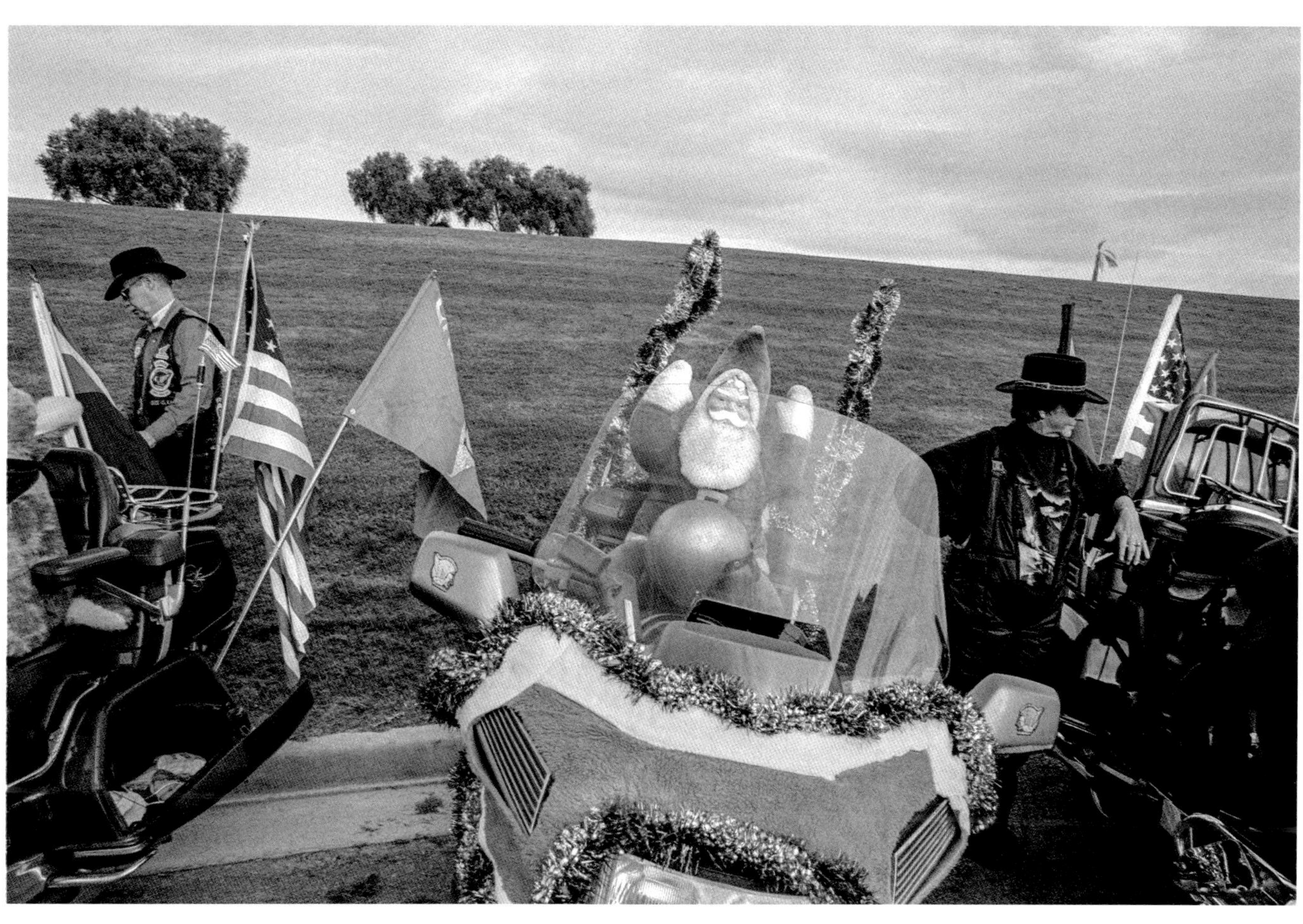

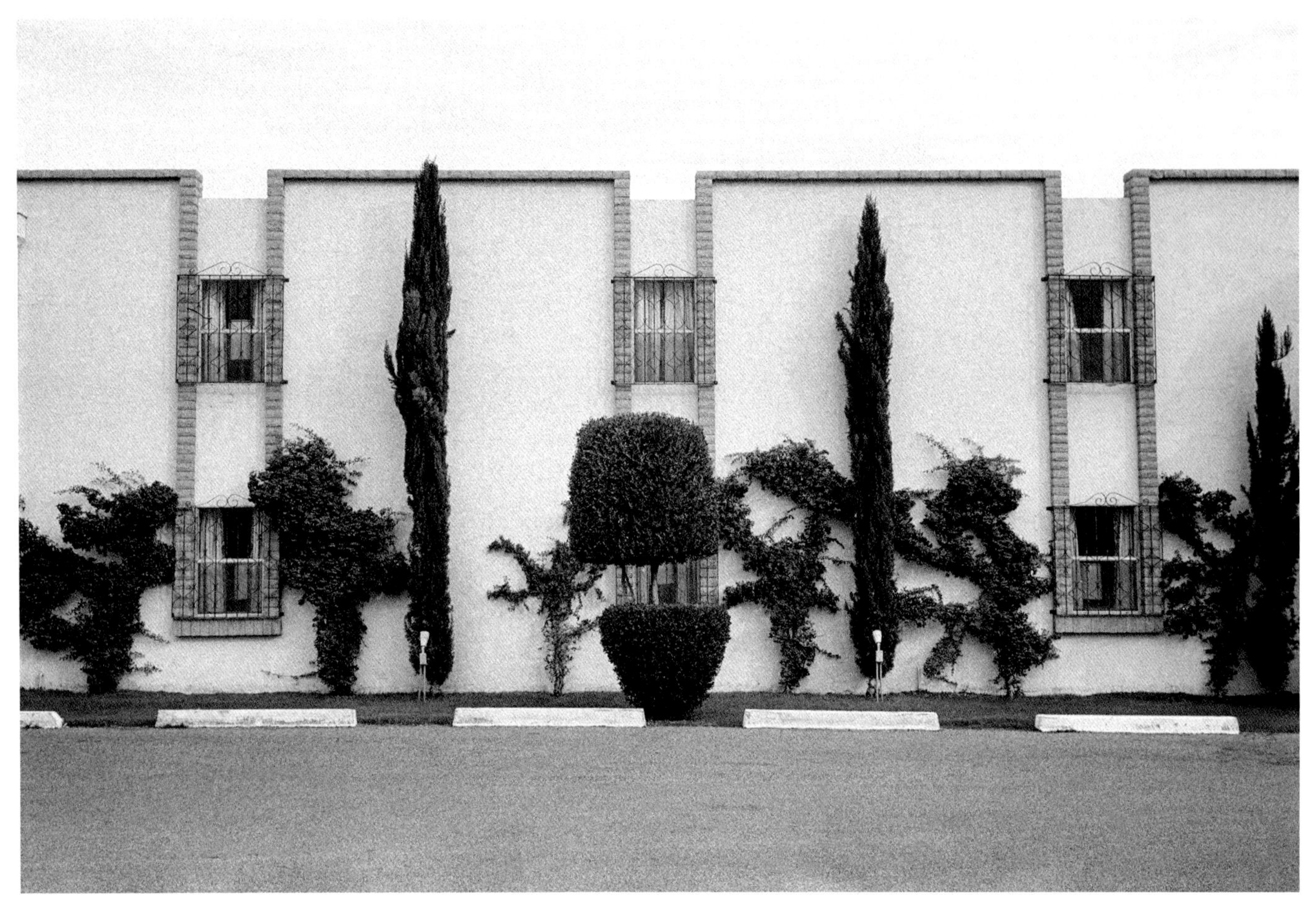

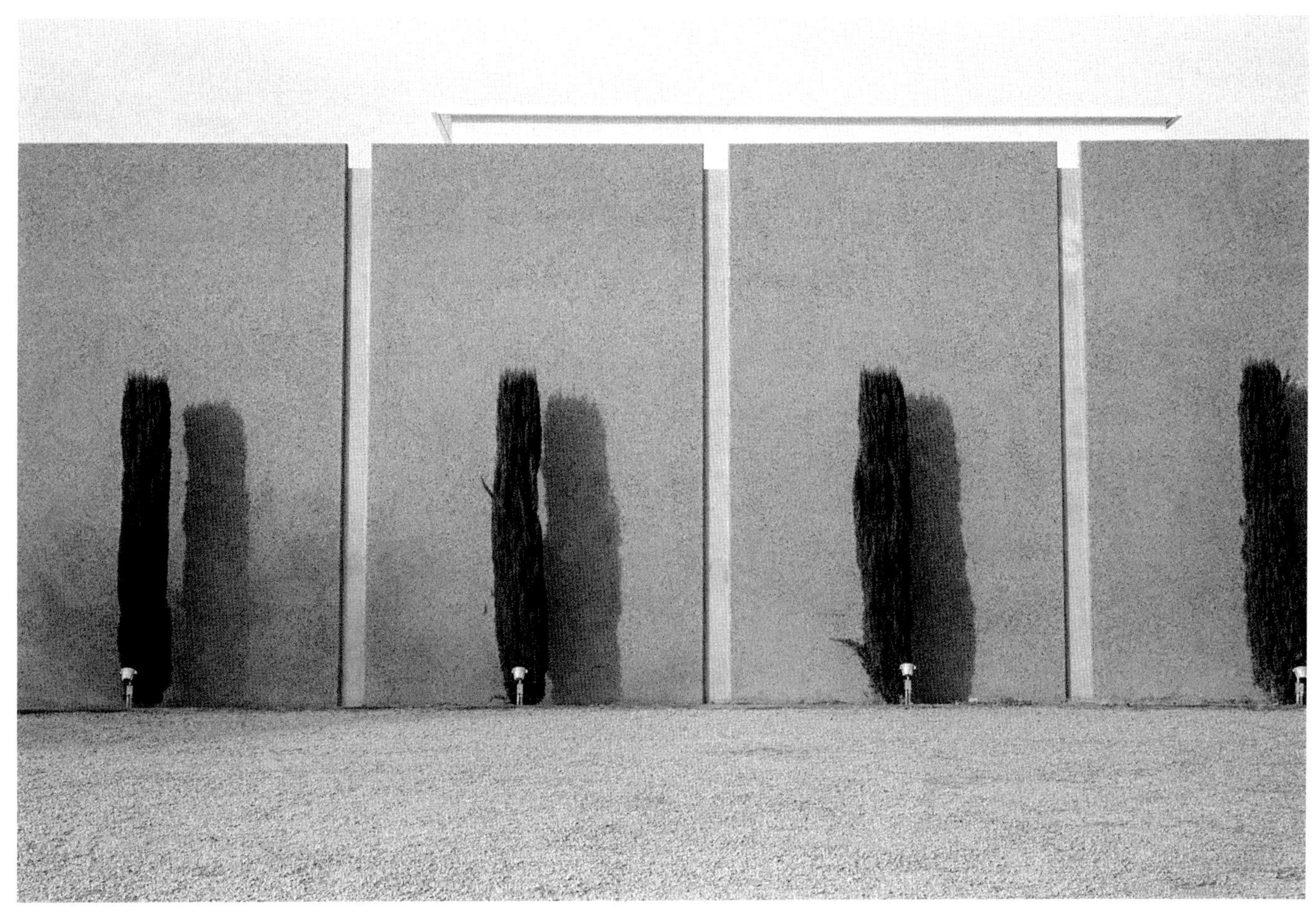

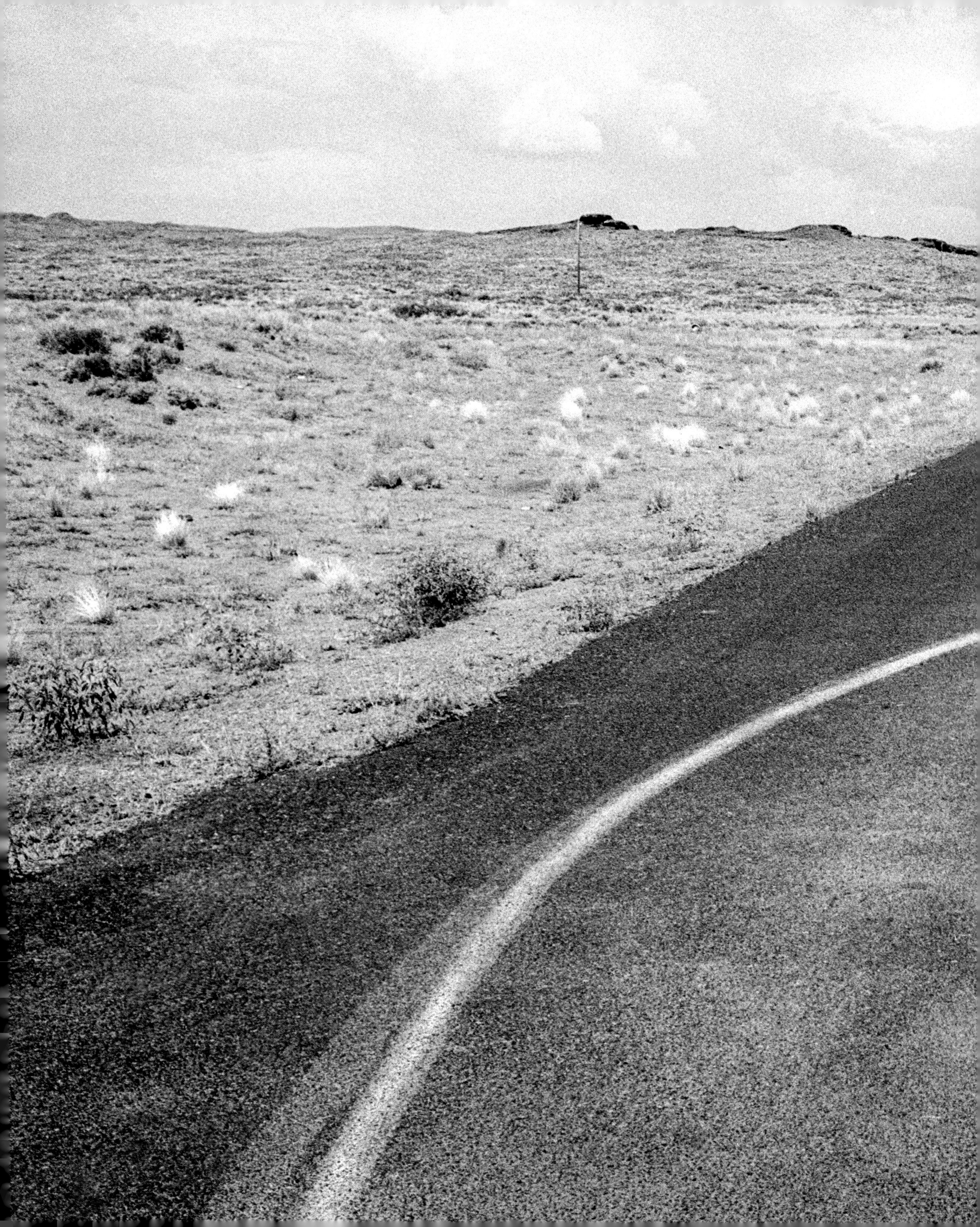

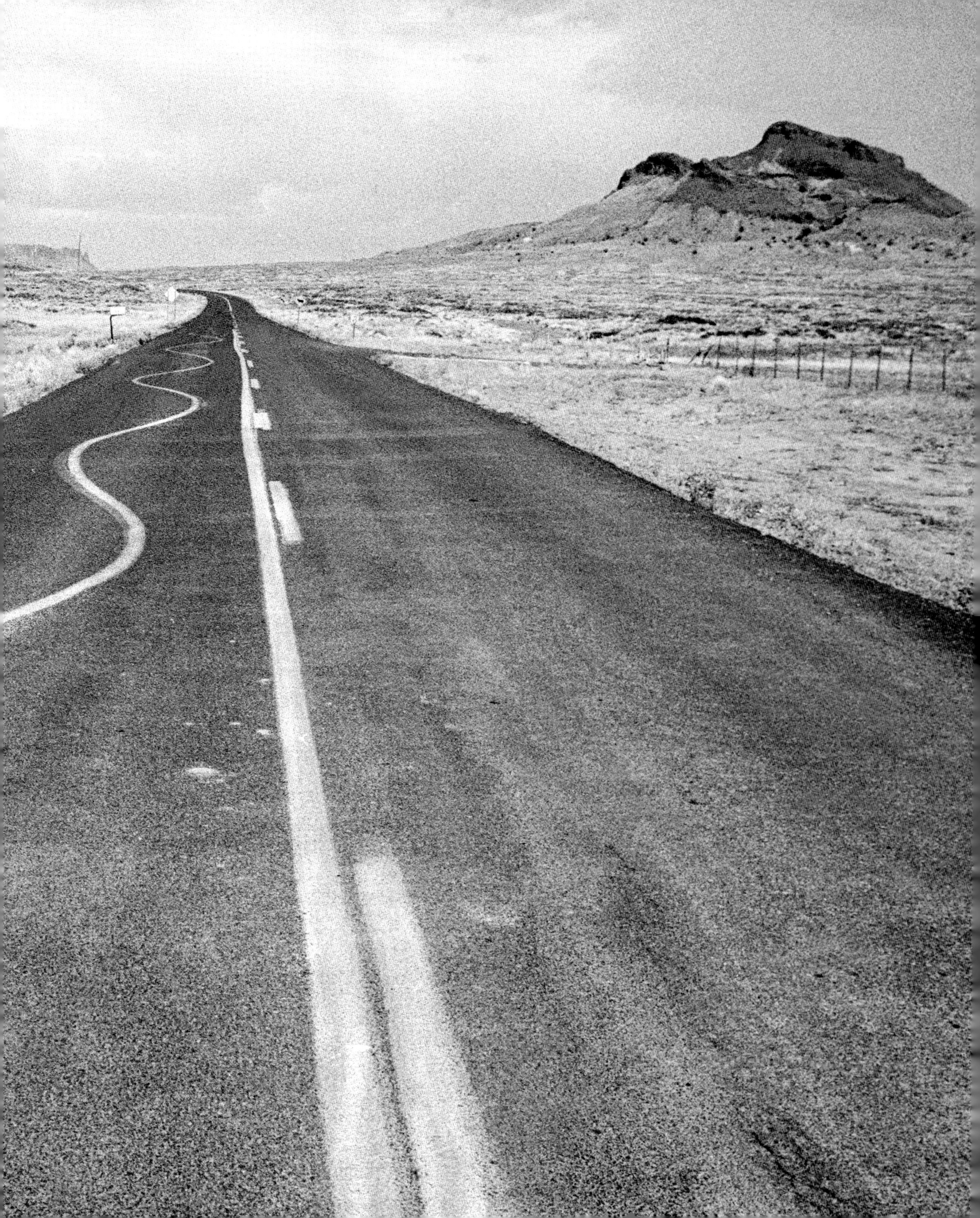

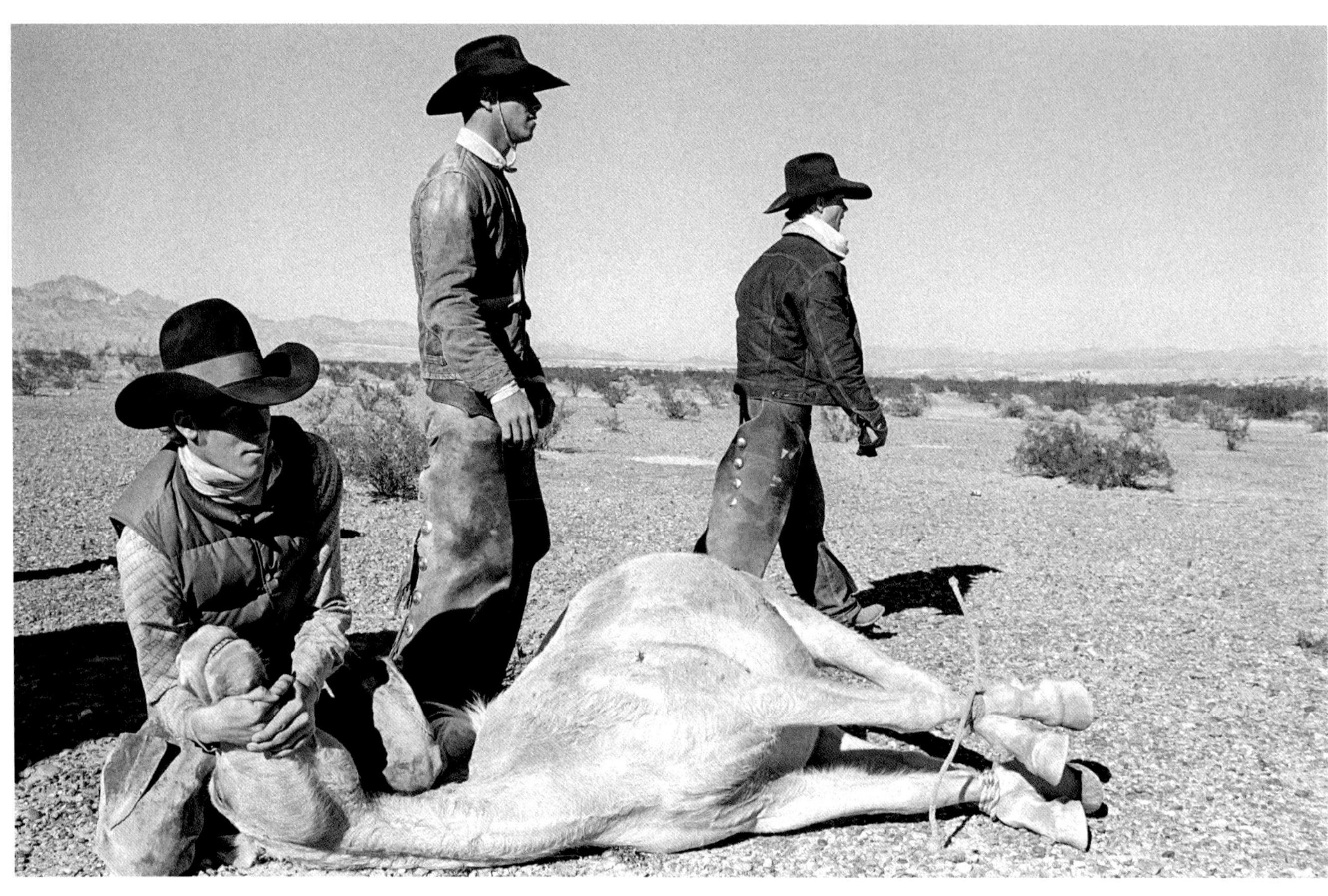

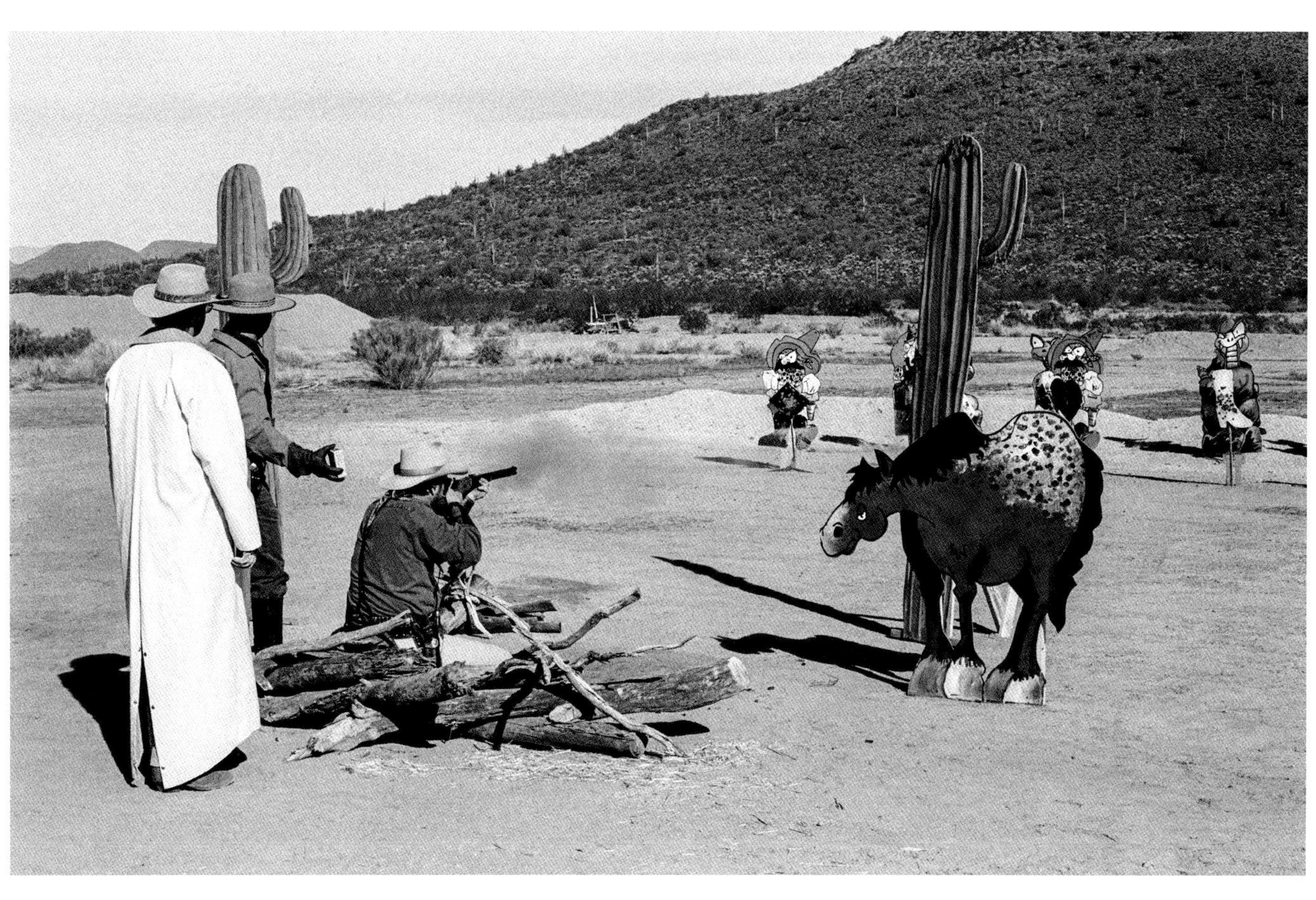

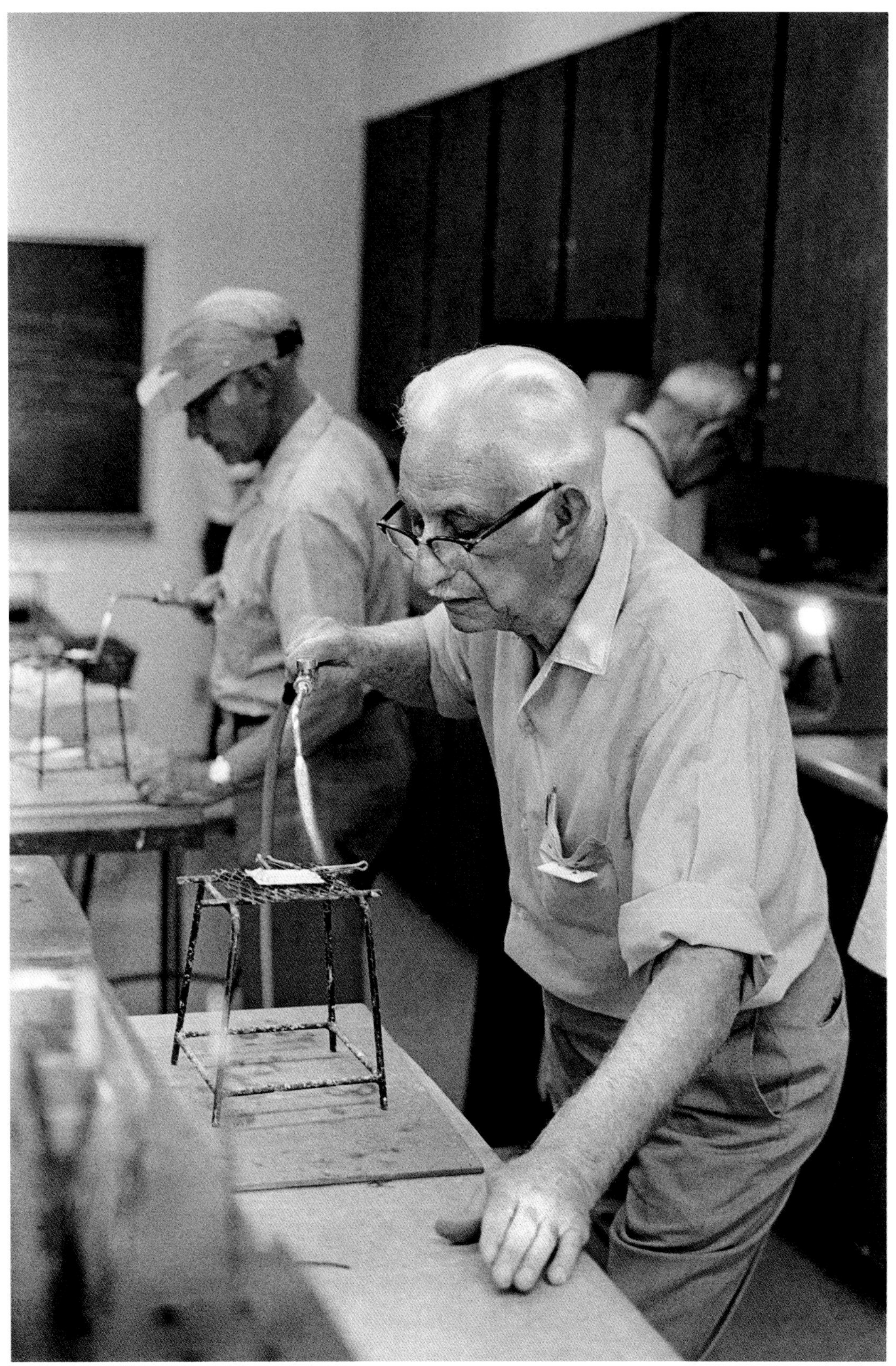

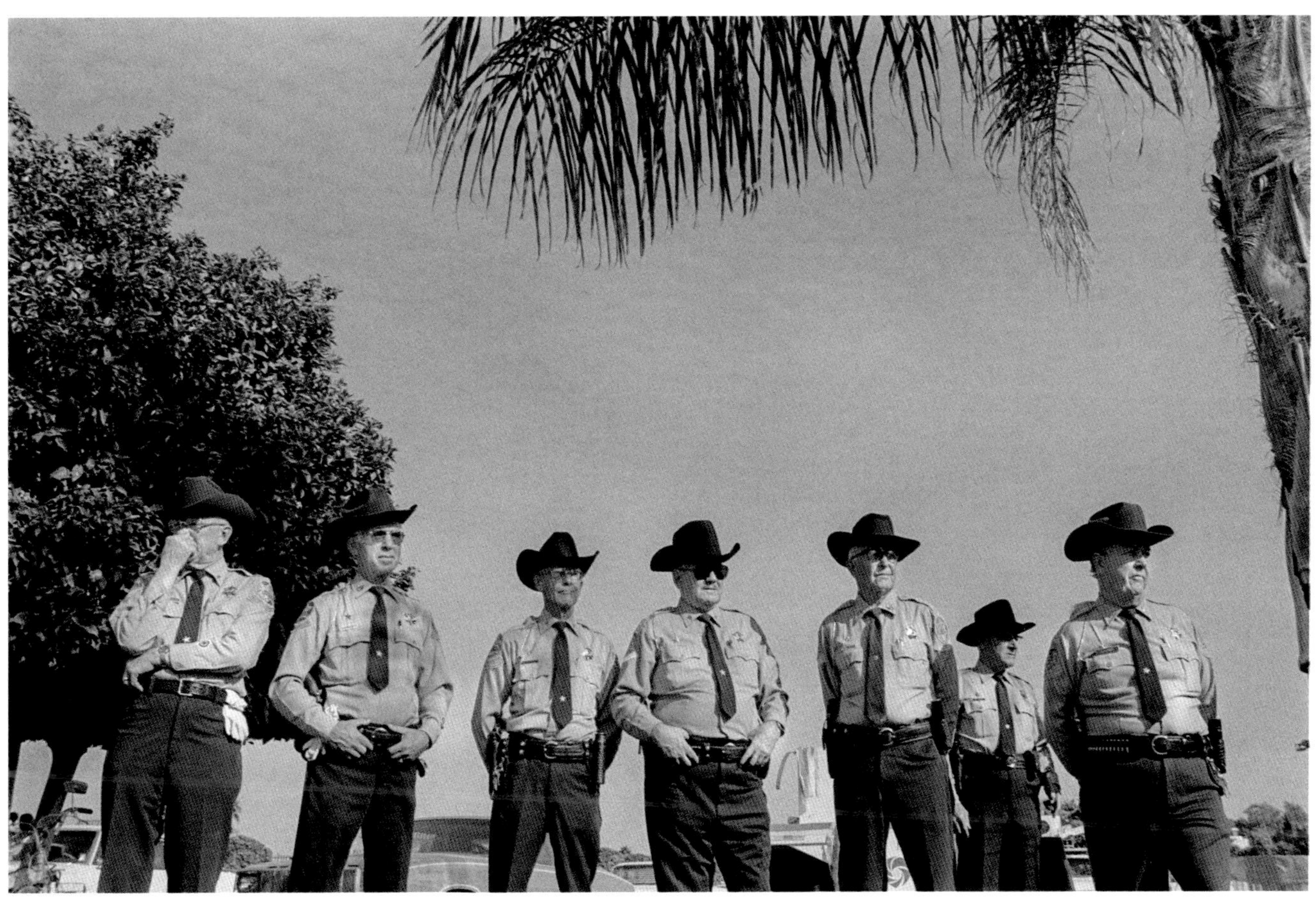

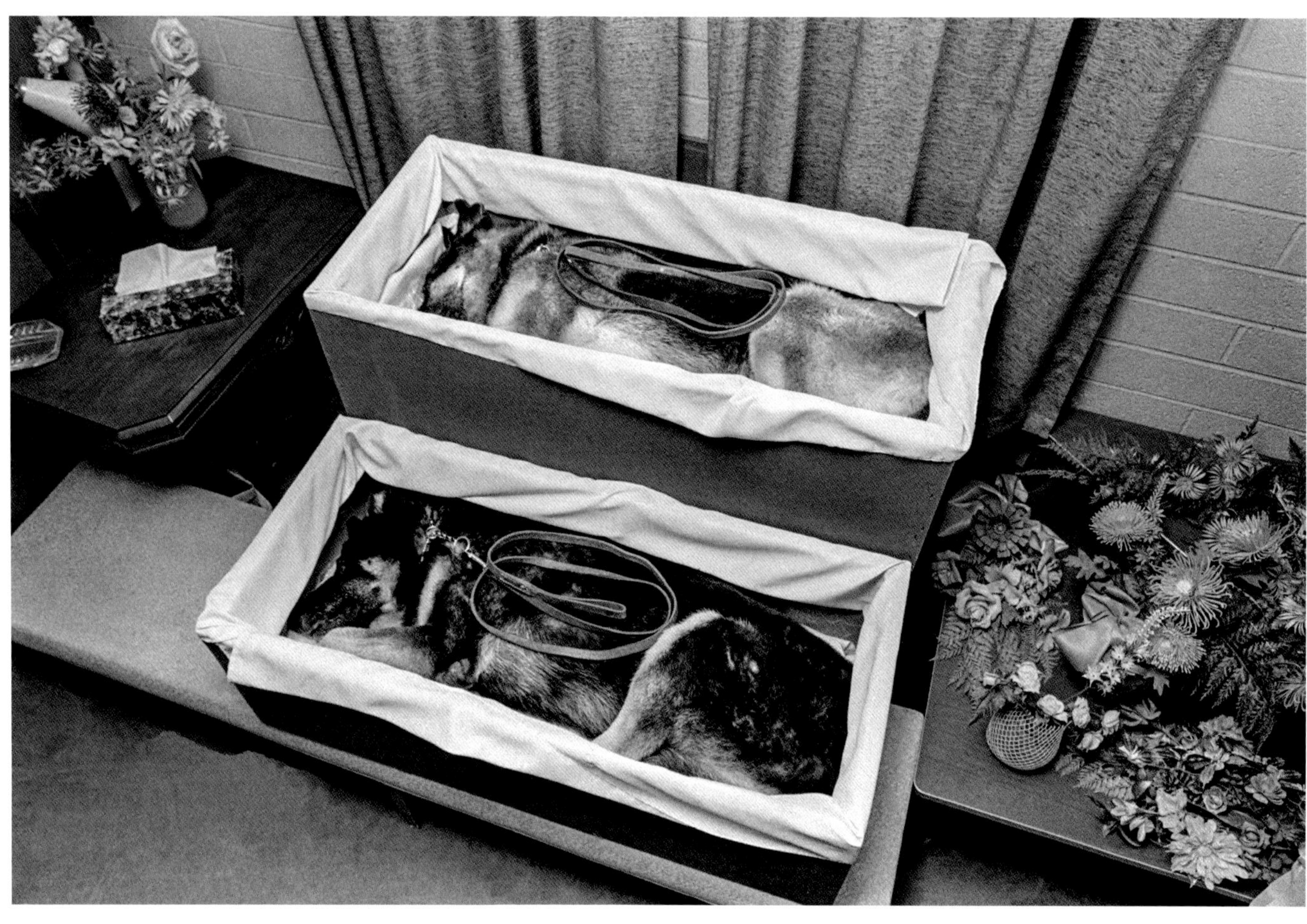

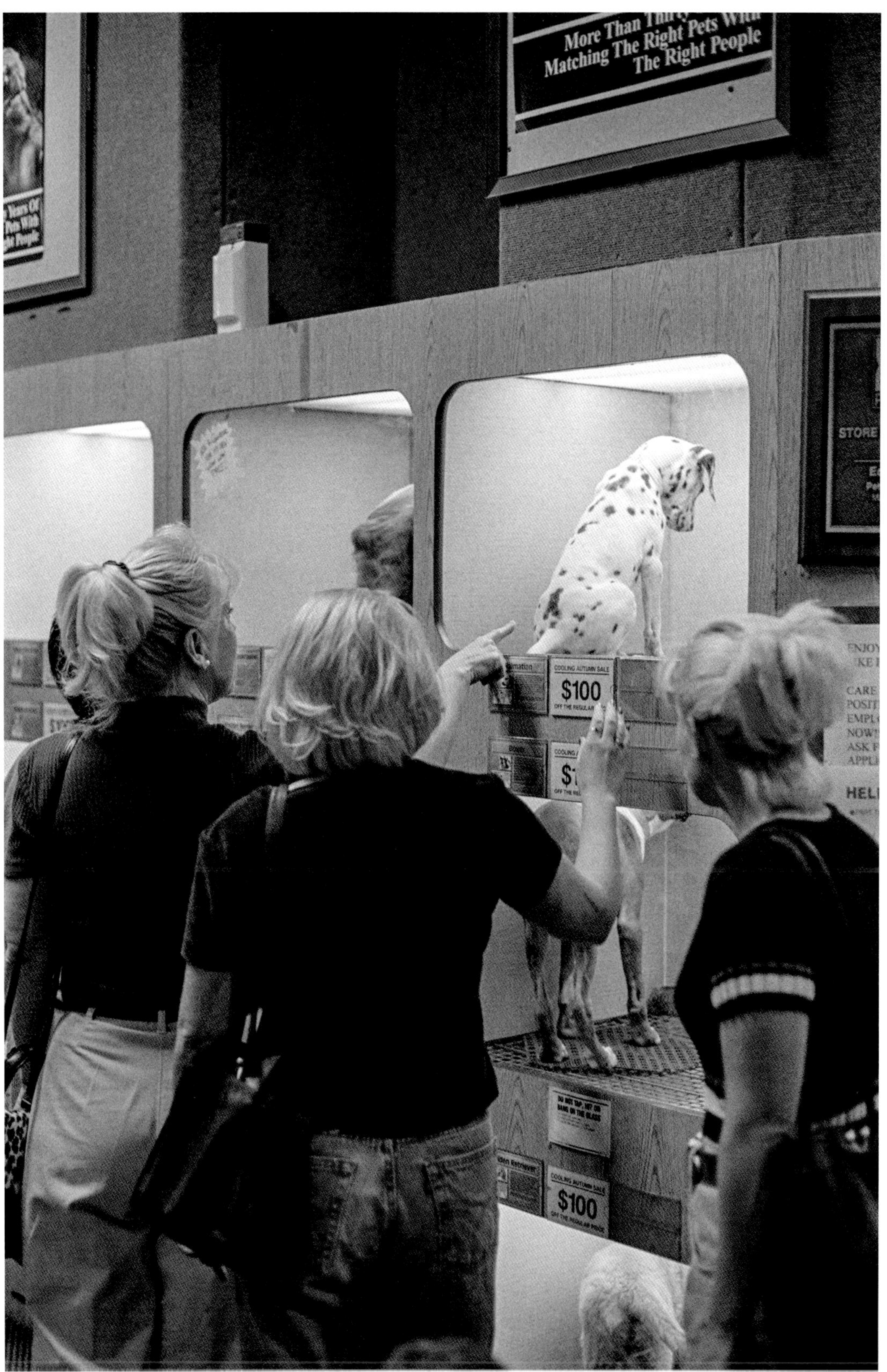

More Than Thirty Years Of
Matching The Right Pets With
The Right People
$100
$100

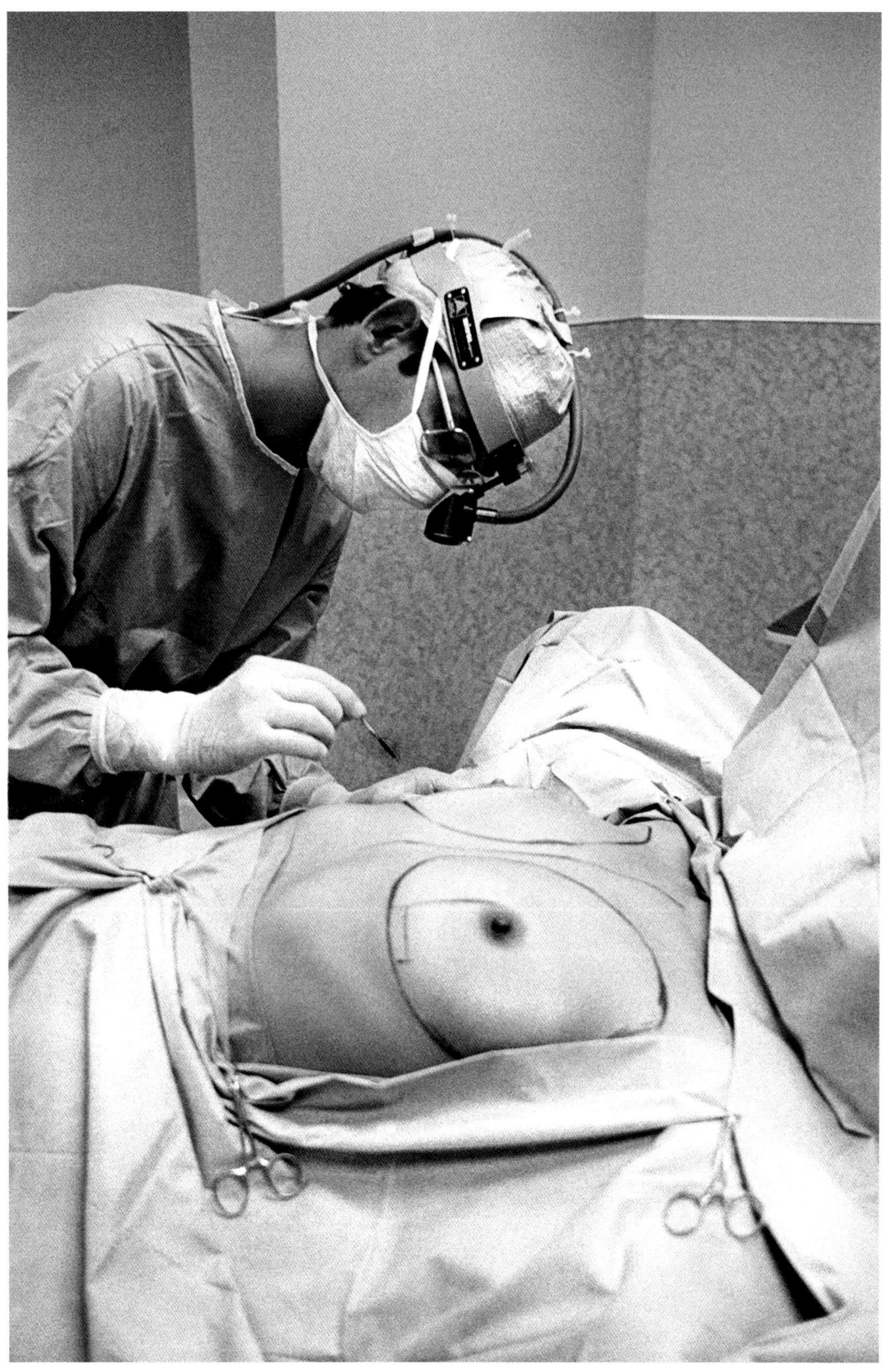

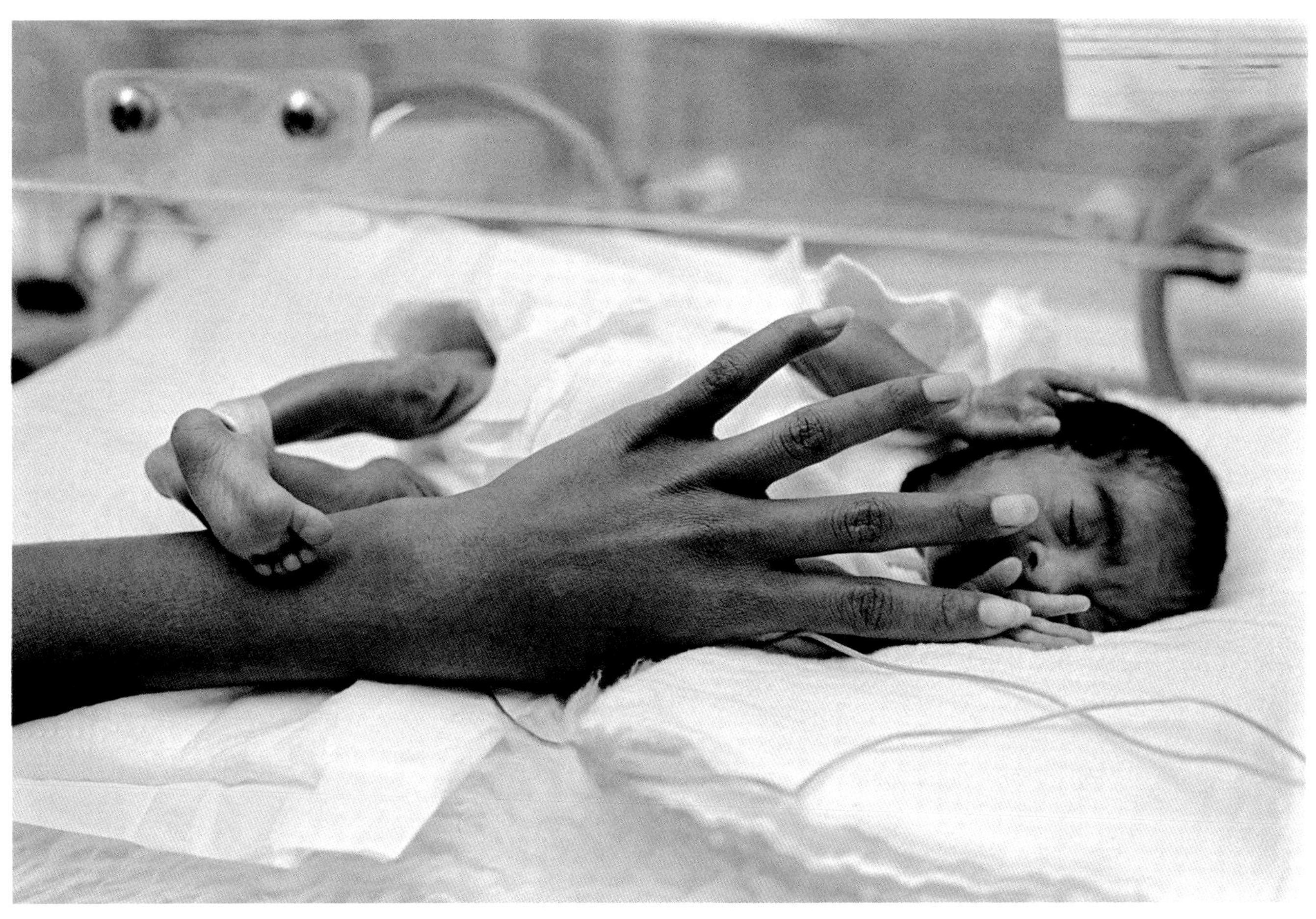

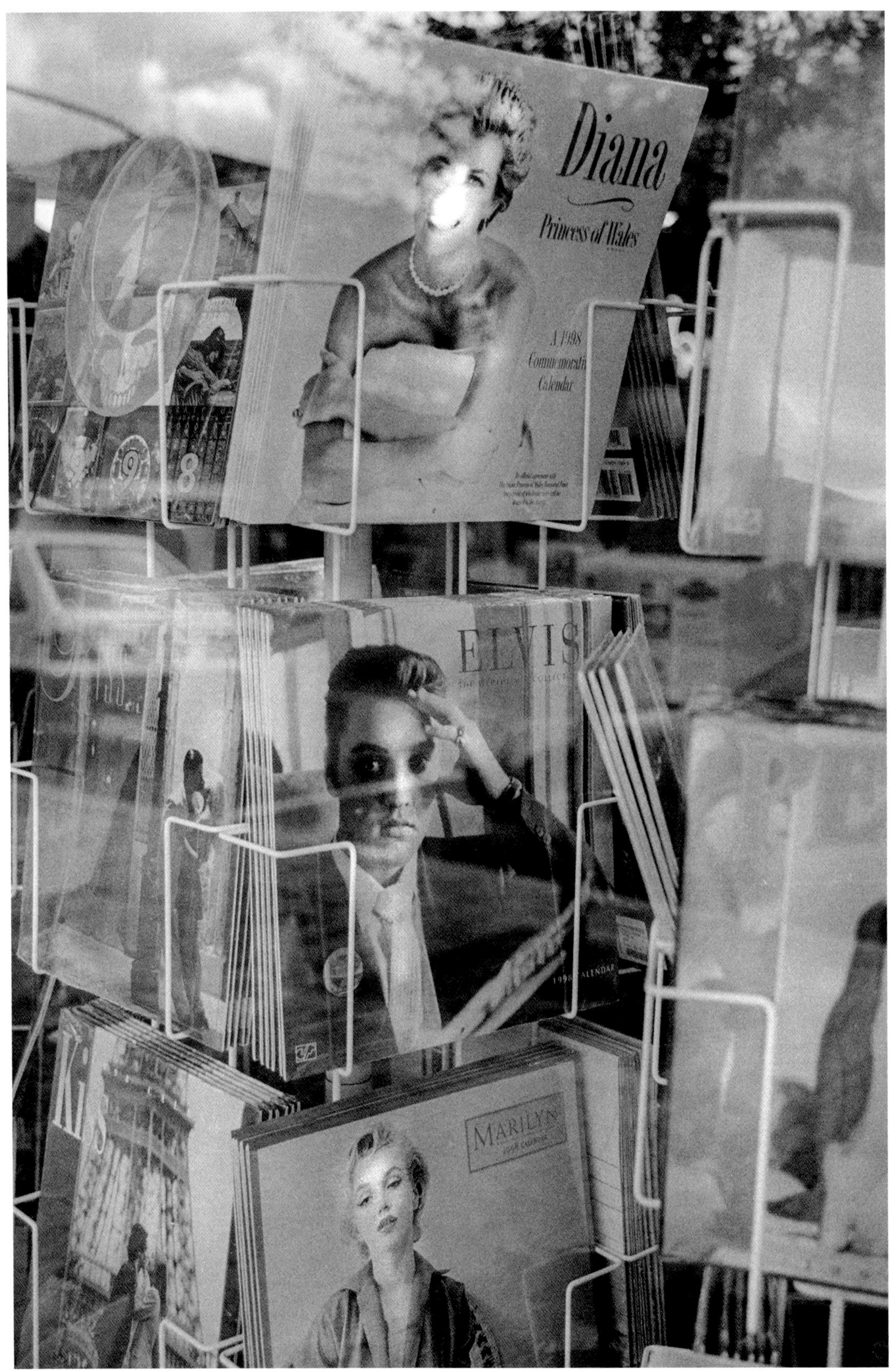

Diana
Princess of Wales
A 1998
Commemorative
Calendar
ELVIS
MARILYN

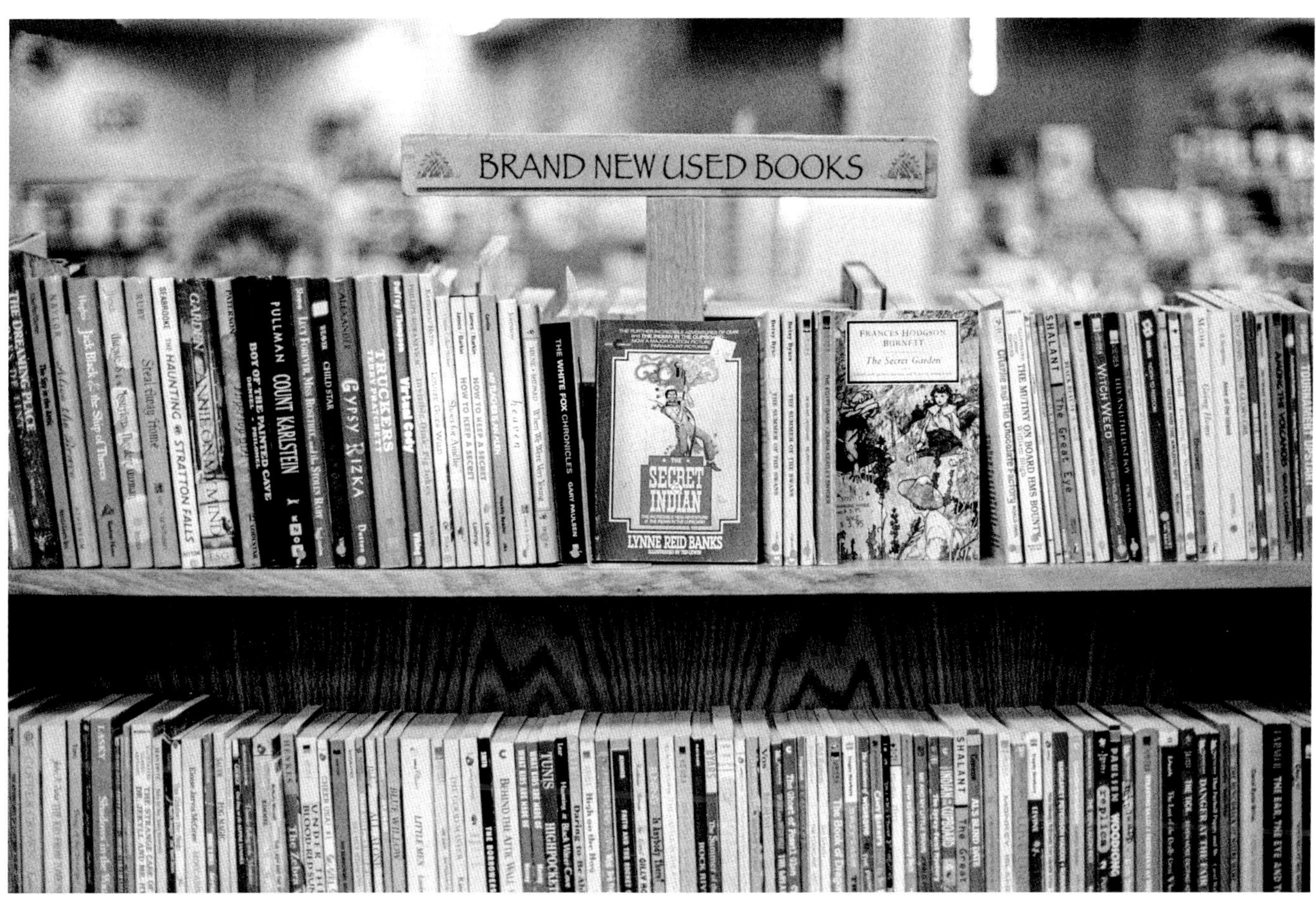

BRAND NEW USED BOOKS

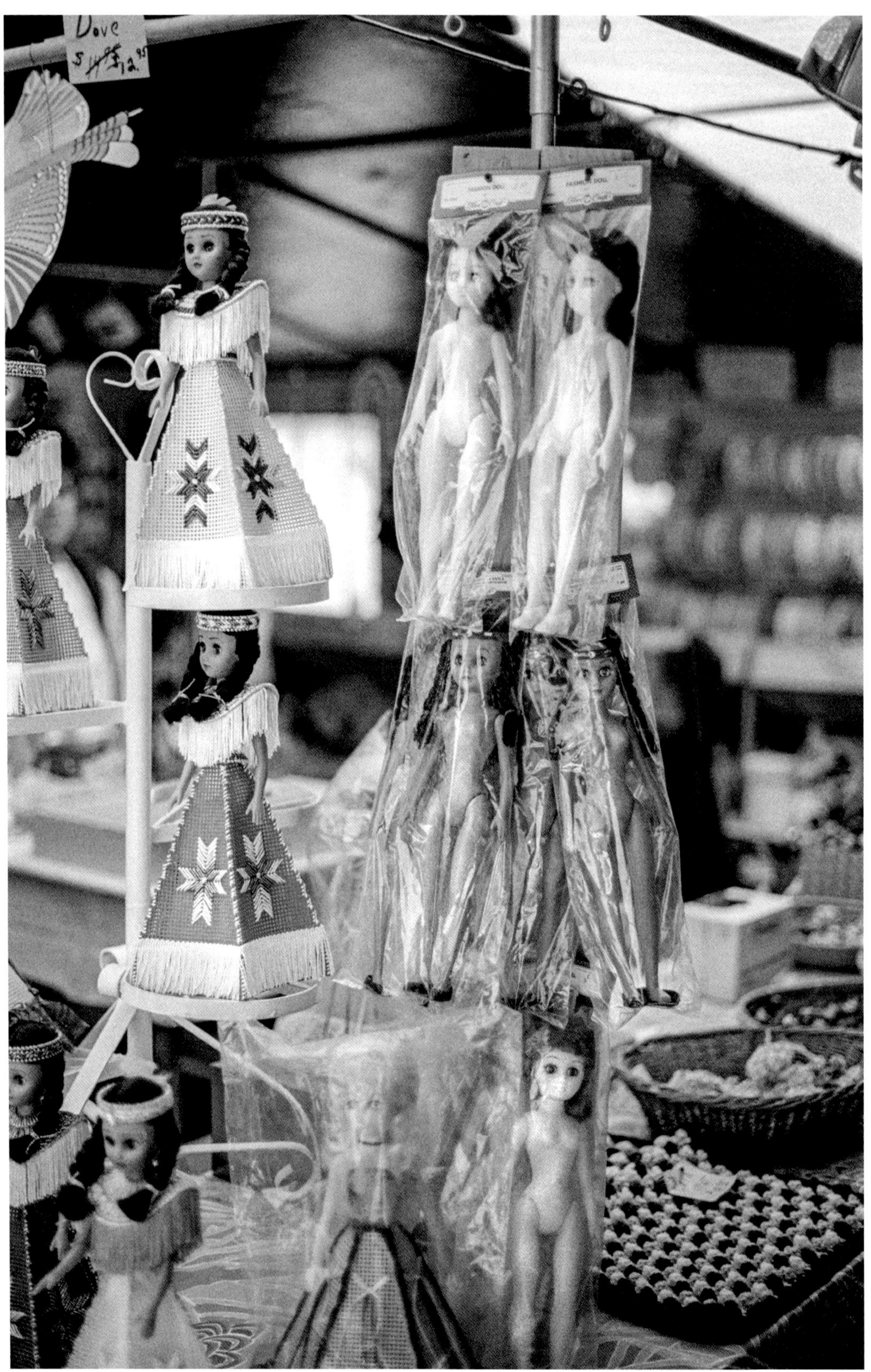

Dove
S 4.98
12.99
FASHION DOLL
FASHION DOLL

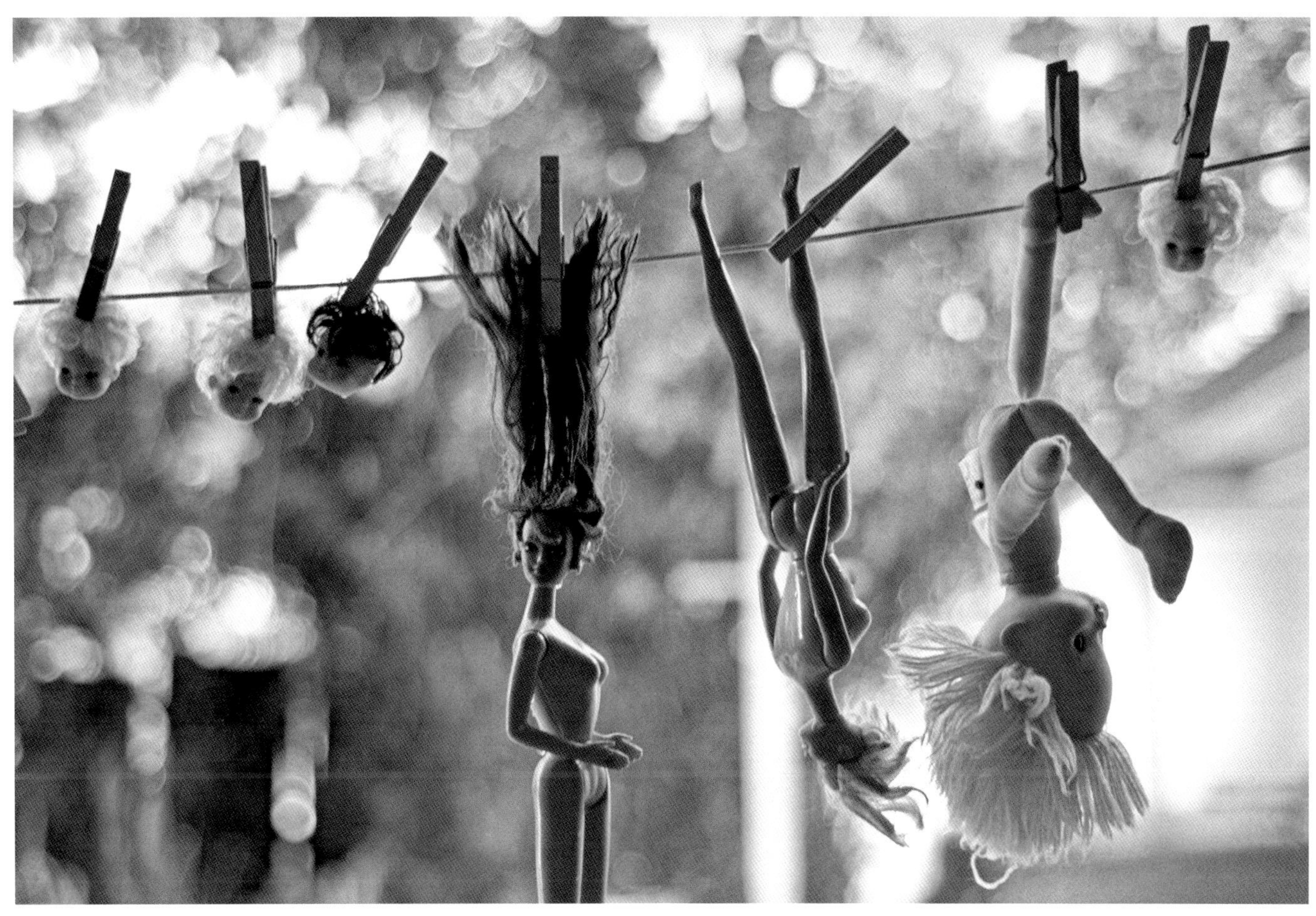

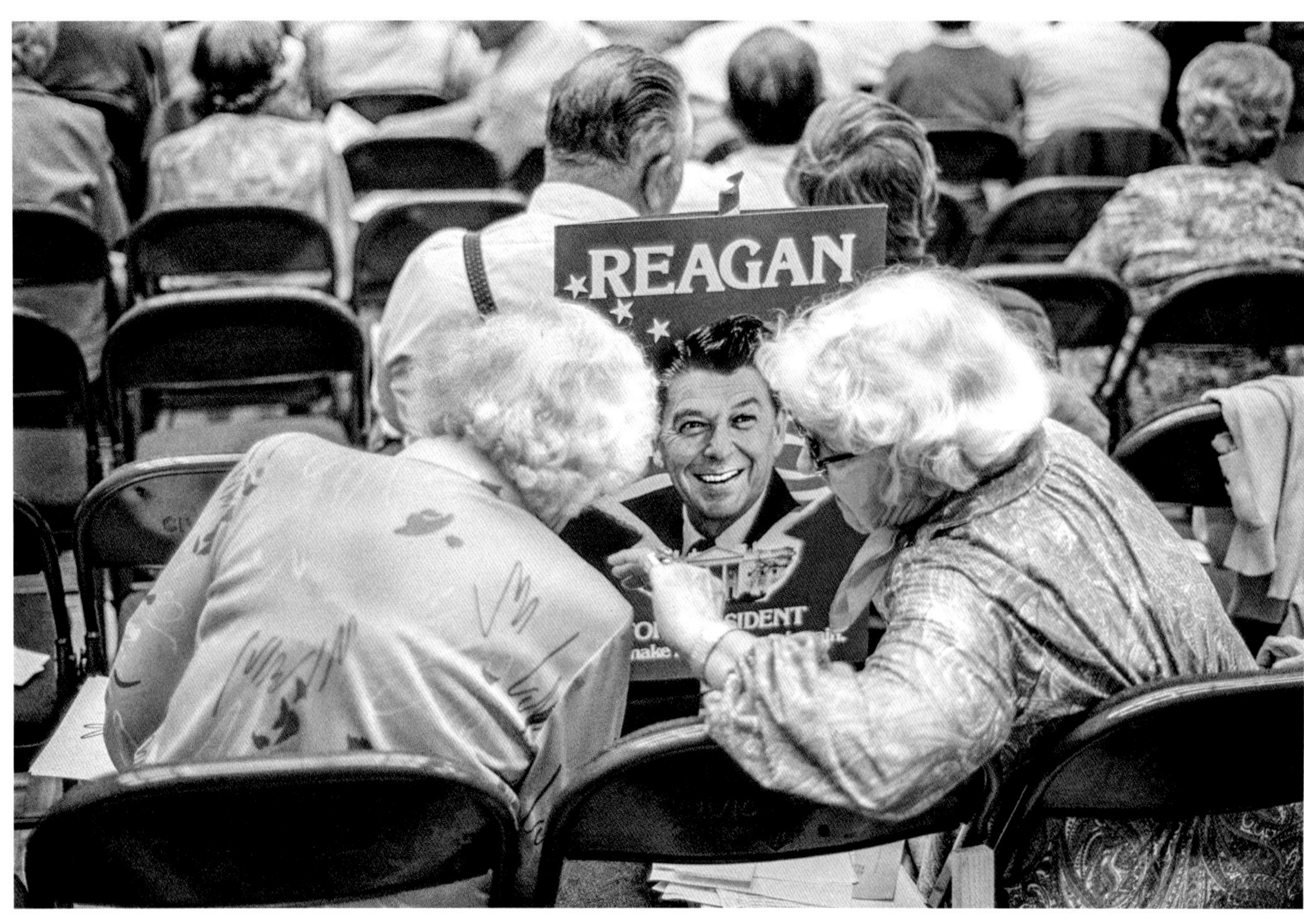

REAGAN
FOR PRESIDENT

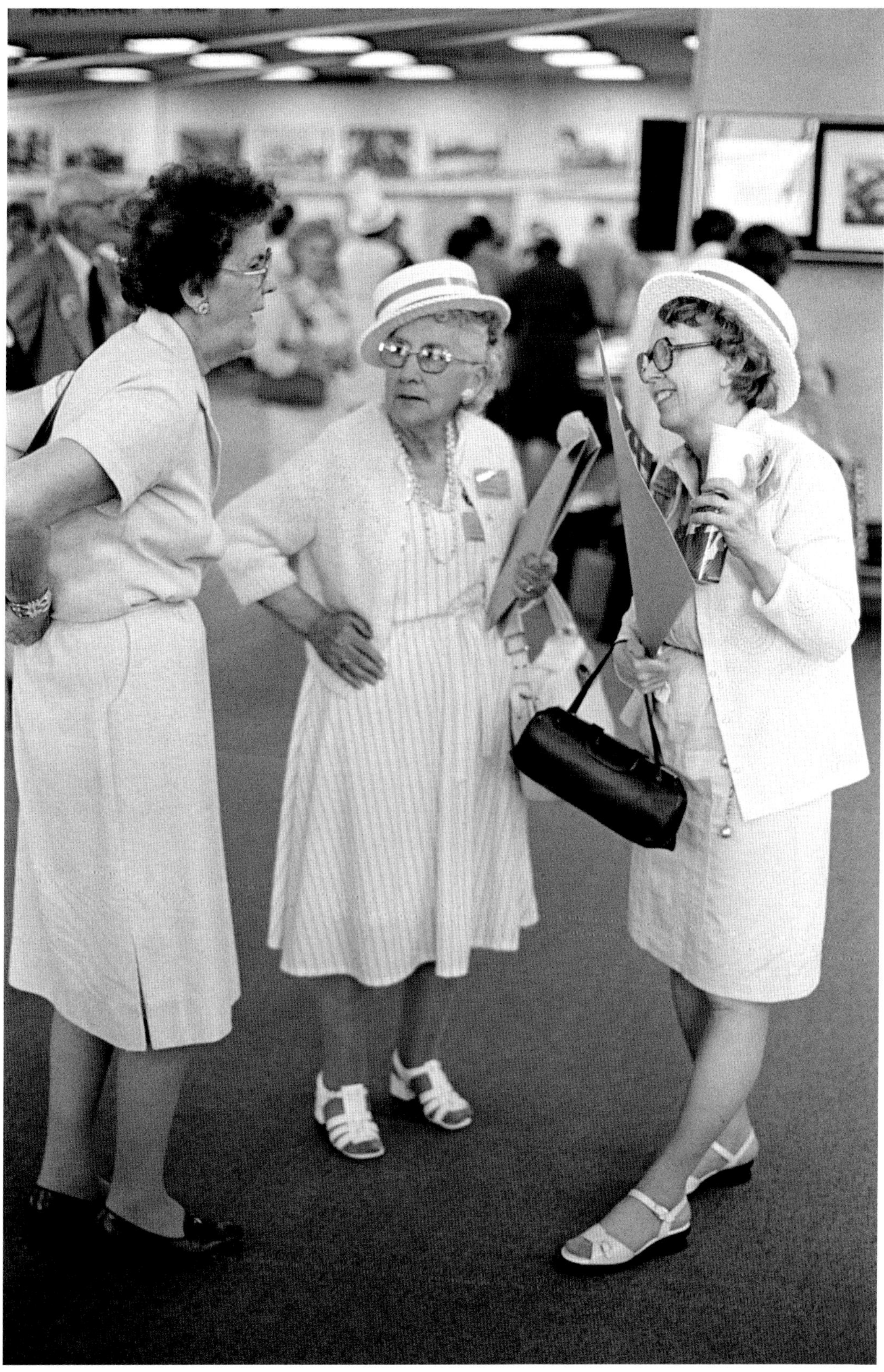

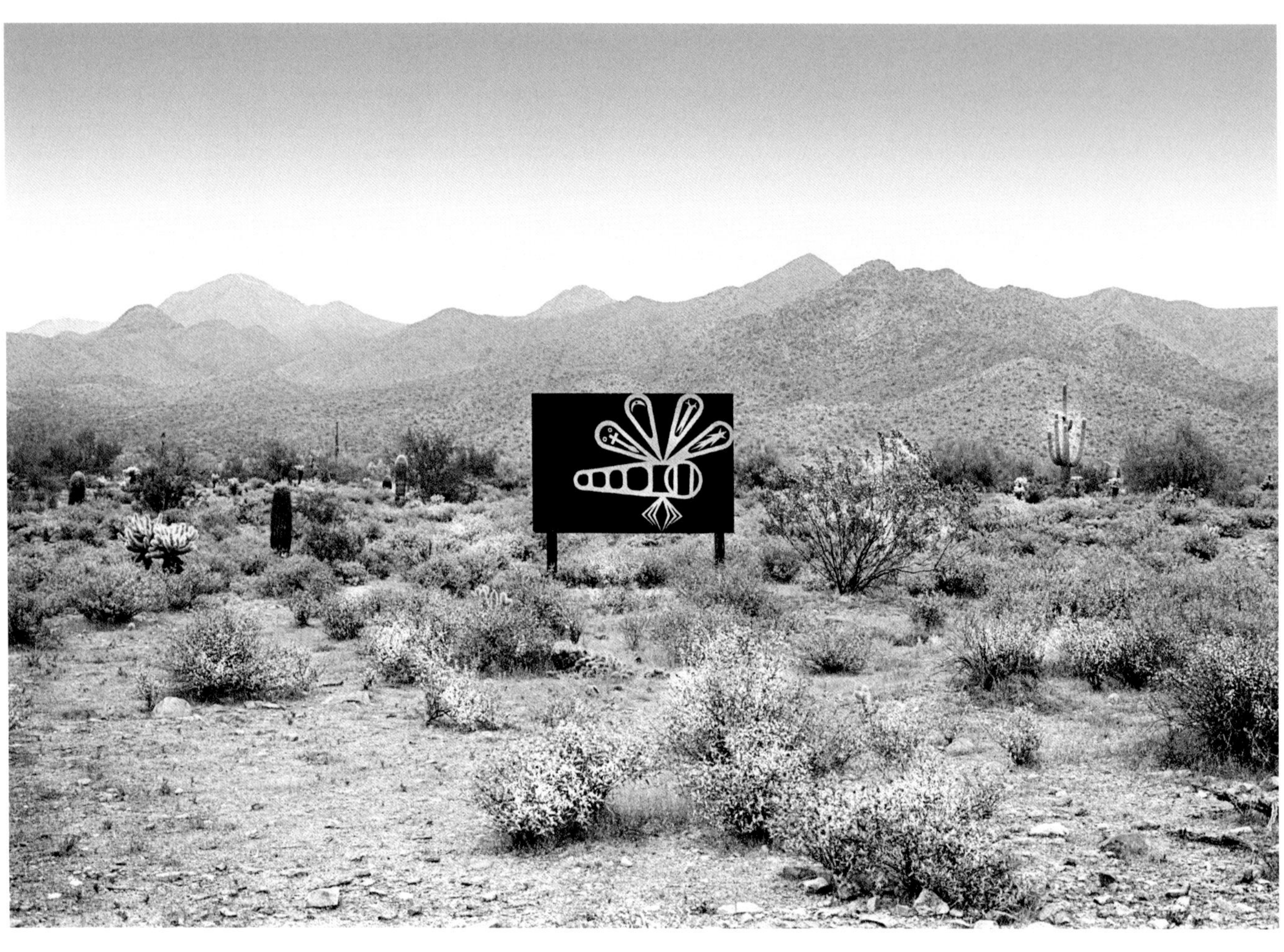

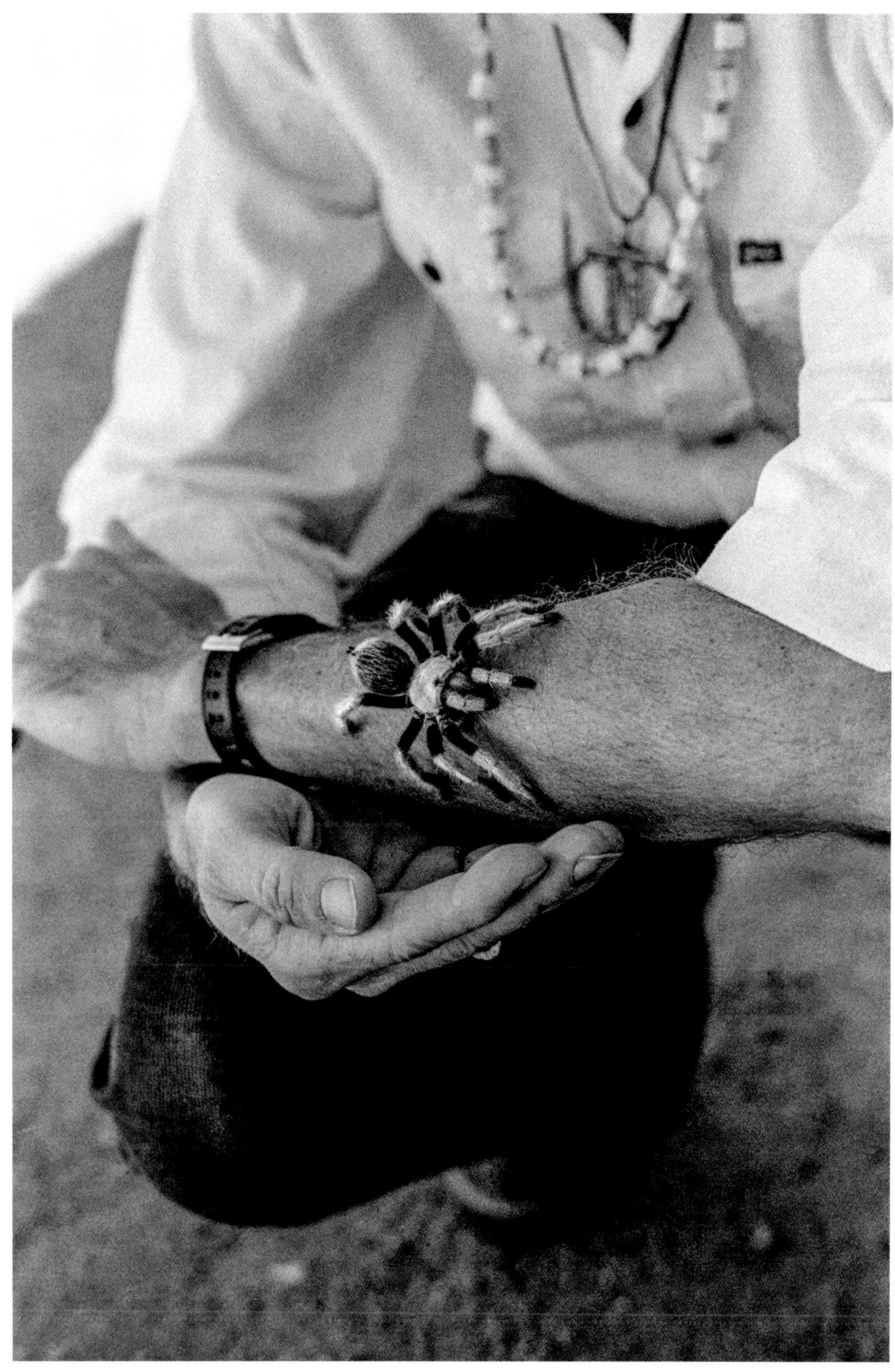

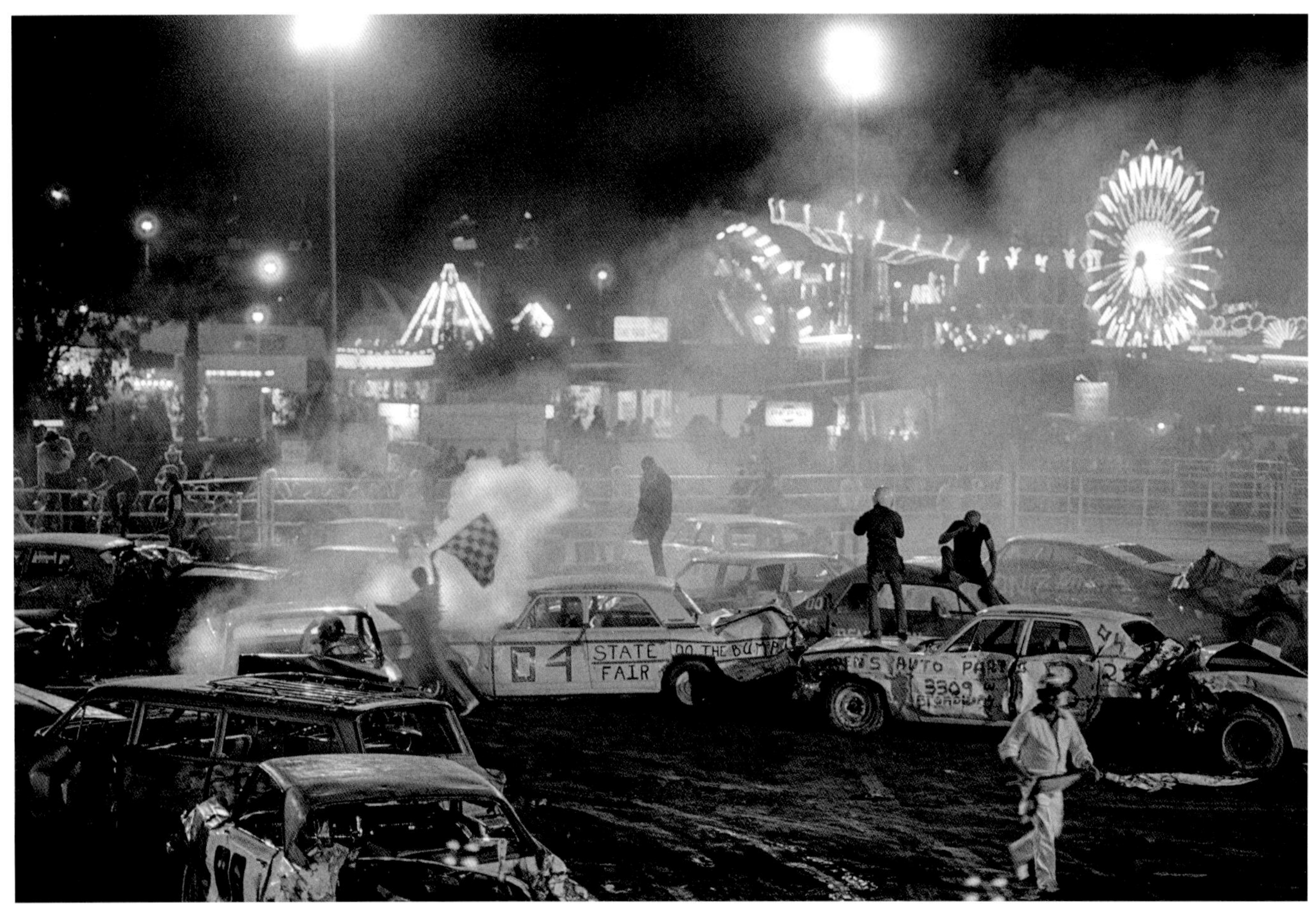

C 4
STATE
FAIR
DO THE BUT
AUTO PARTS
3309 W

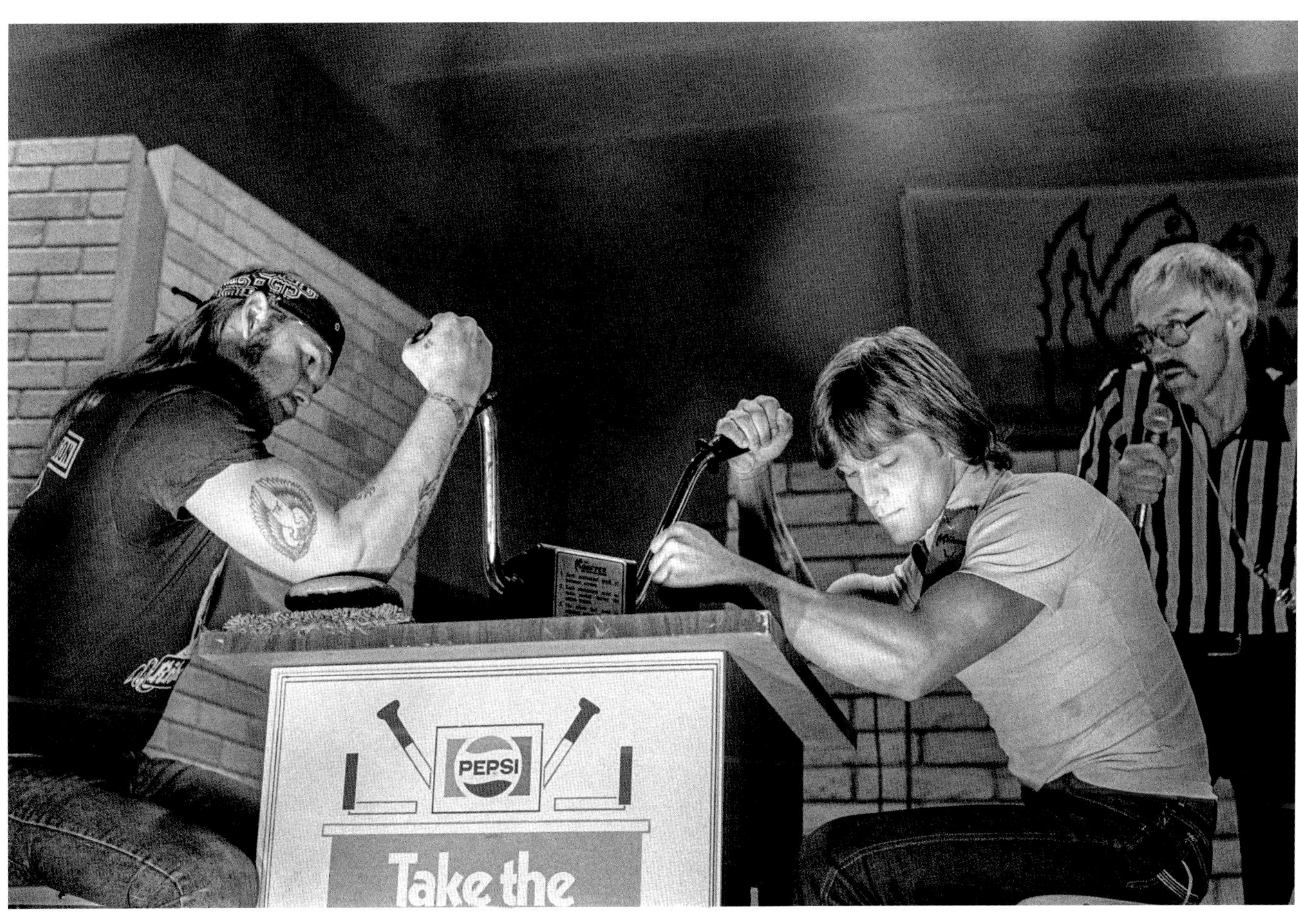

PEPSI
Take the

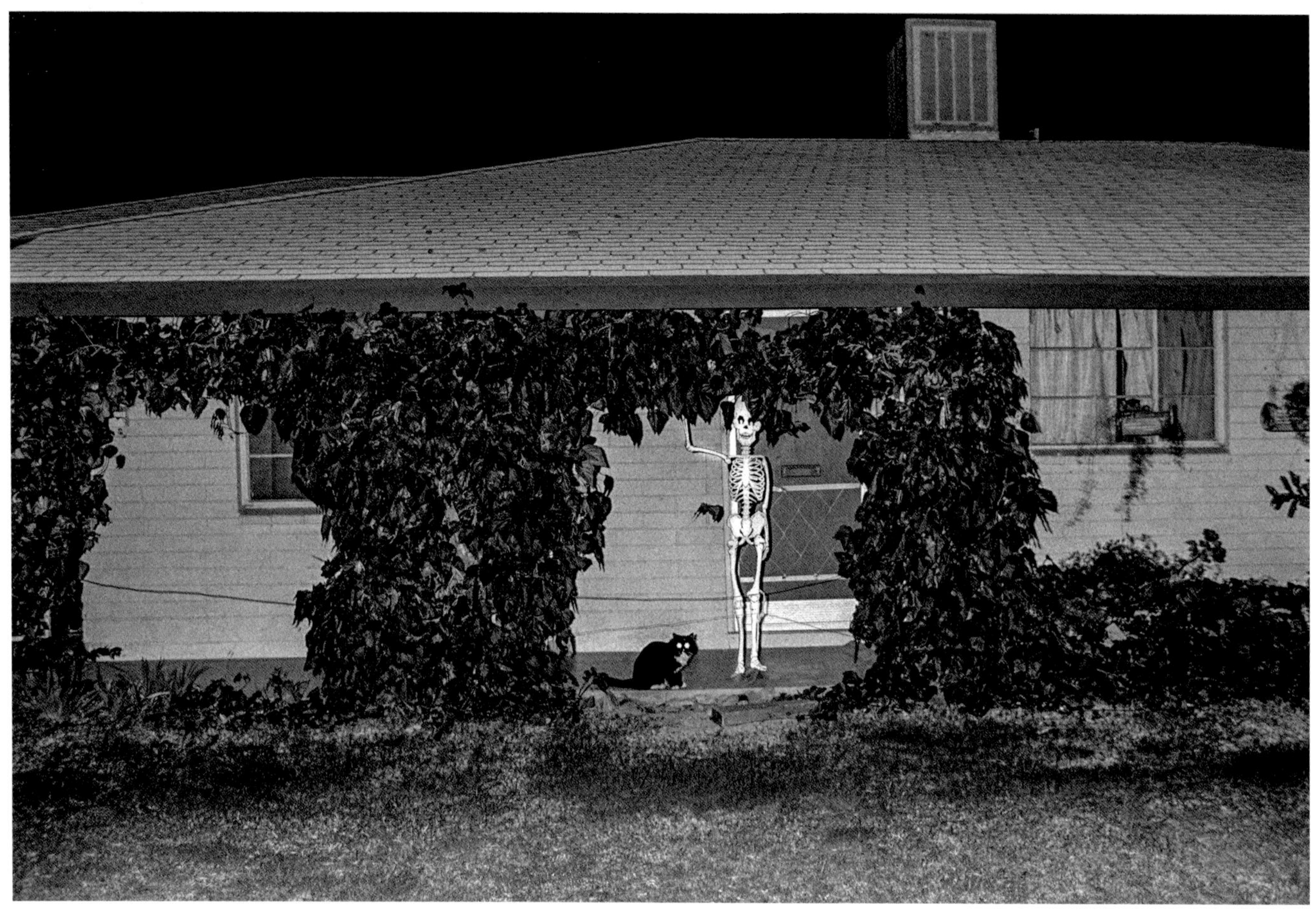

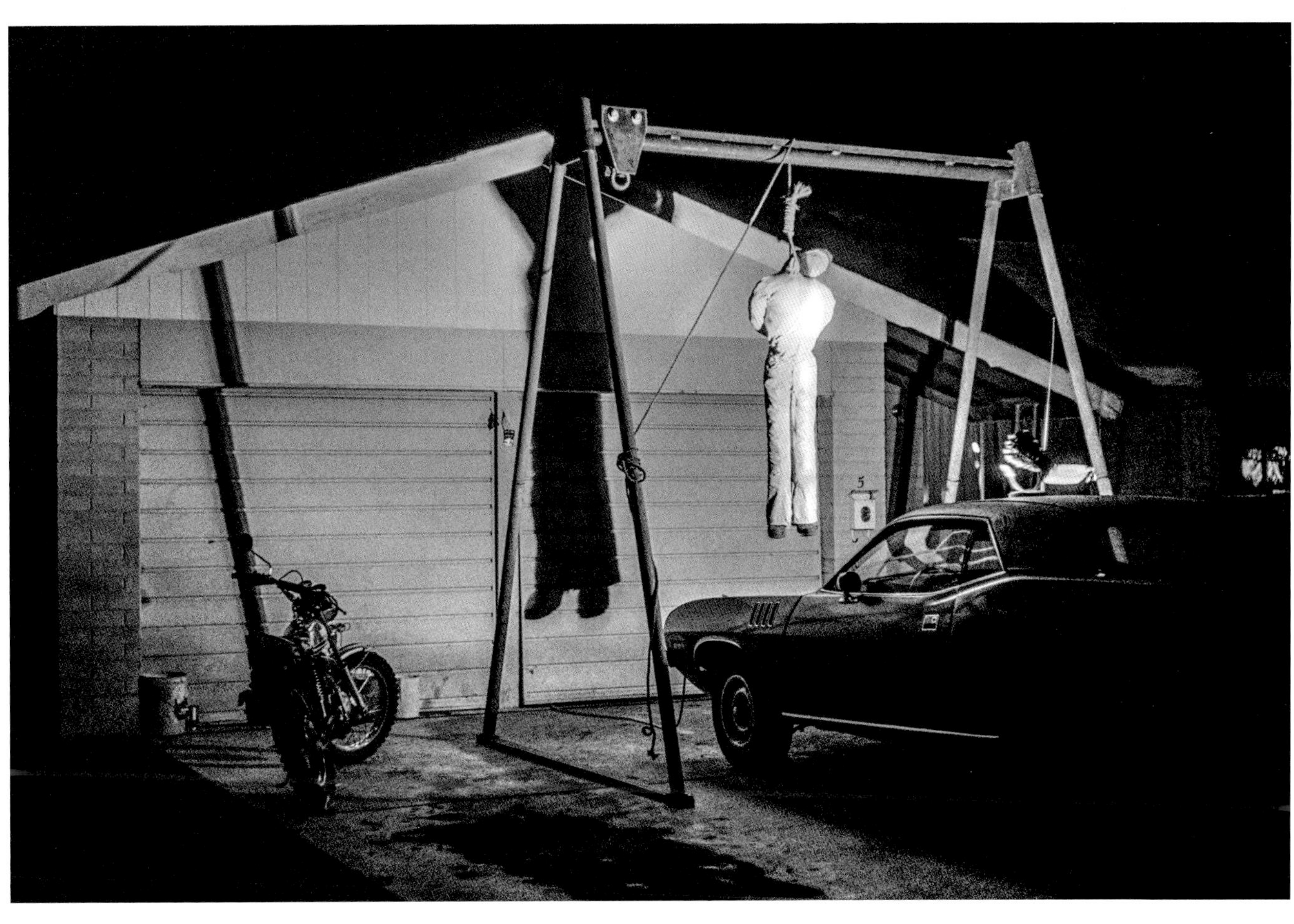

5

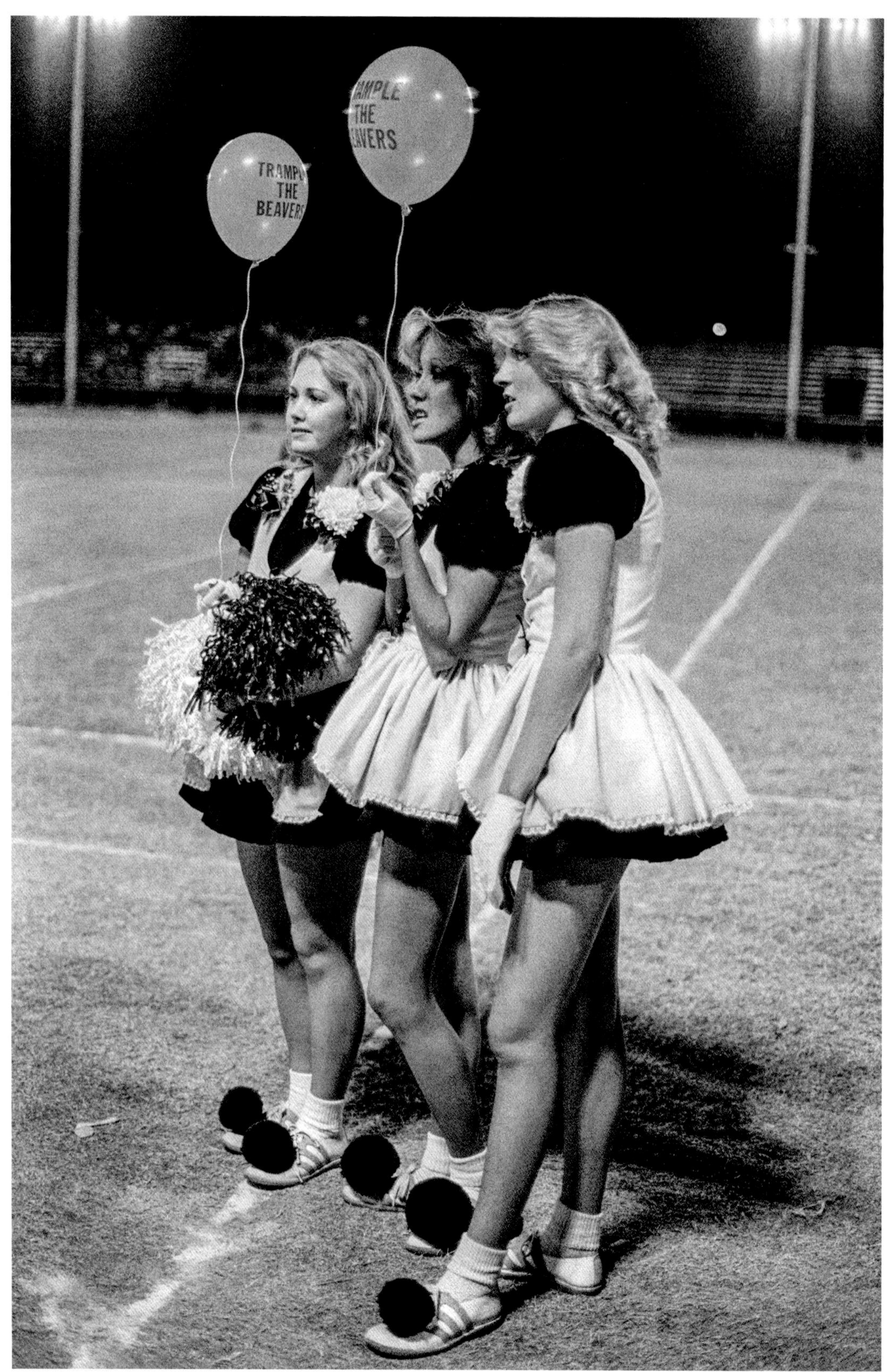
TRAMPLE
THE
BEAVERS
TRAMPLE
THE
BEAVERS

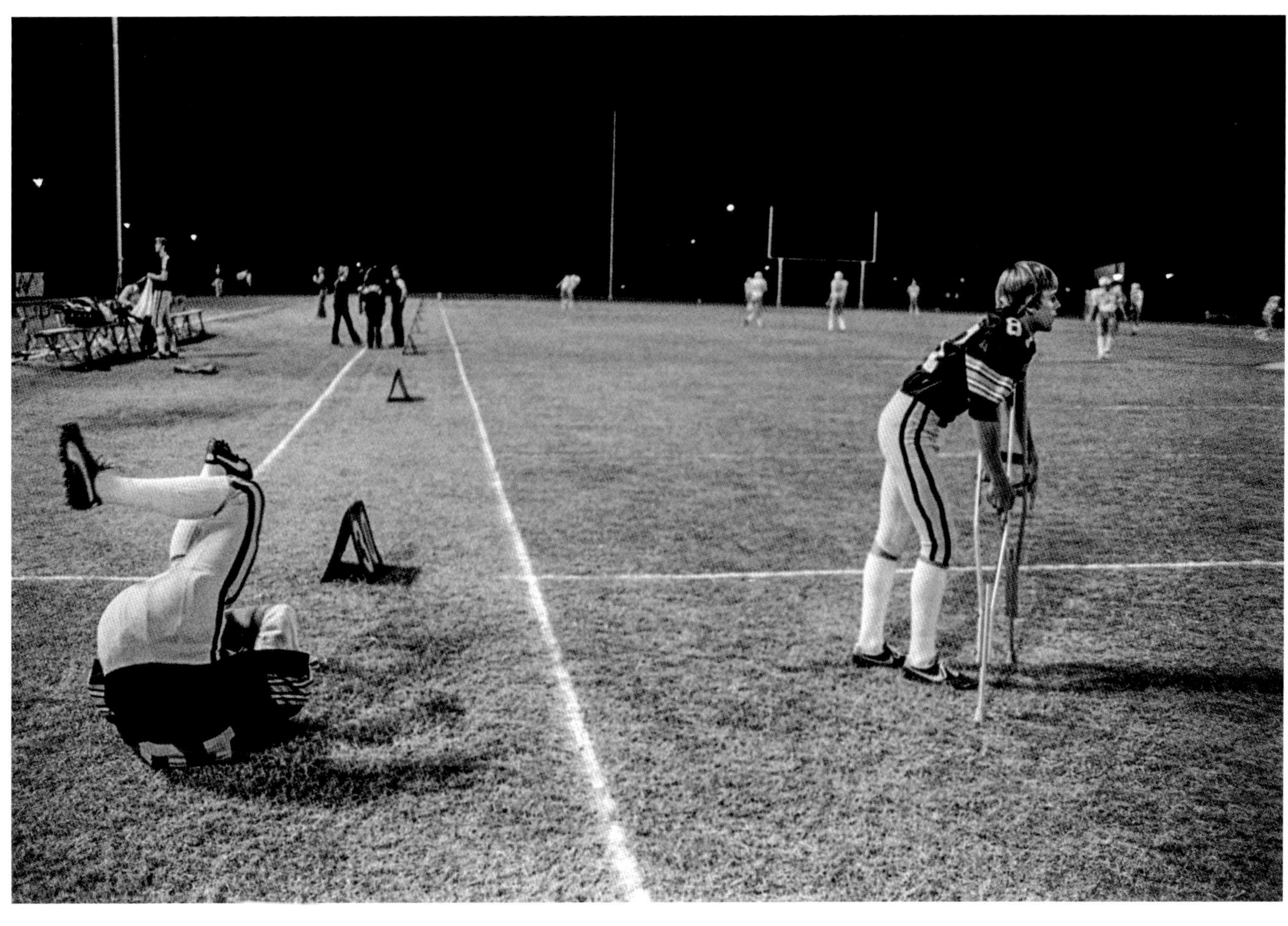

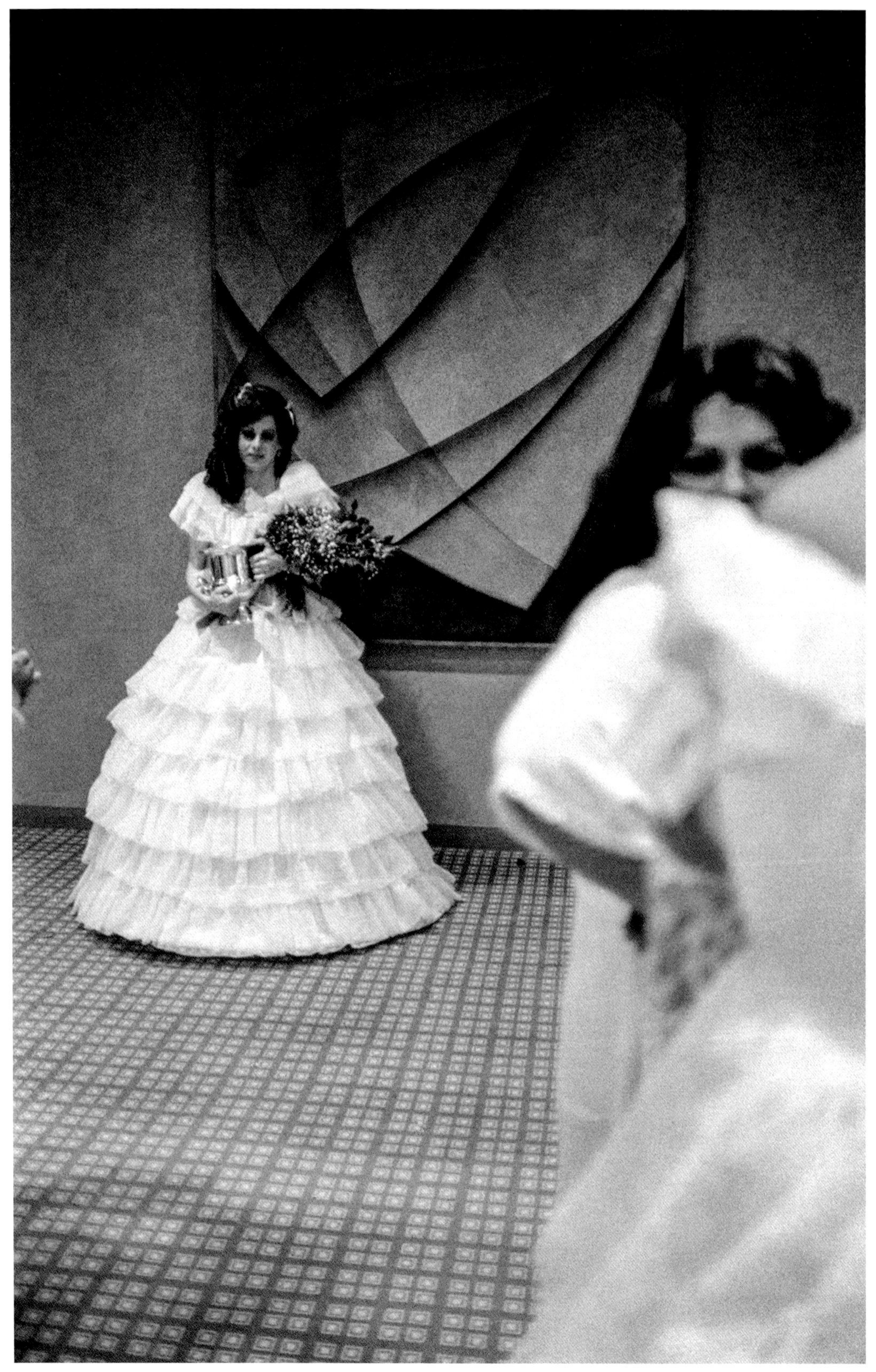

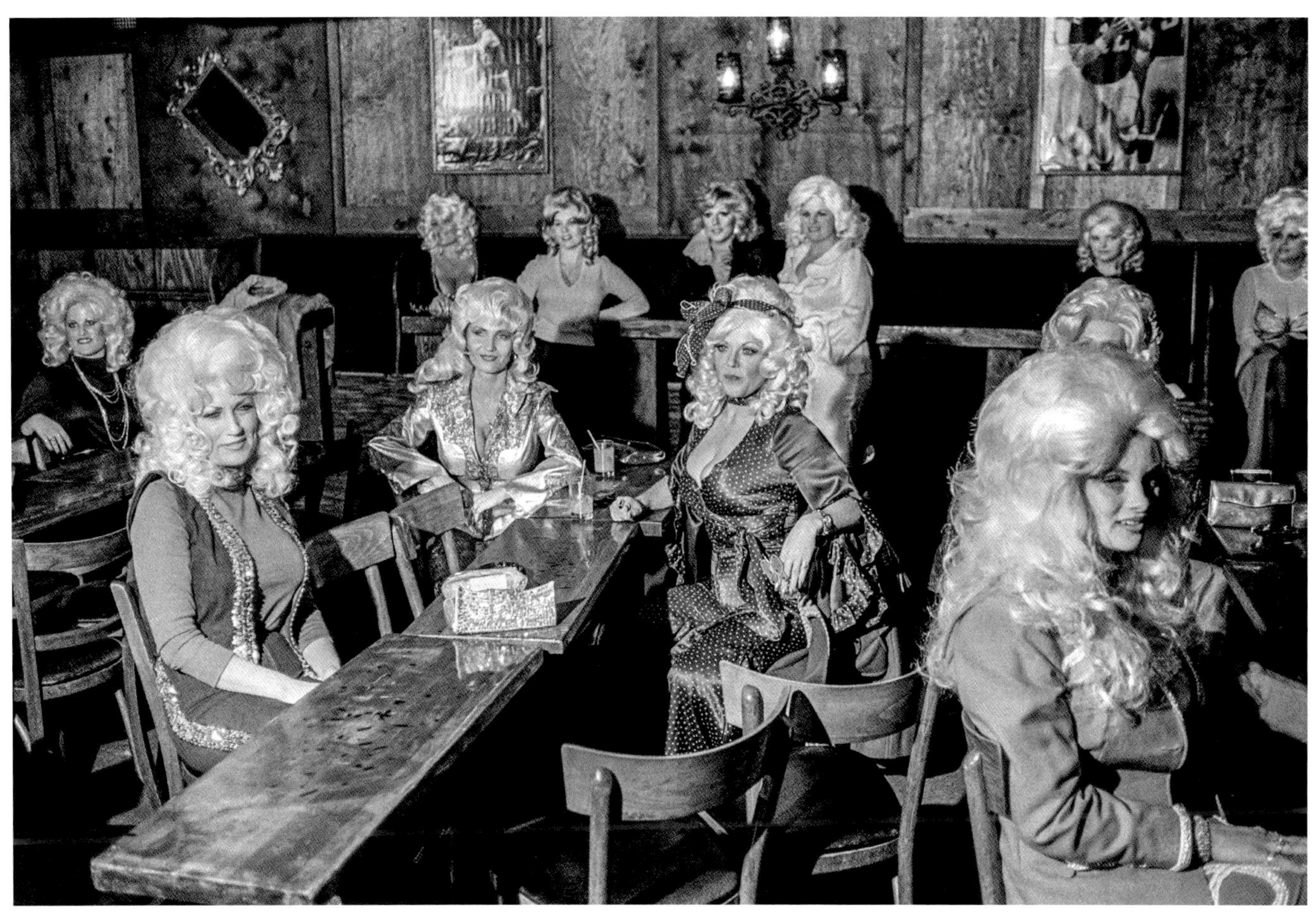

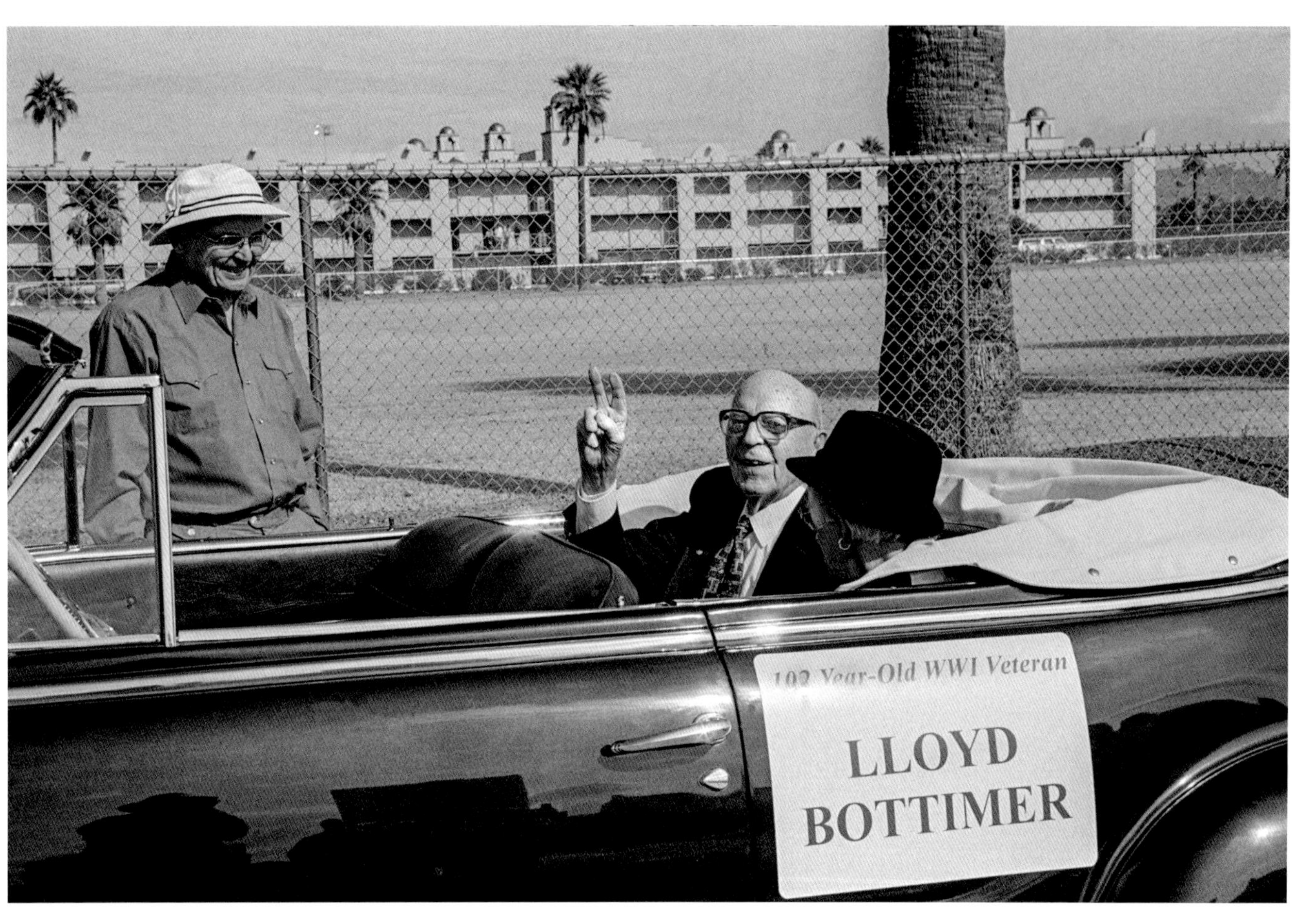
102 Year-Old WWI Veteran
LLOYD
BOTTIMER

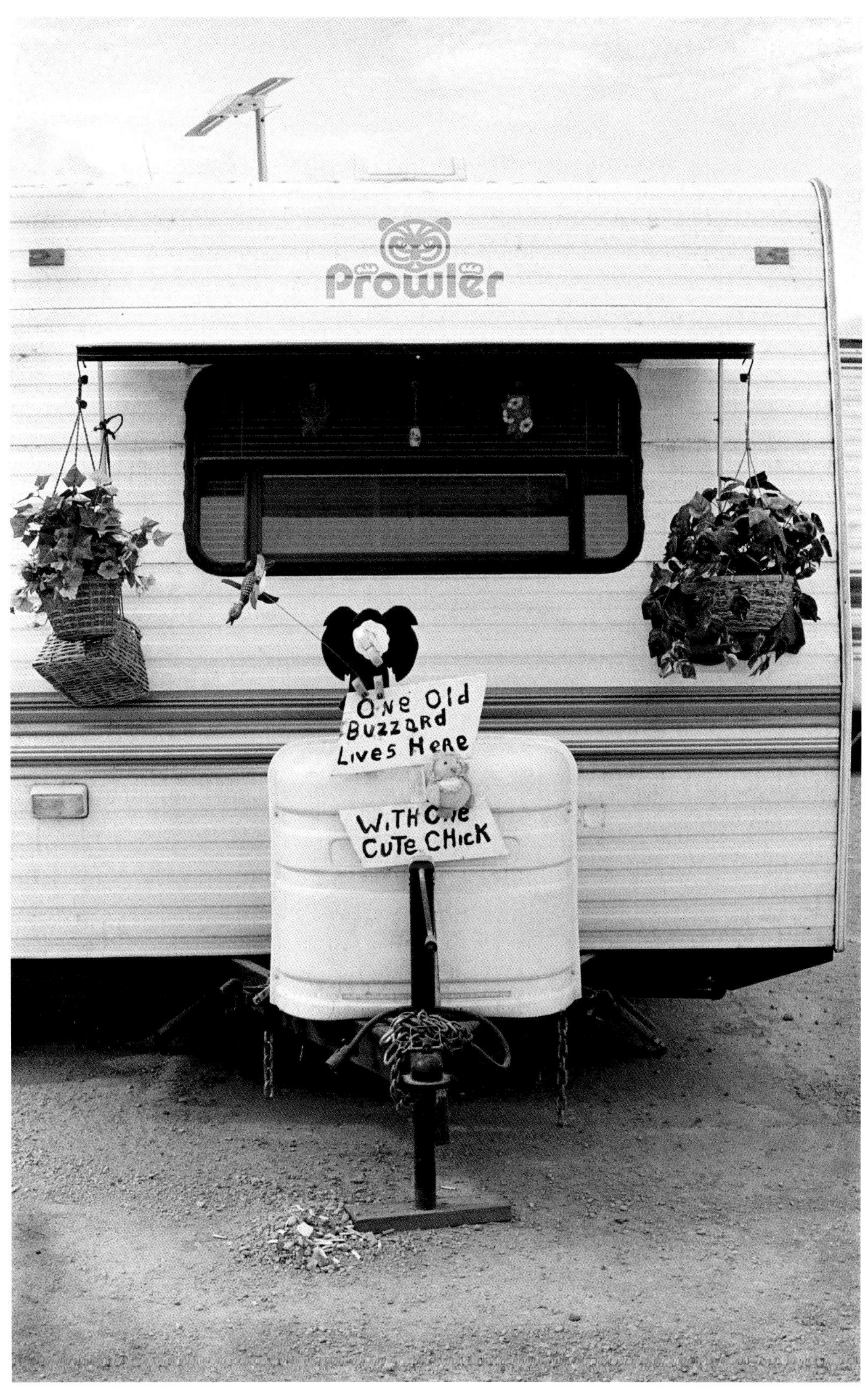
Prowler
One Old
Buzzard
Lives Here
With One
Cute Chick

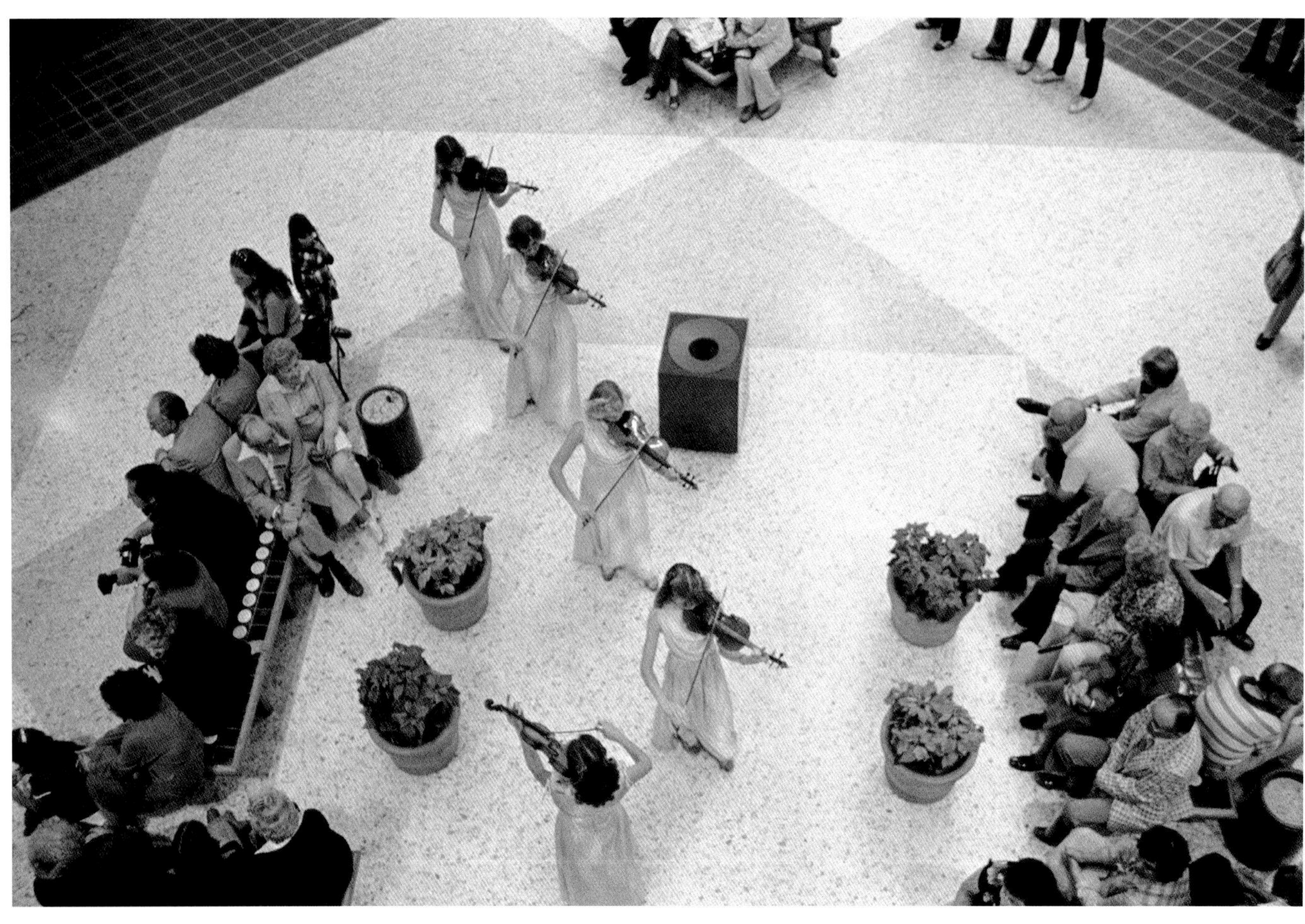

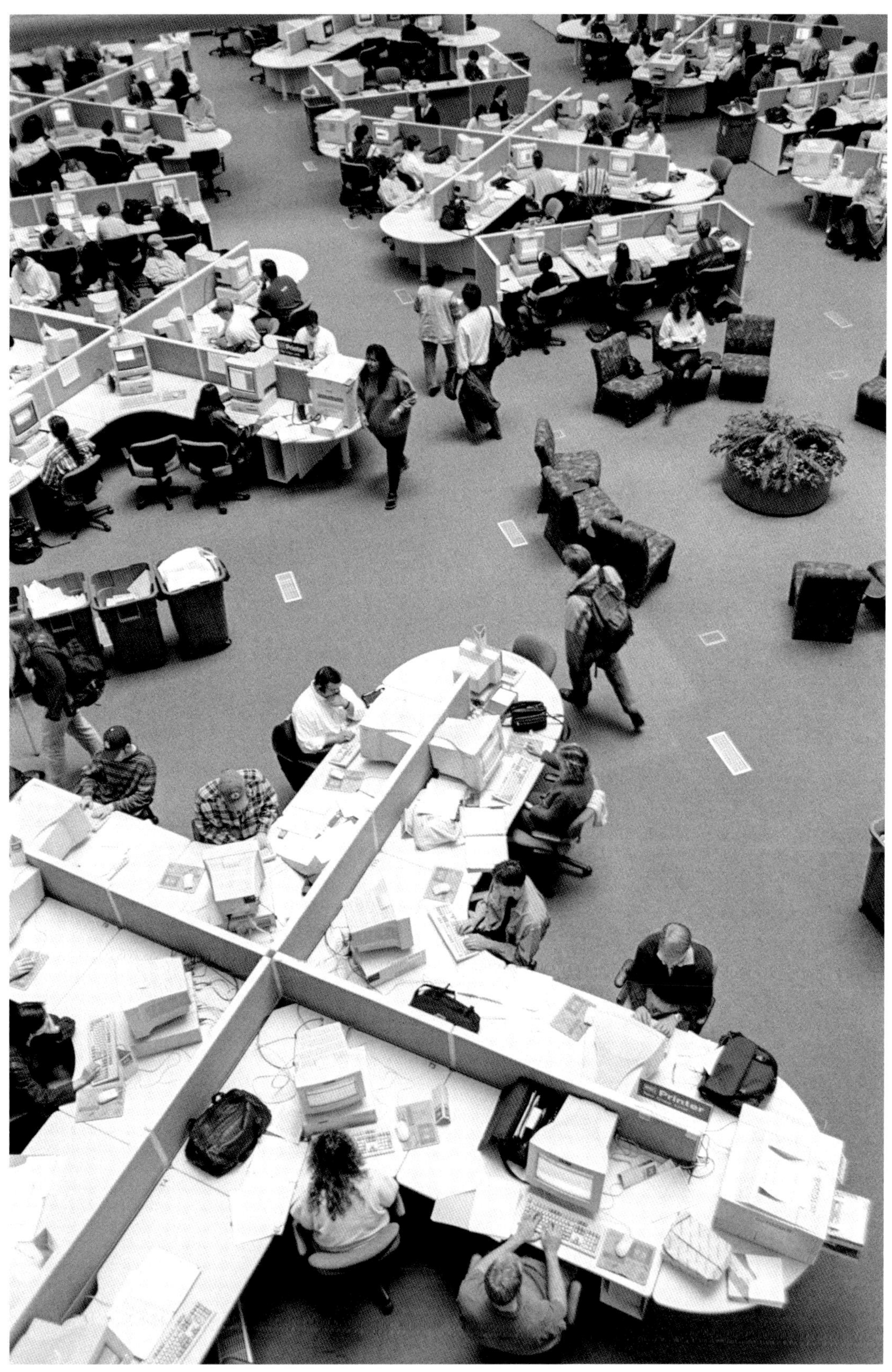

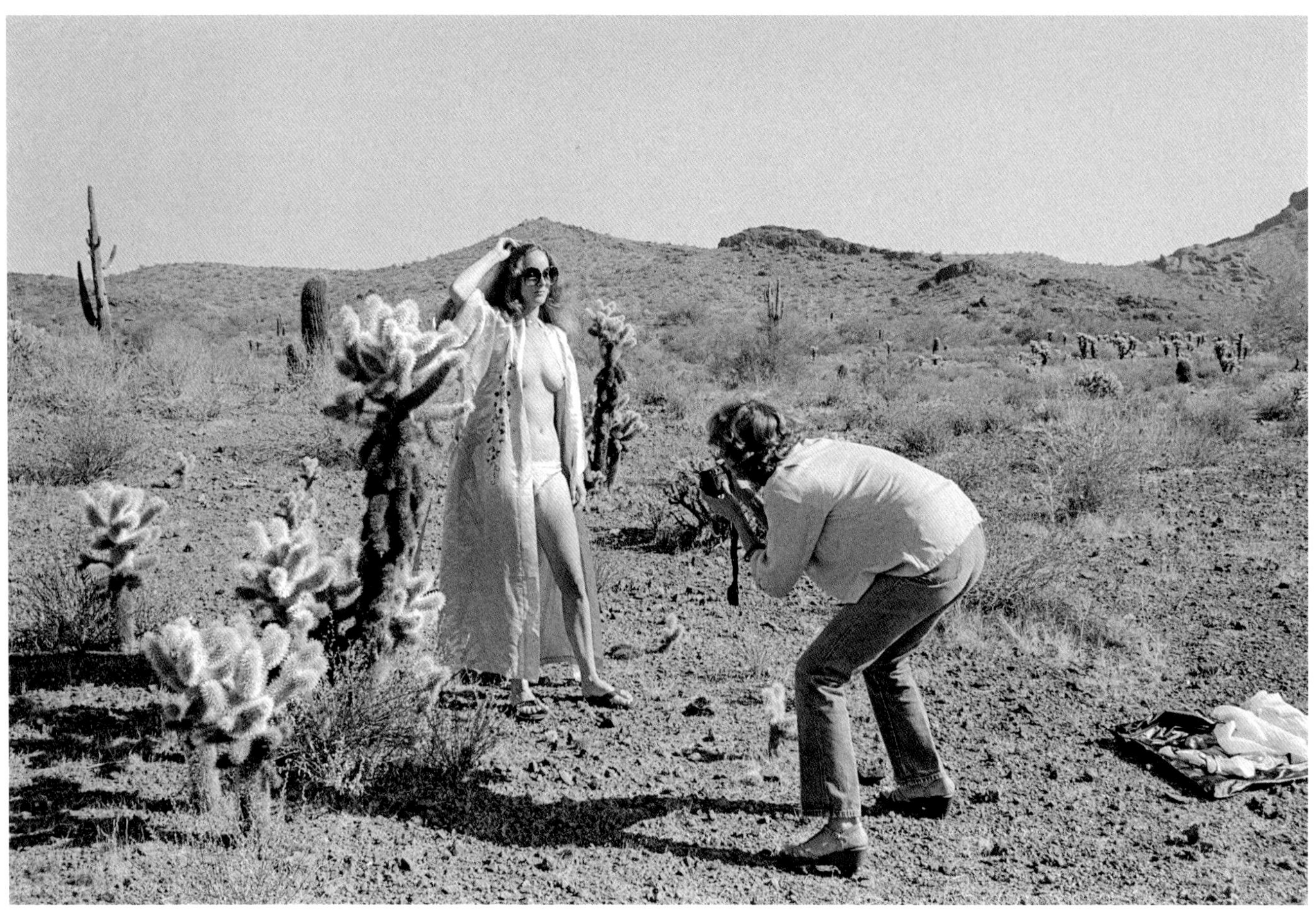

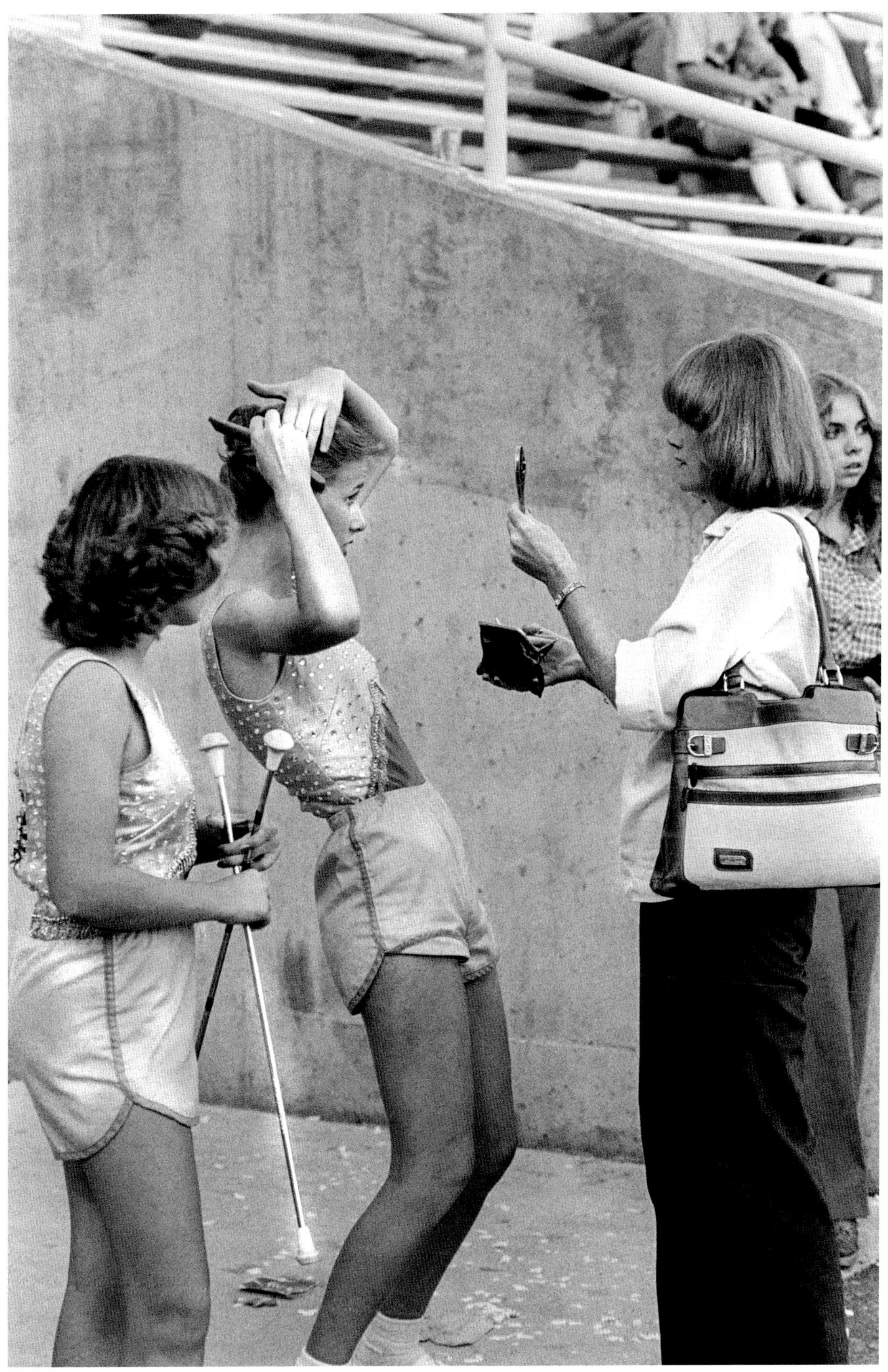

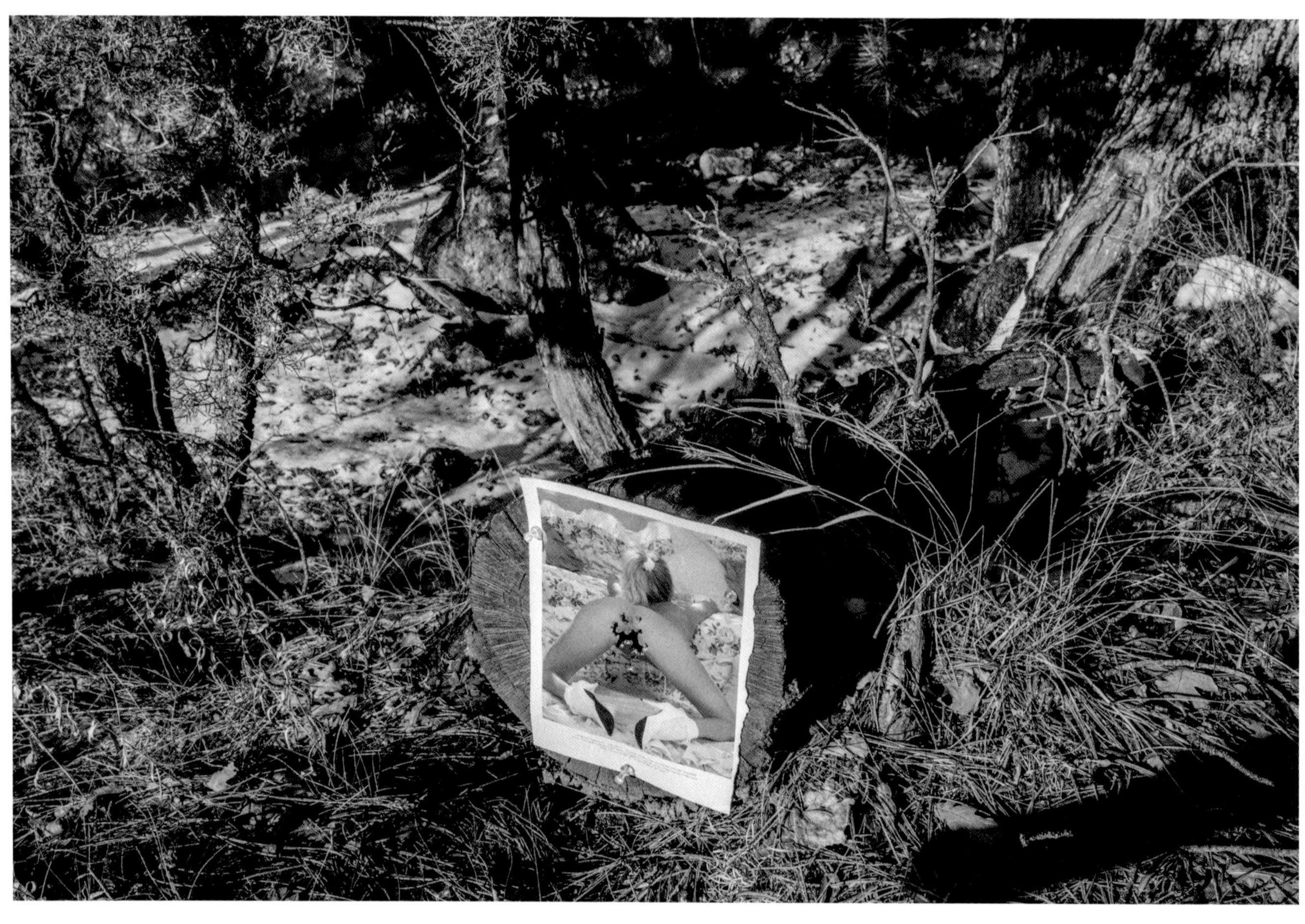

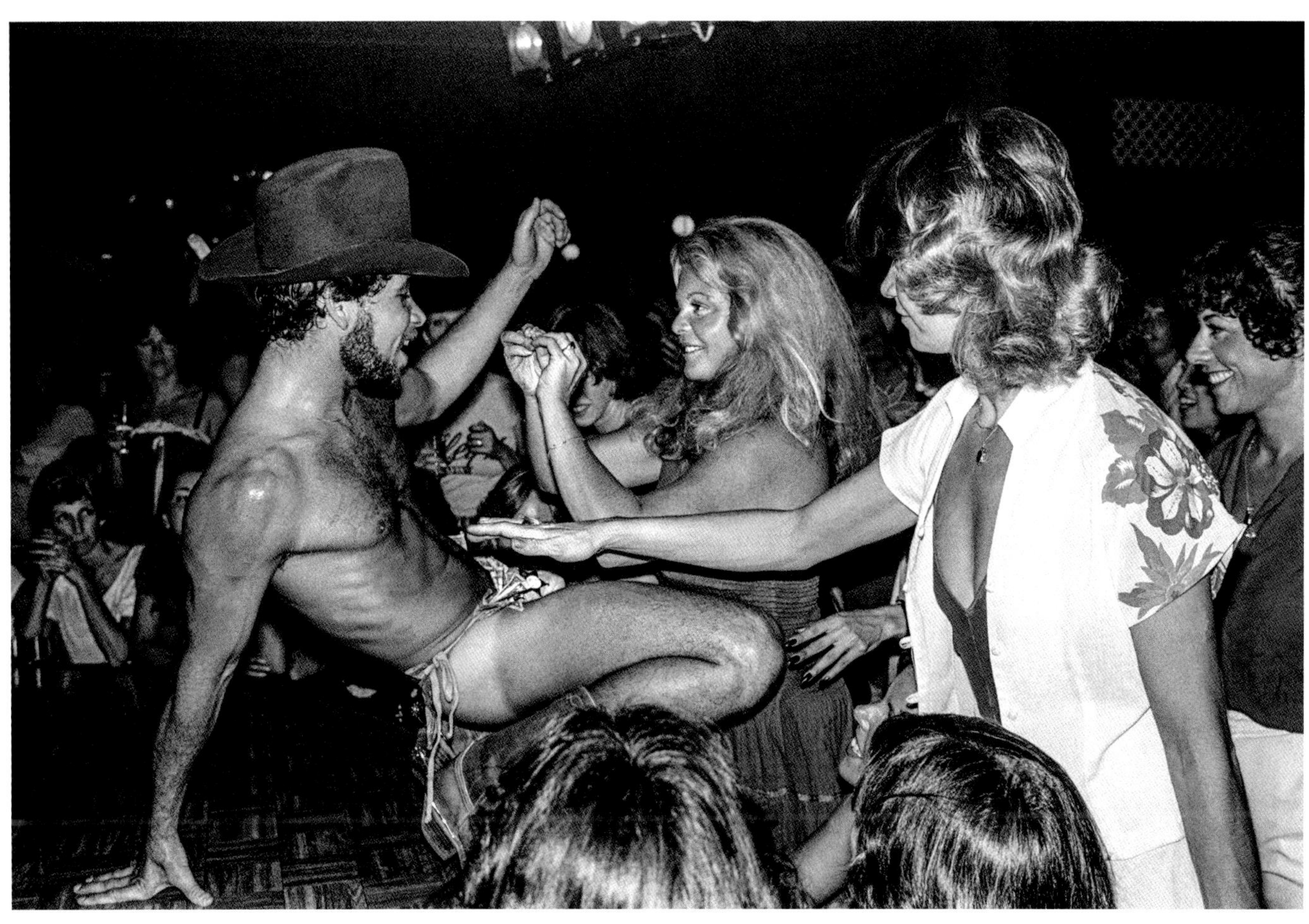

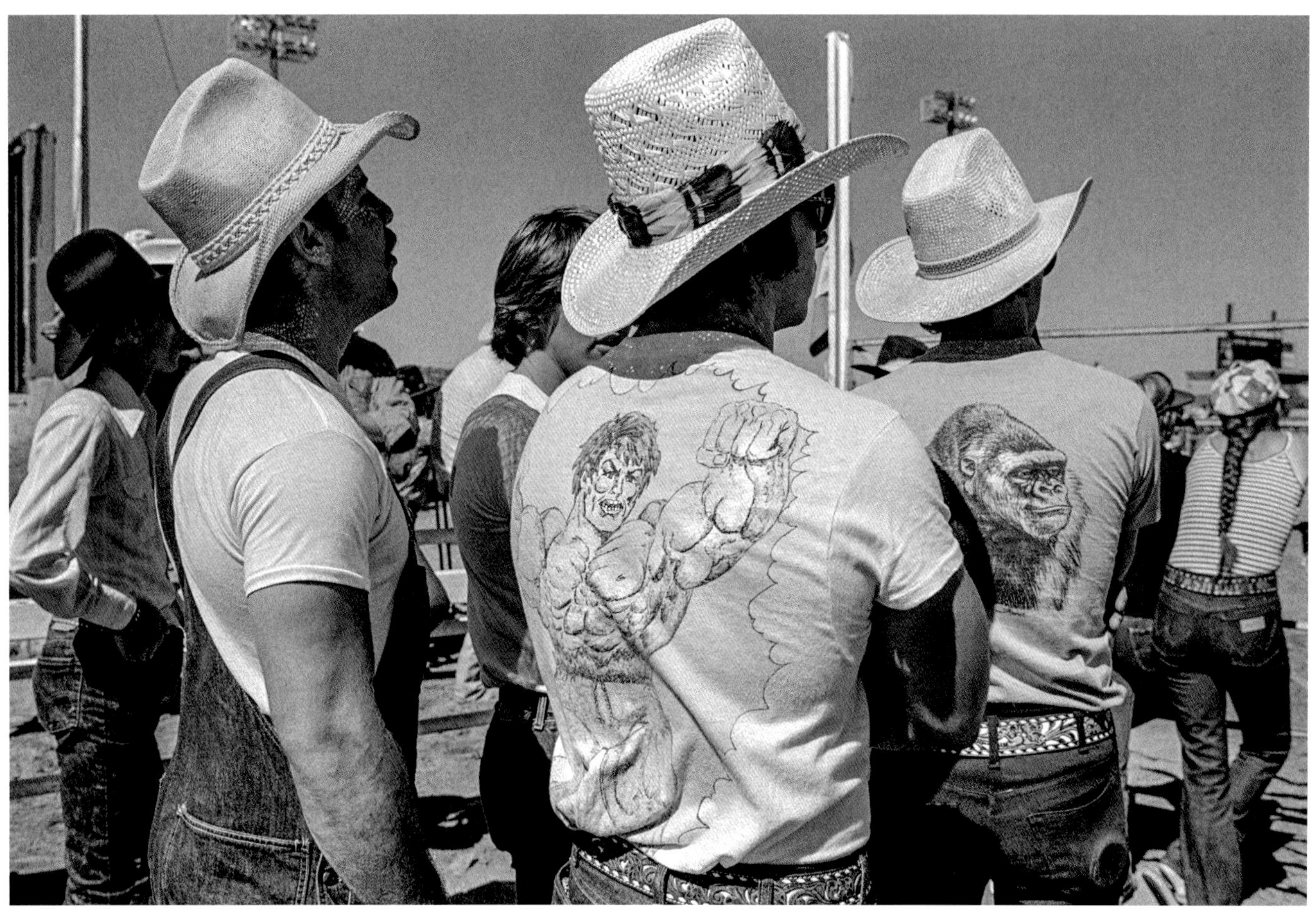

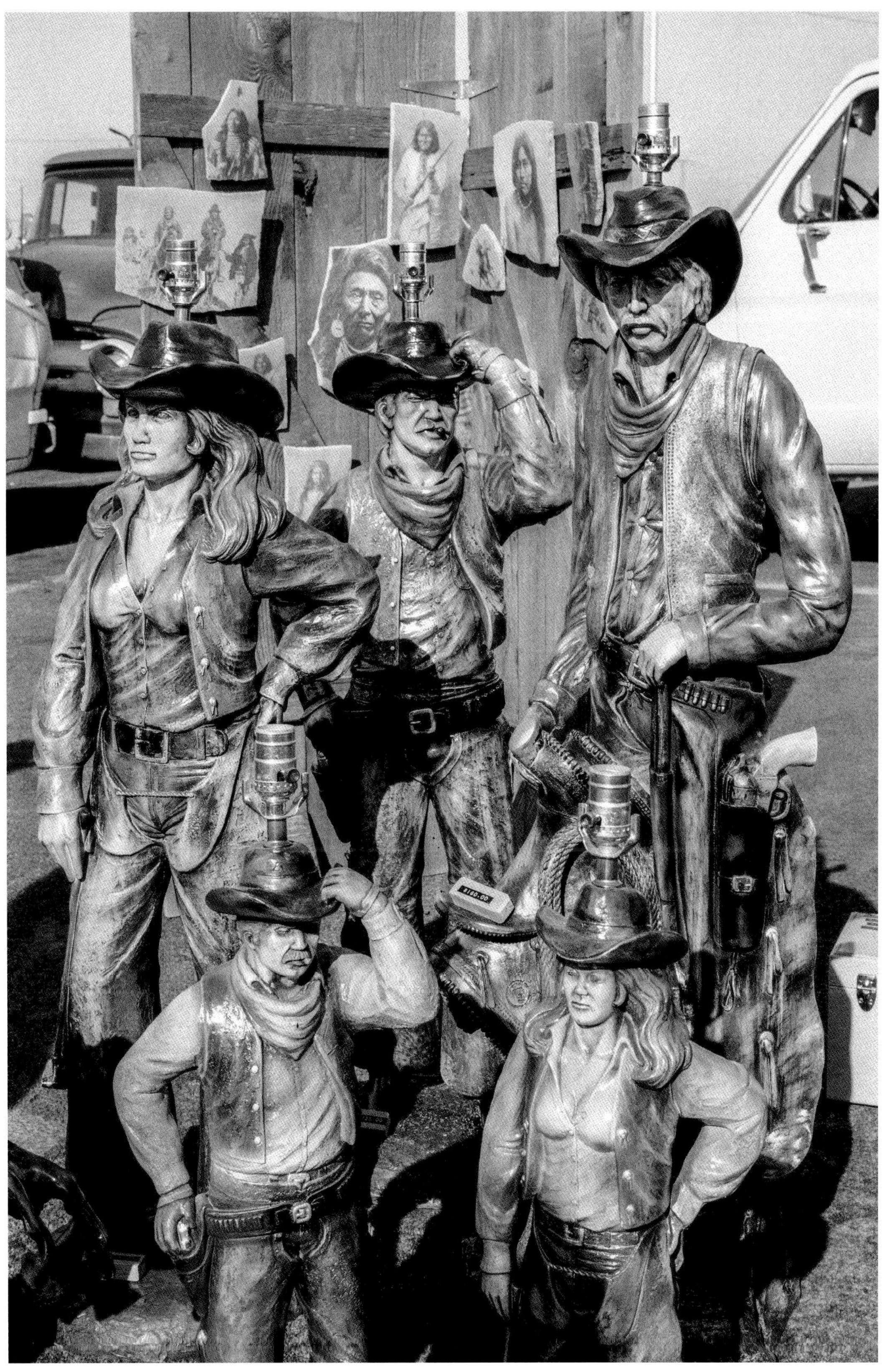

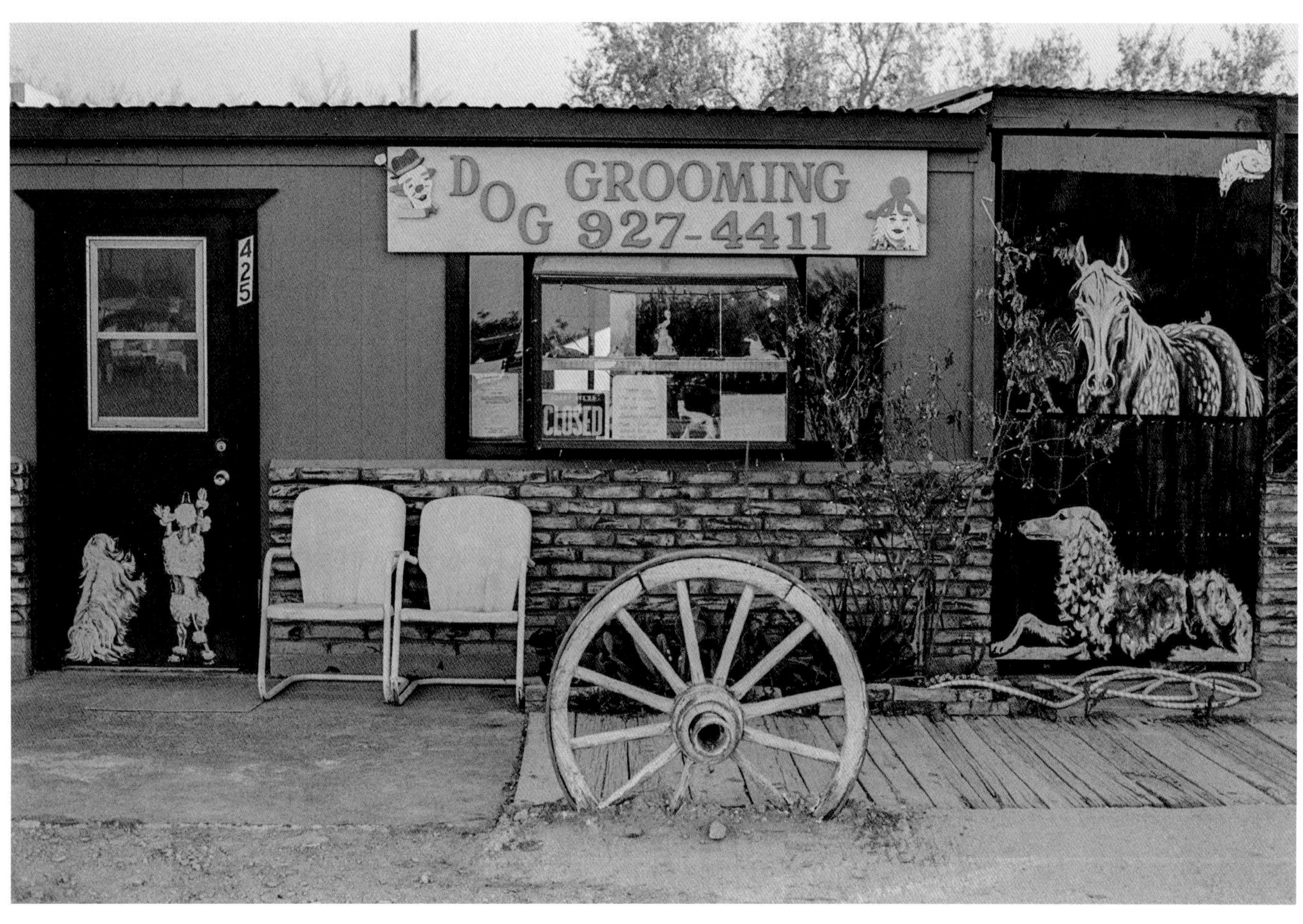

DOG GROOMING
927-4411
425
CLOSED

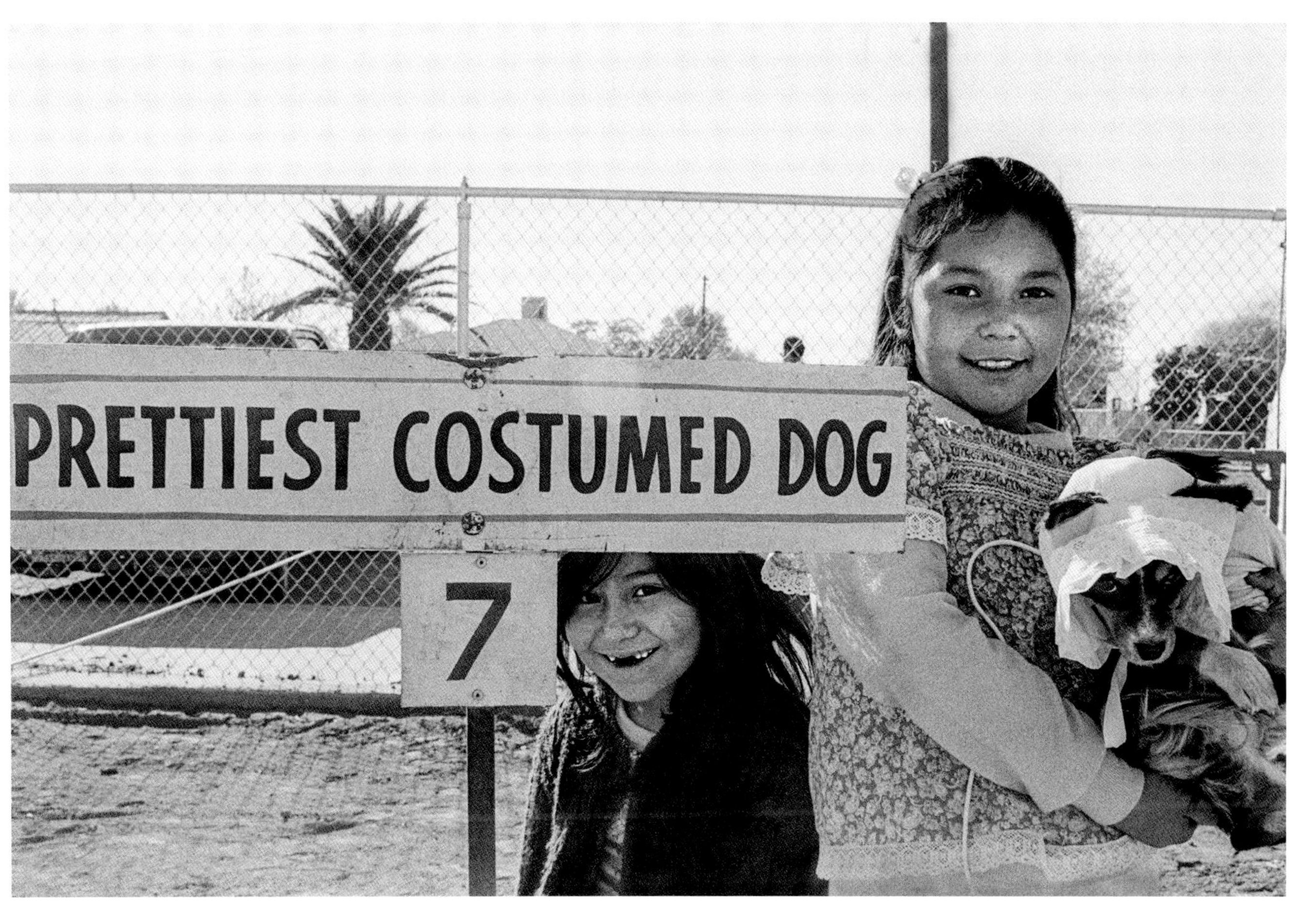
PRETTIEST COSTUMED DOG
7

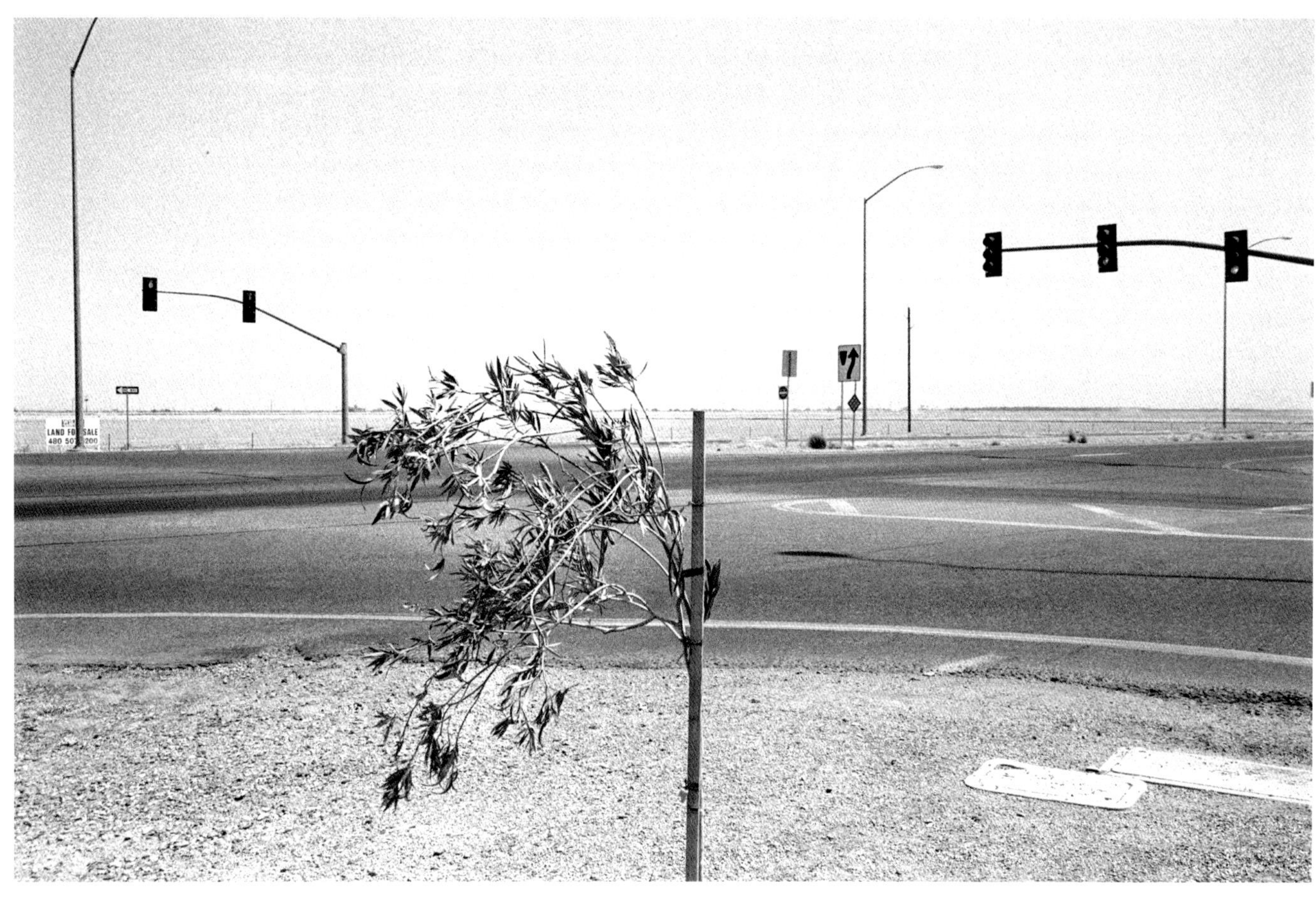

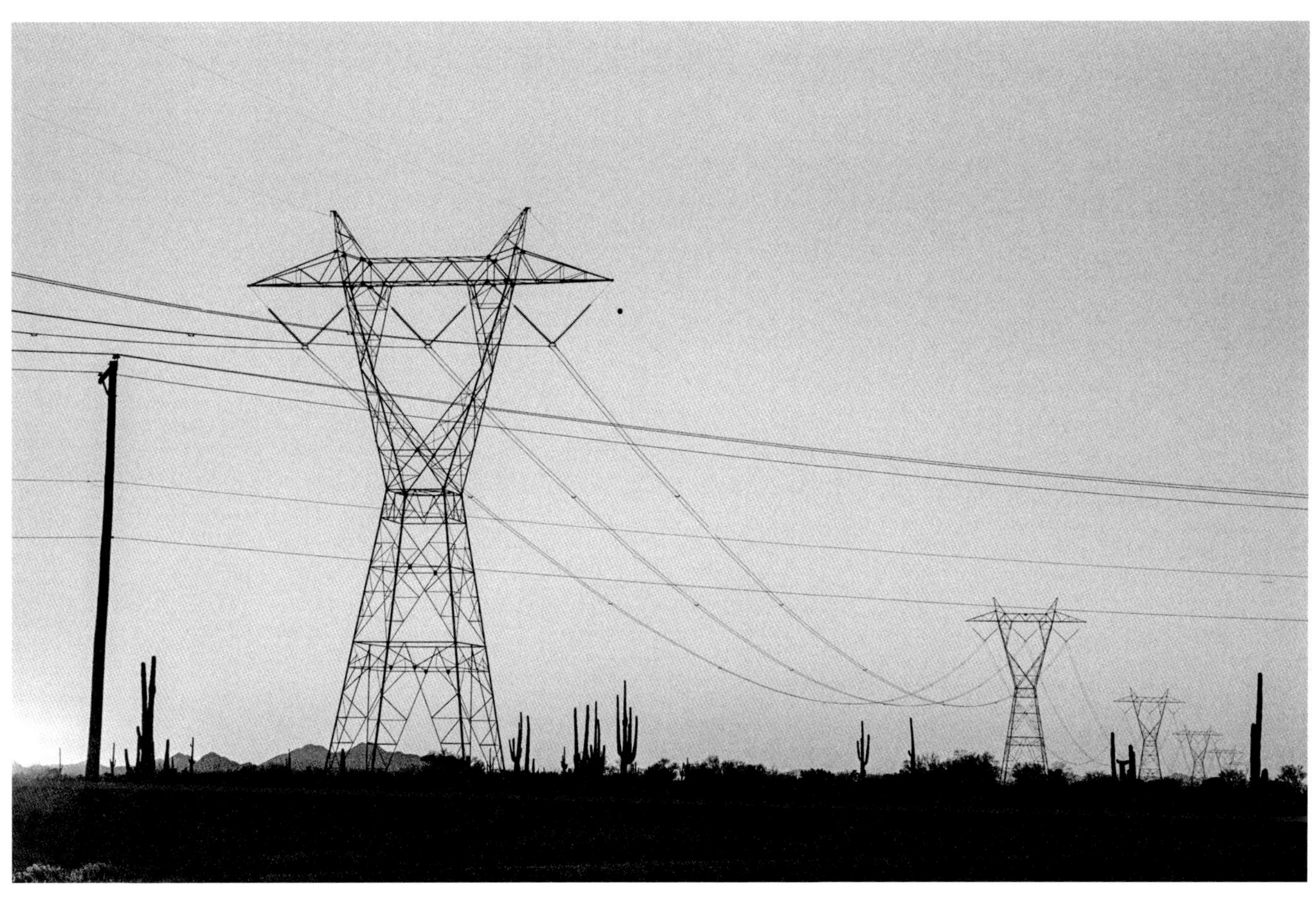

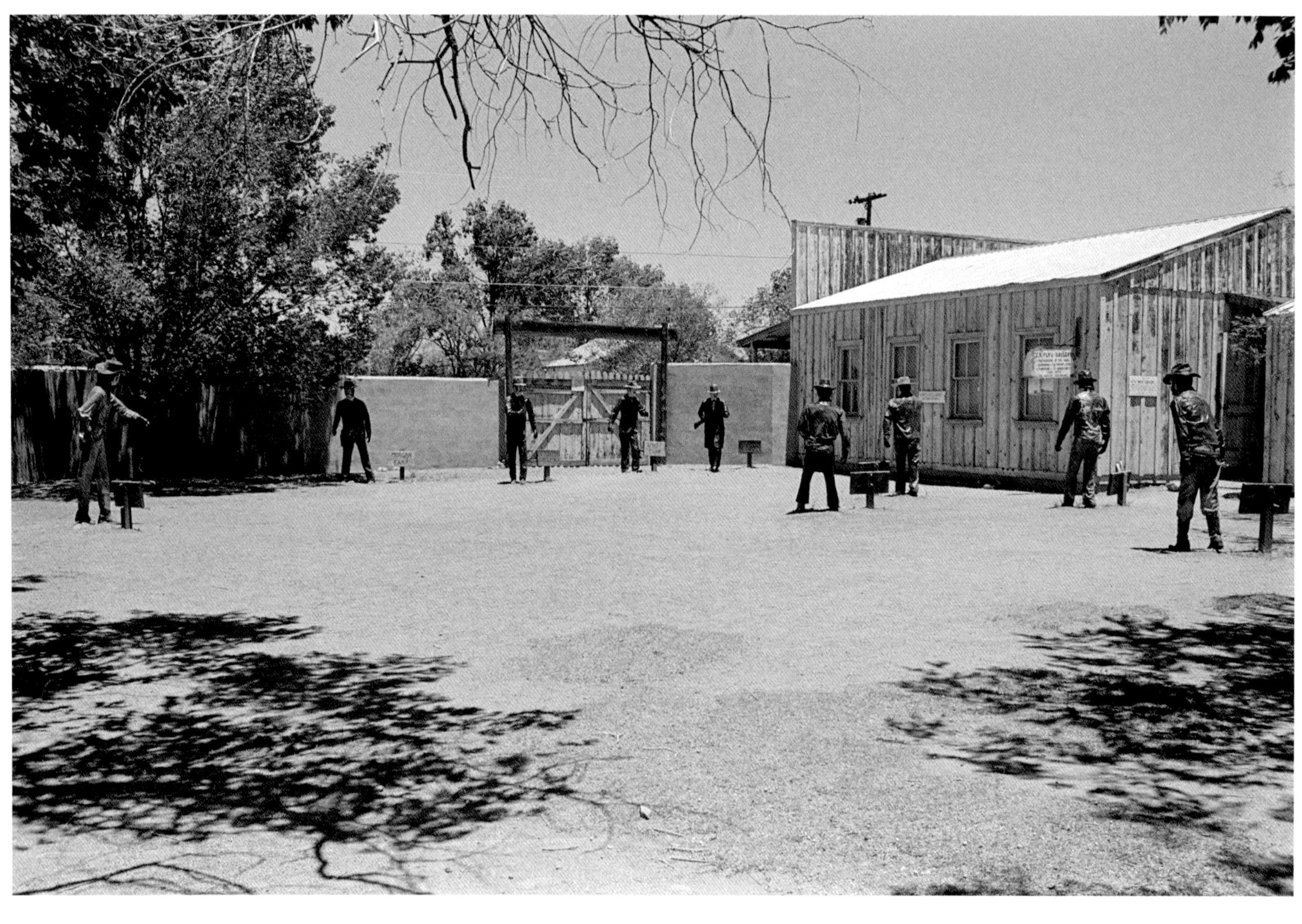

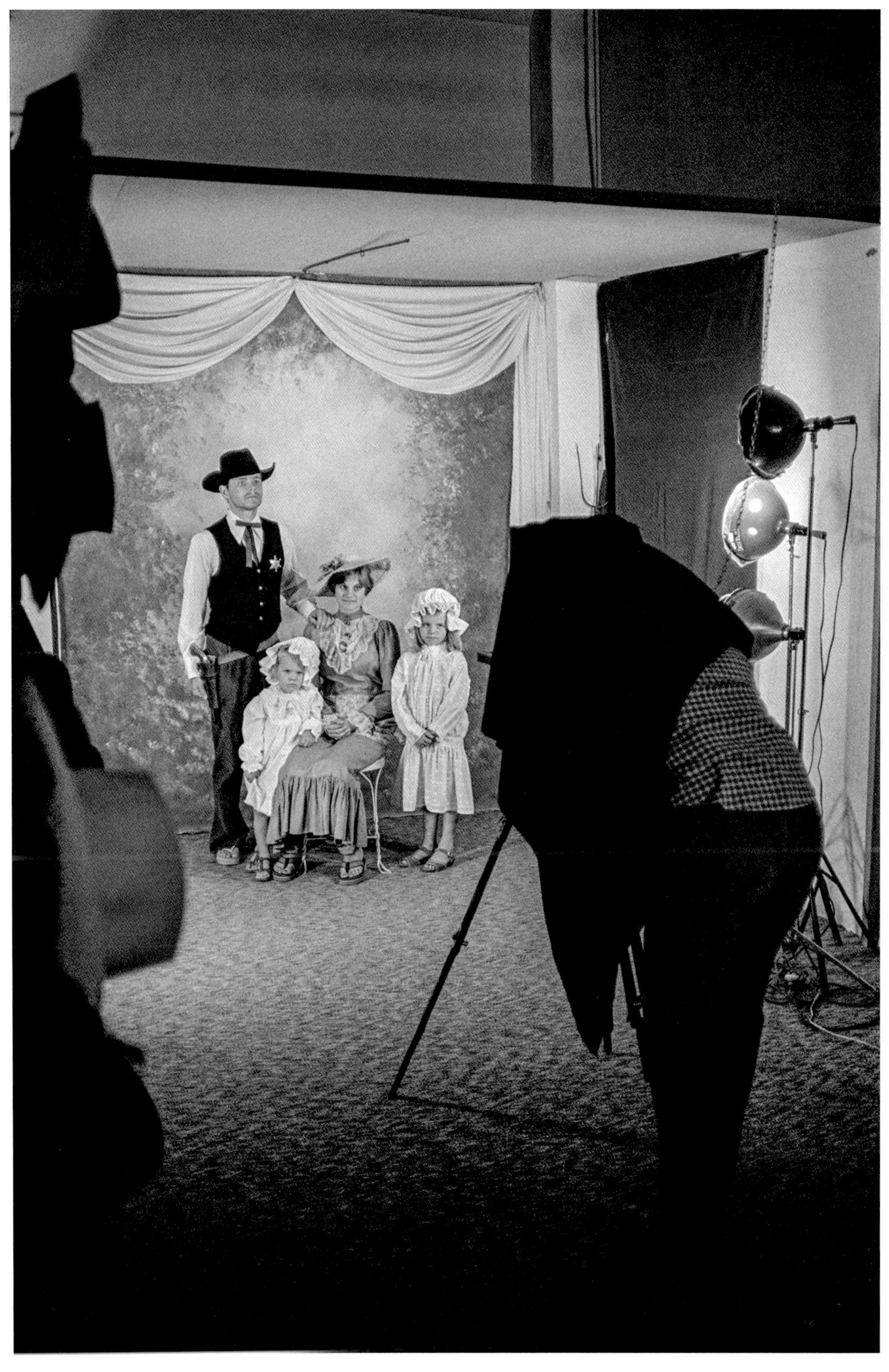

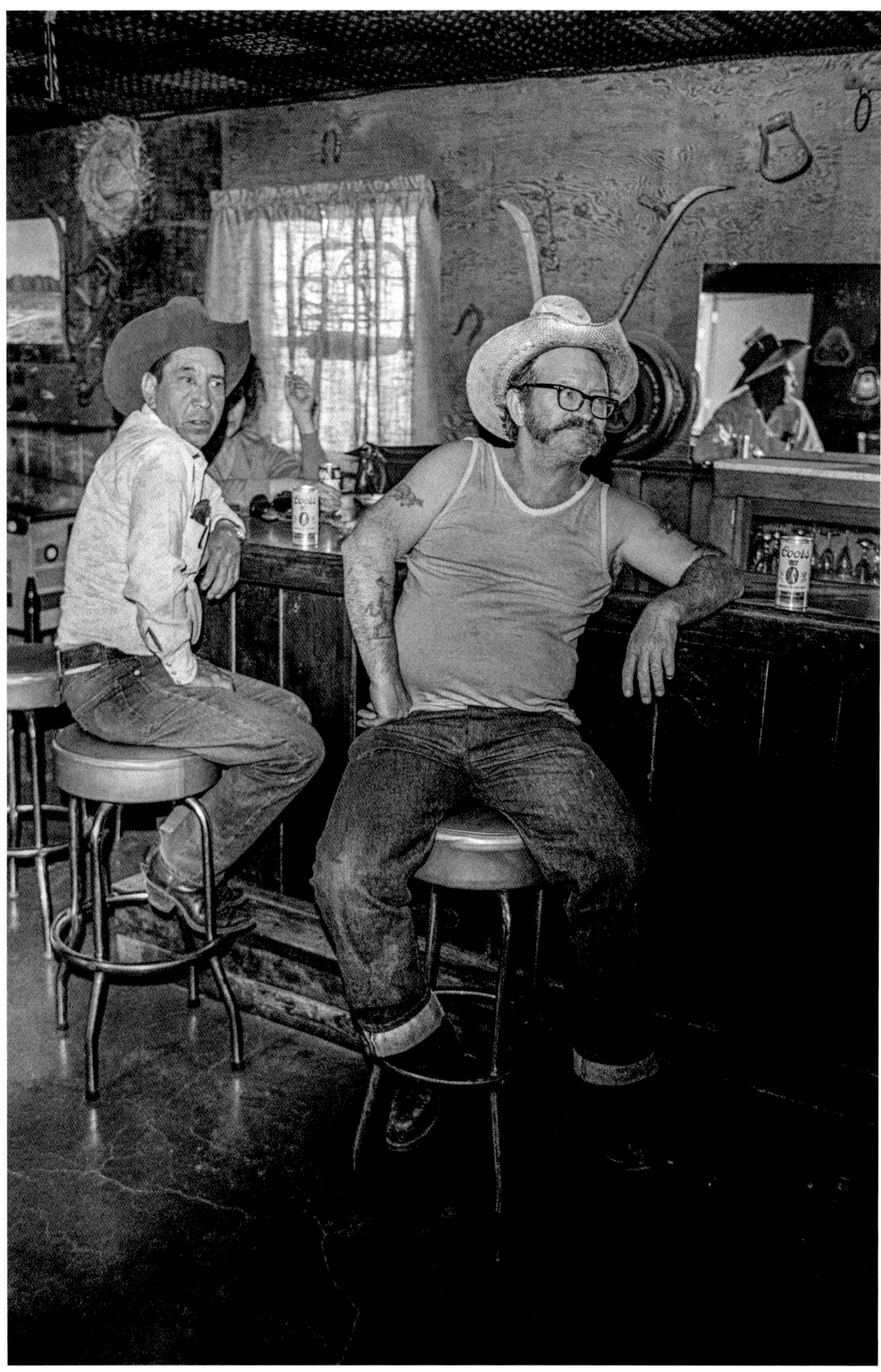

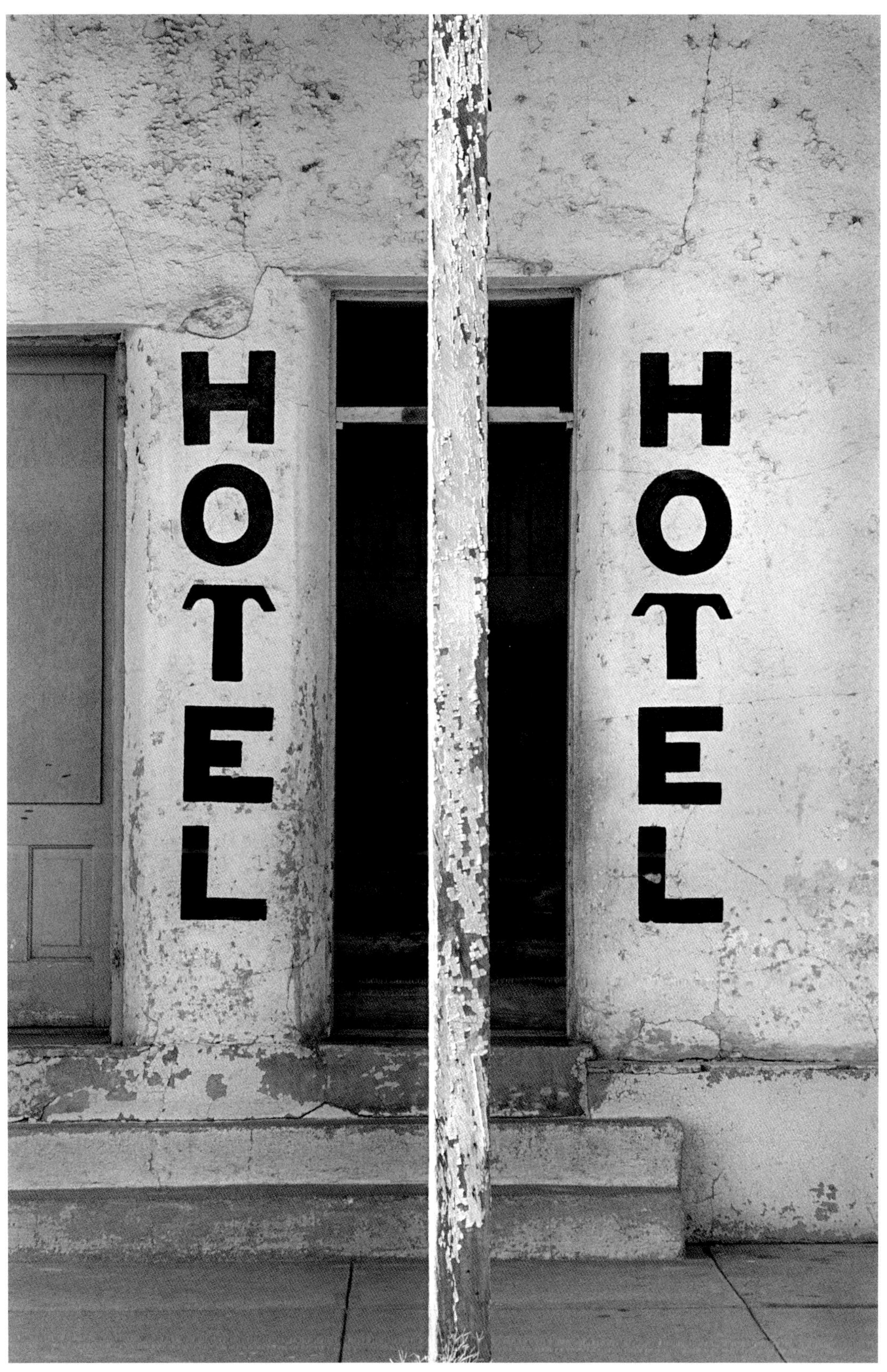
HOTEL
HOTEL

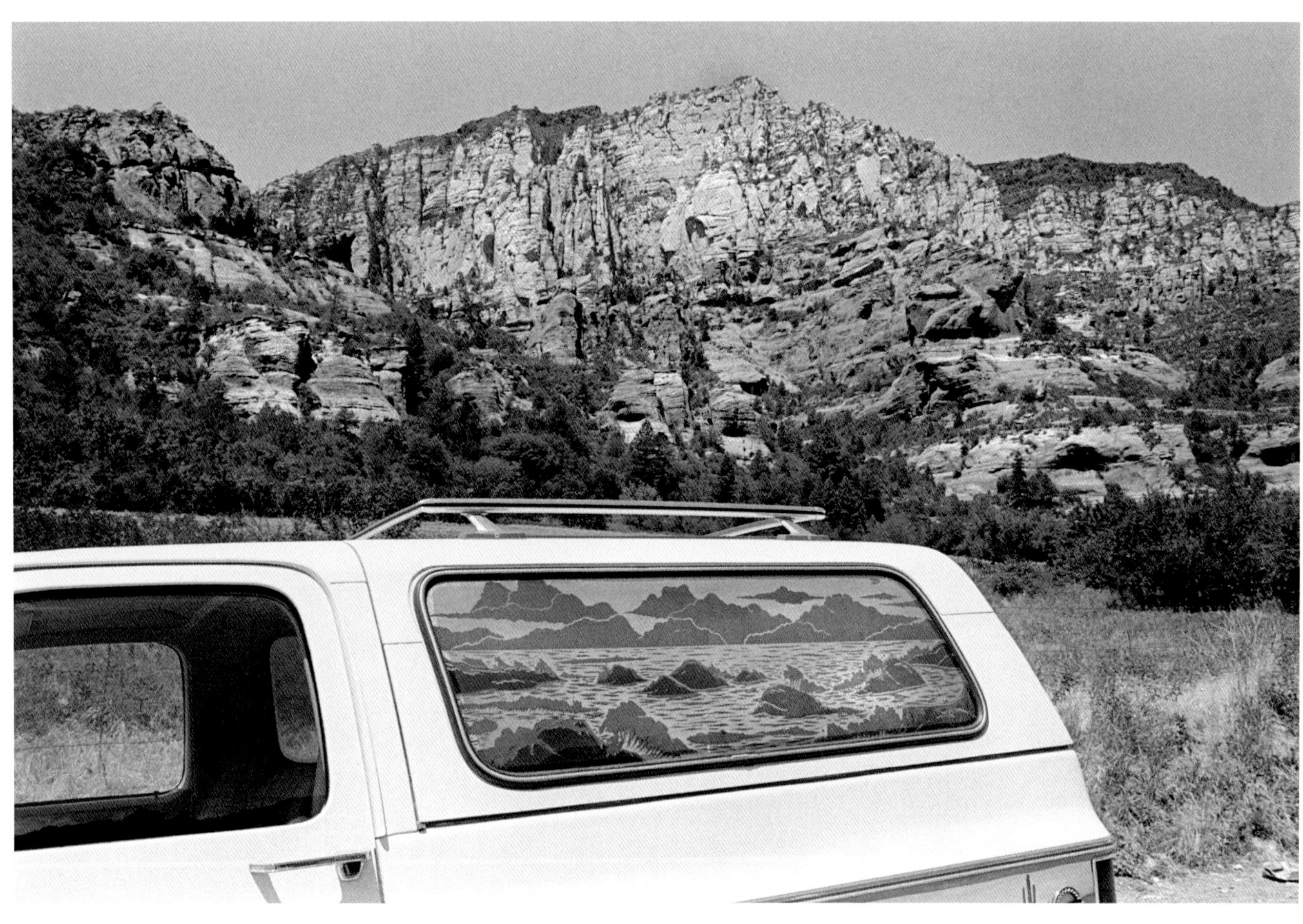

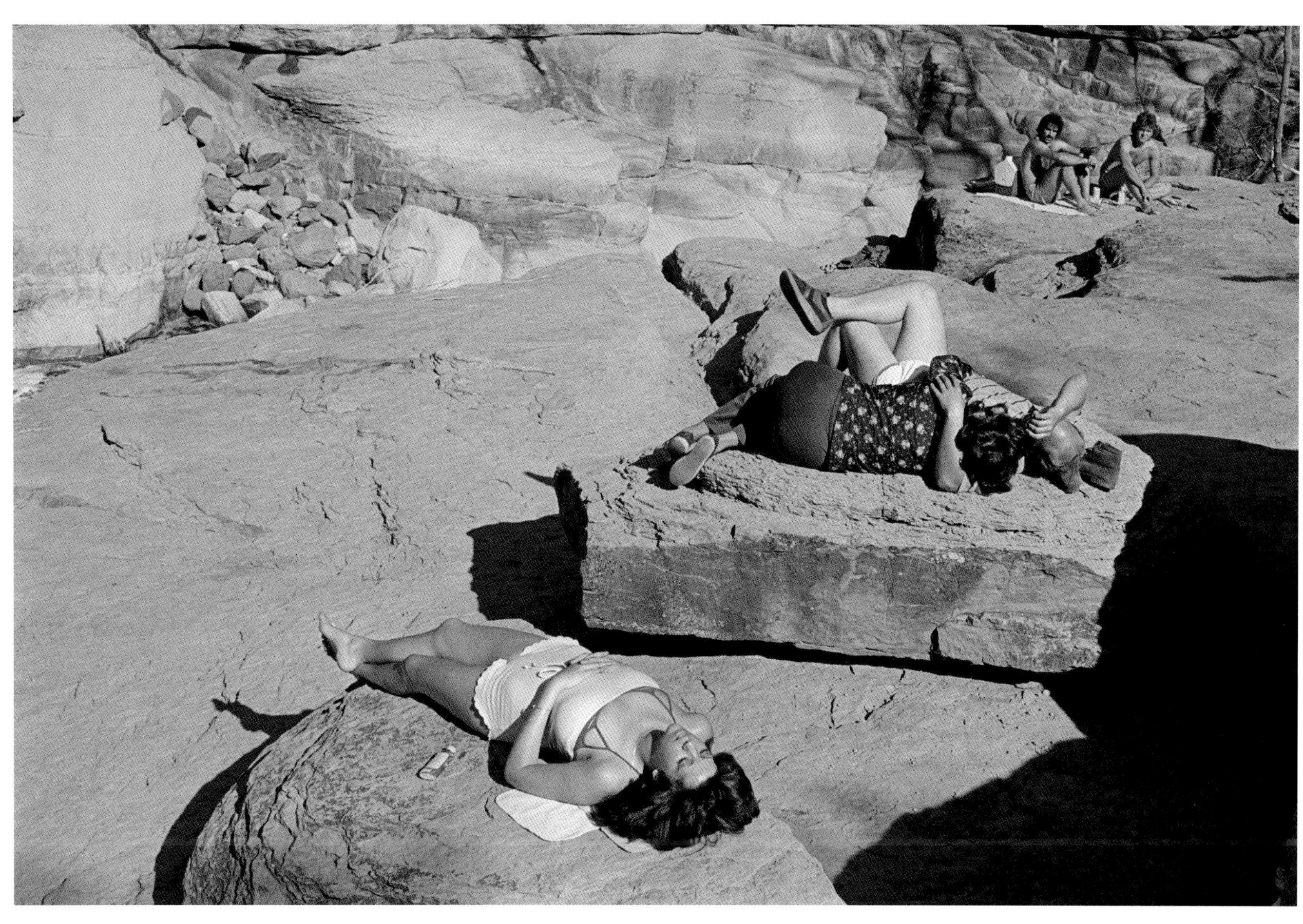

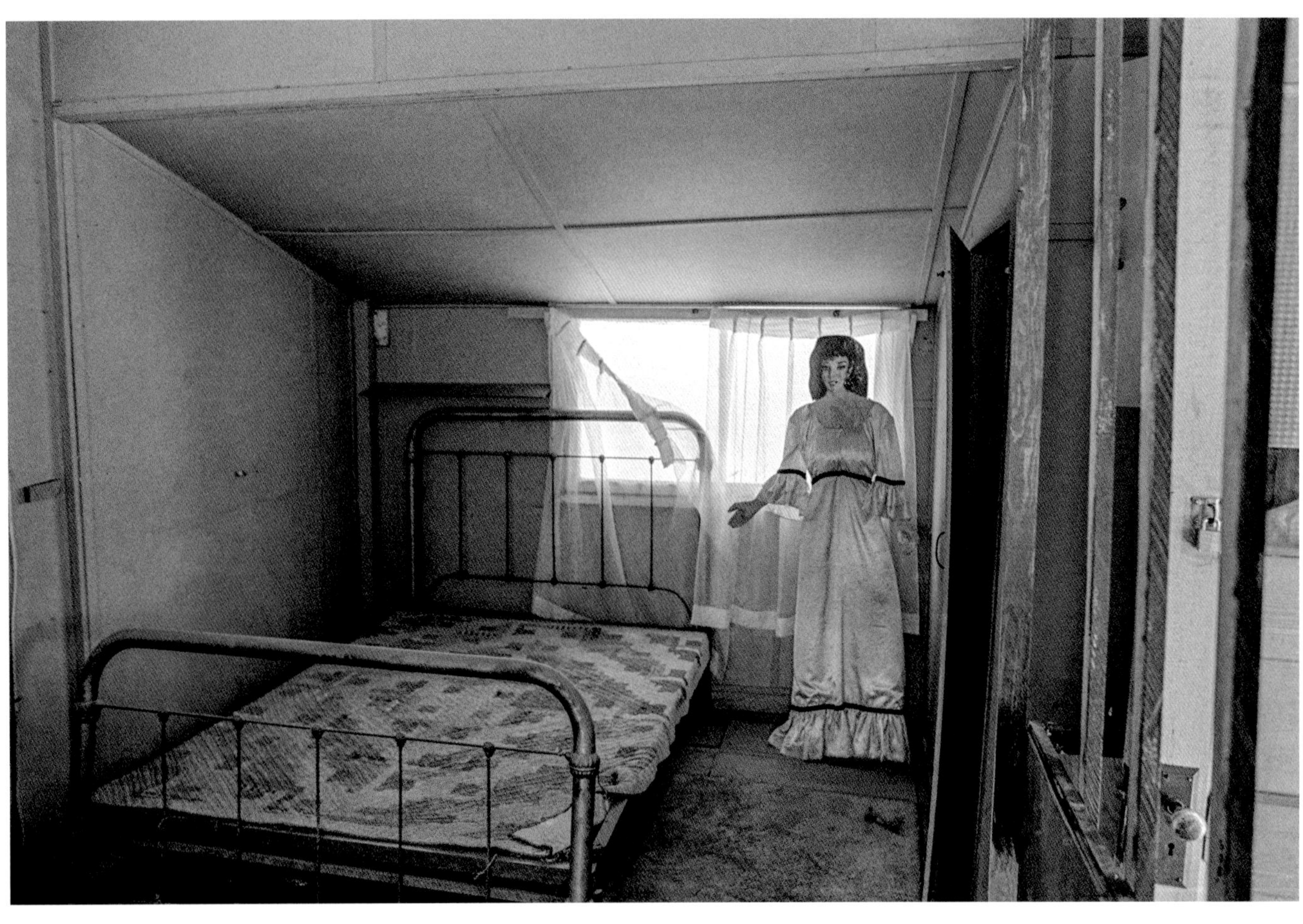

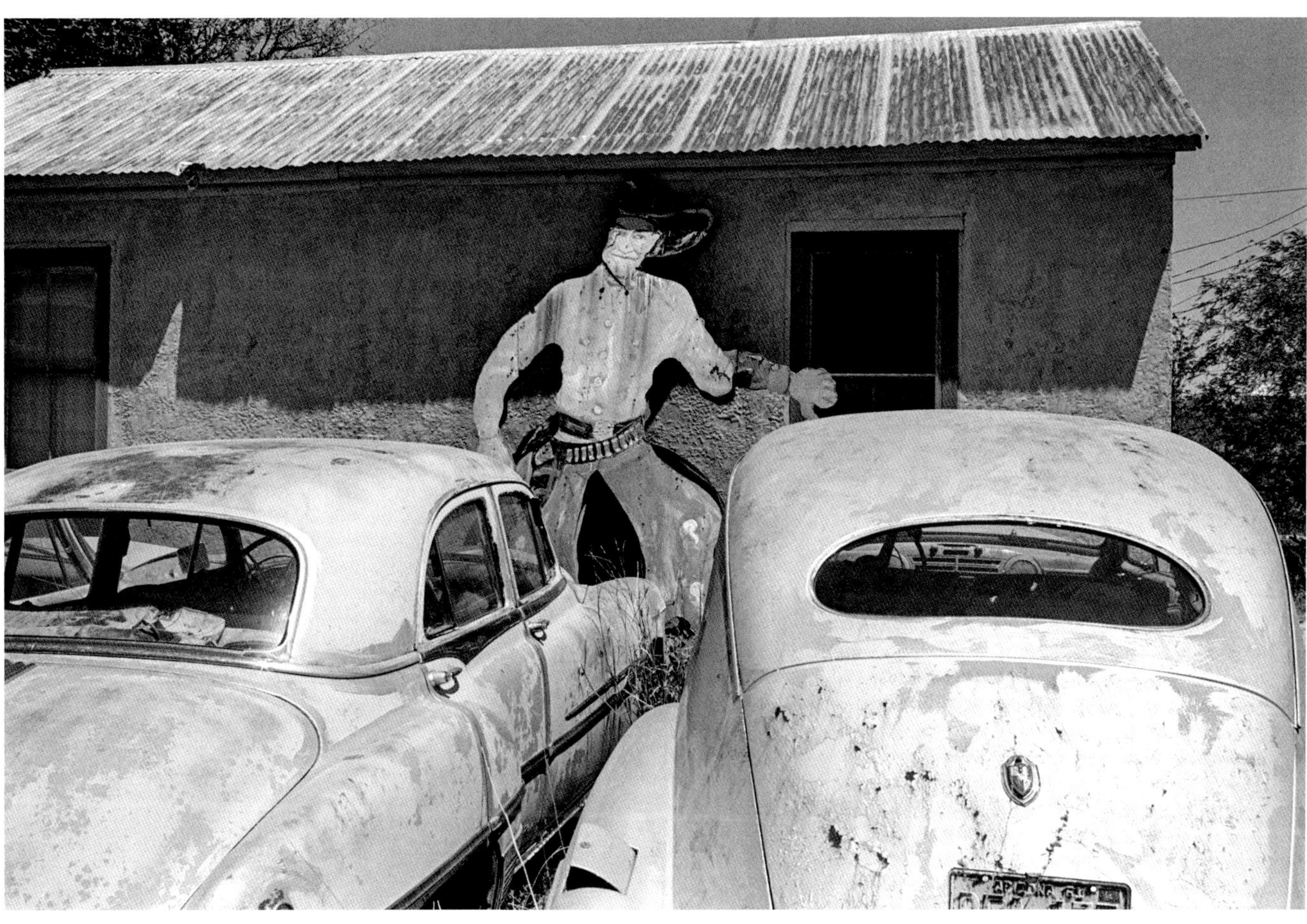

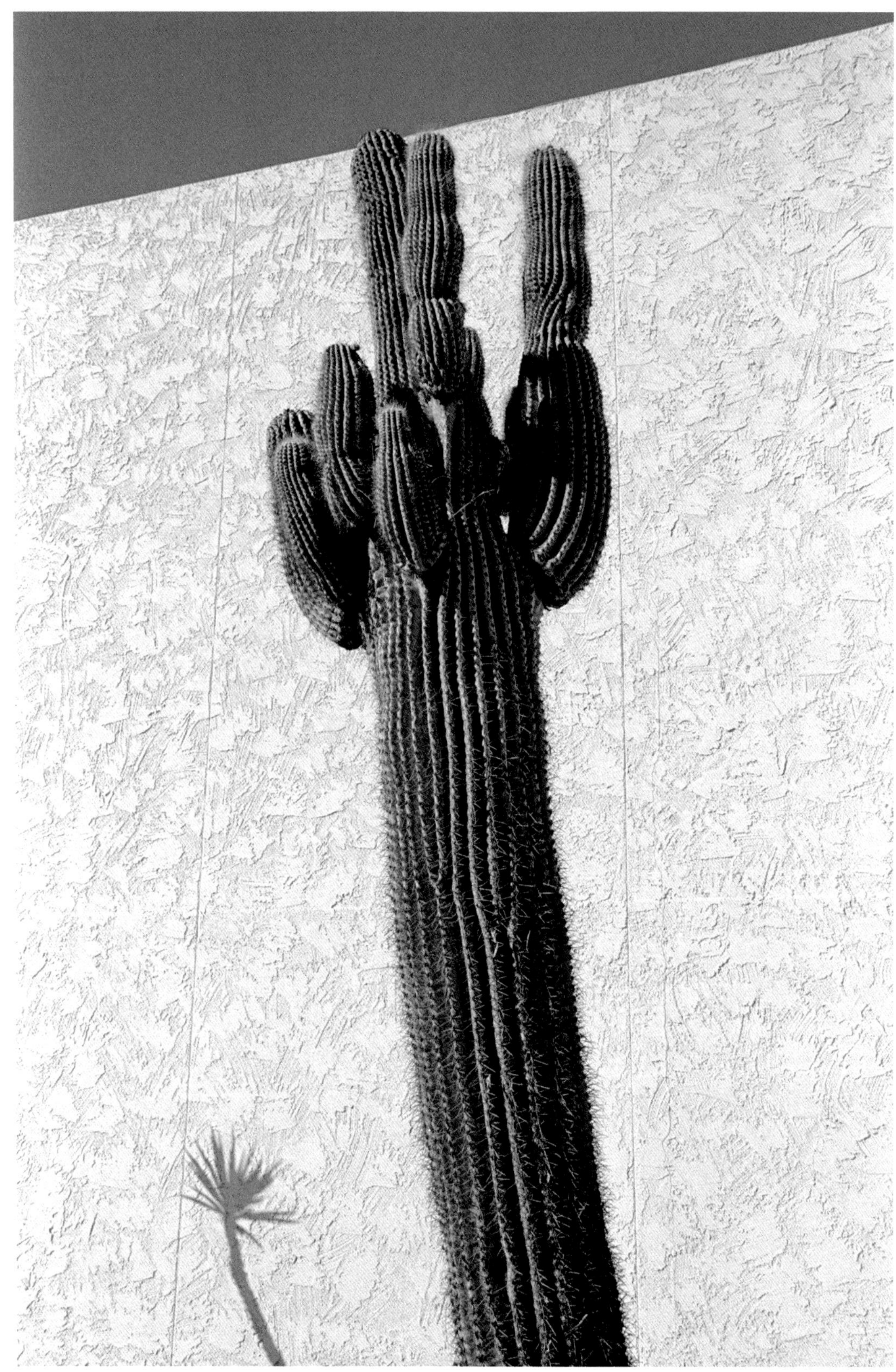

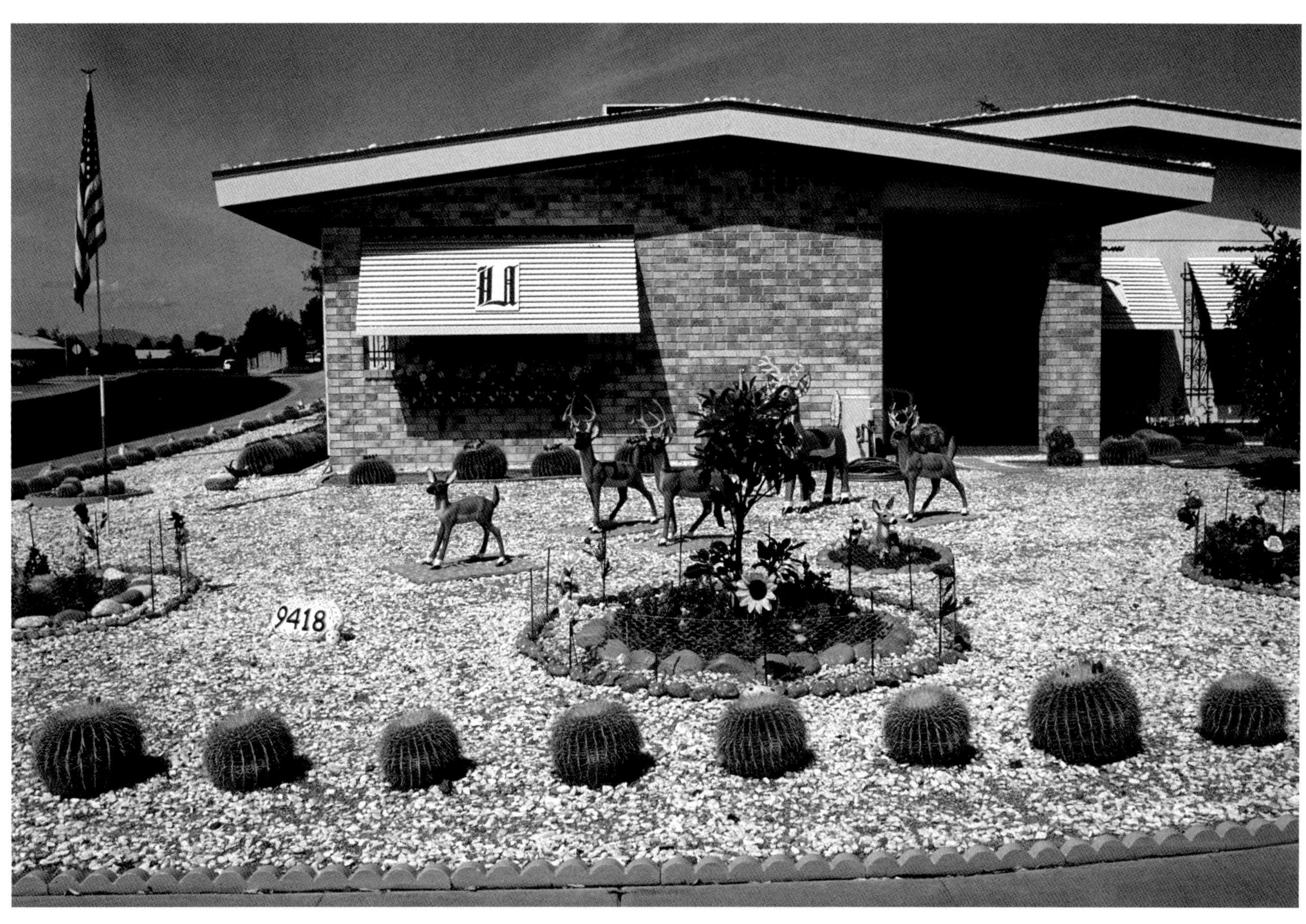

9418

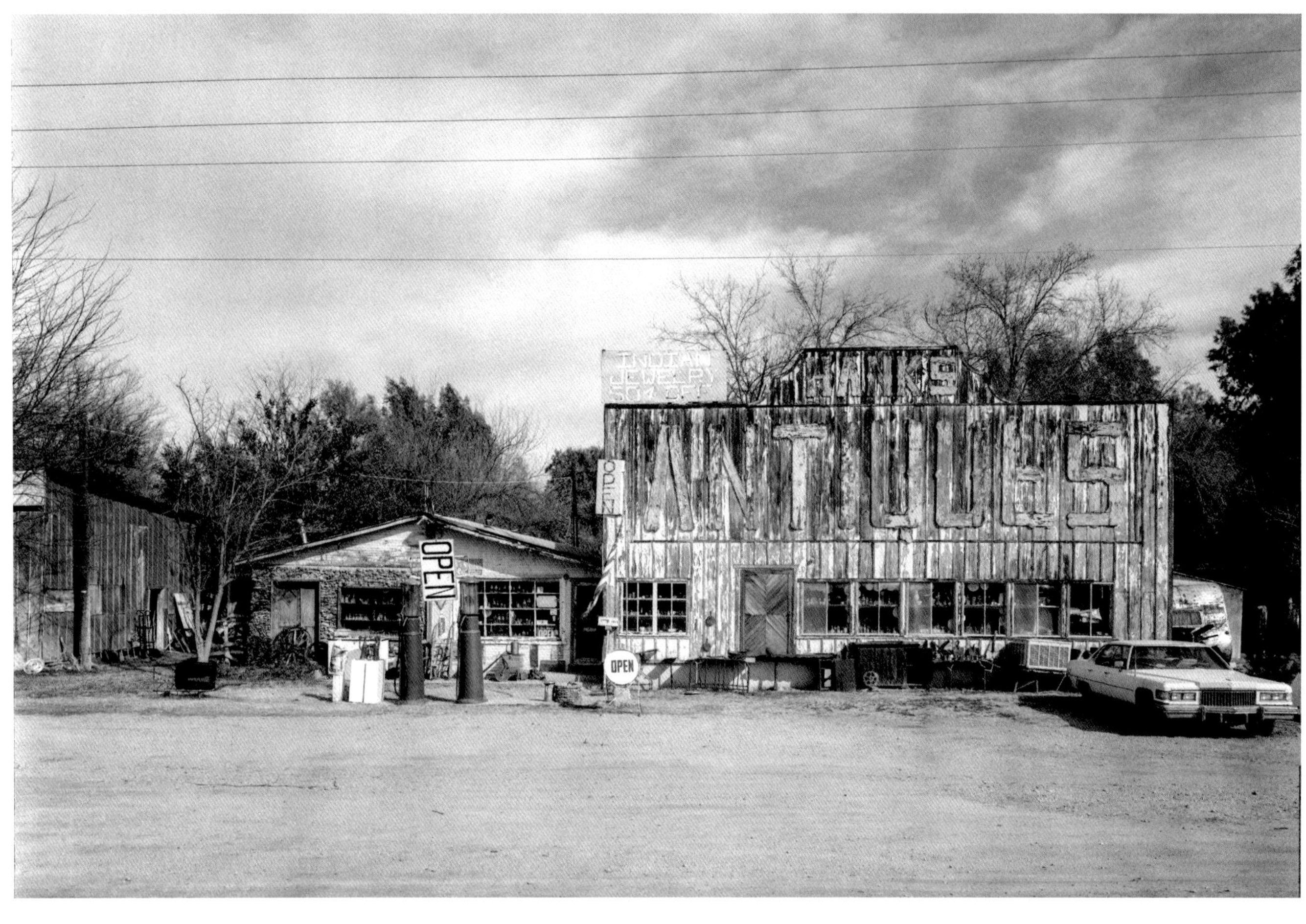

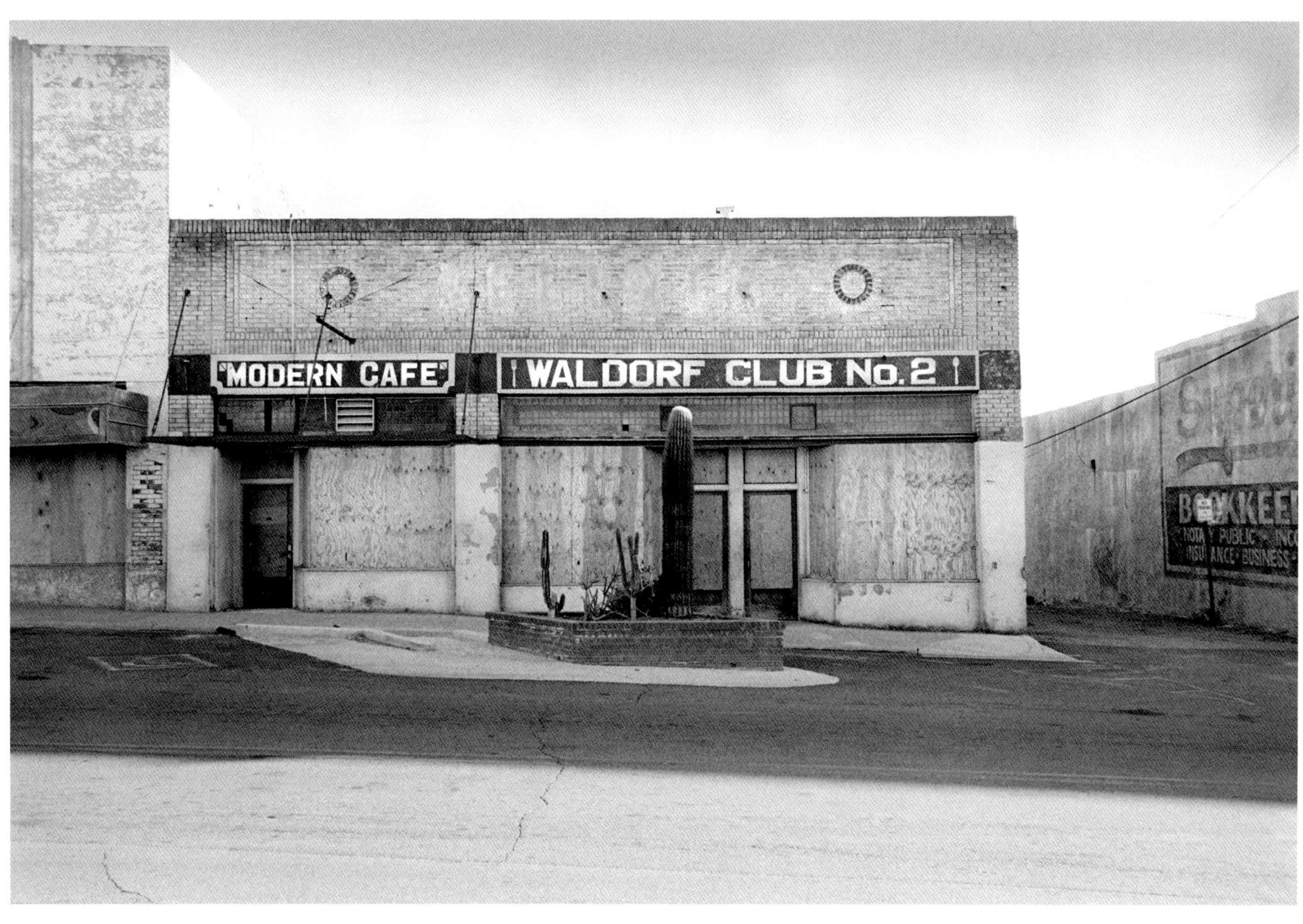

"MODERN CAFE"
WALDORF CLUB No. 2
BOOKKEE
NOTARY PUBLIC
INSURANCE BUSINESS

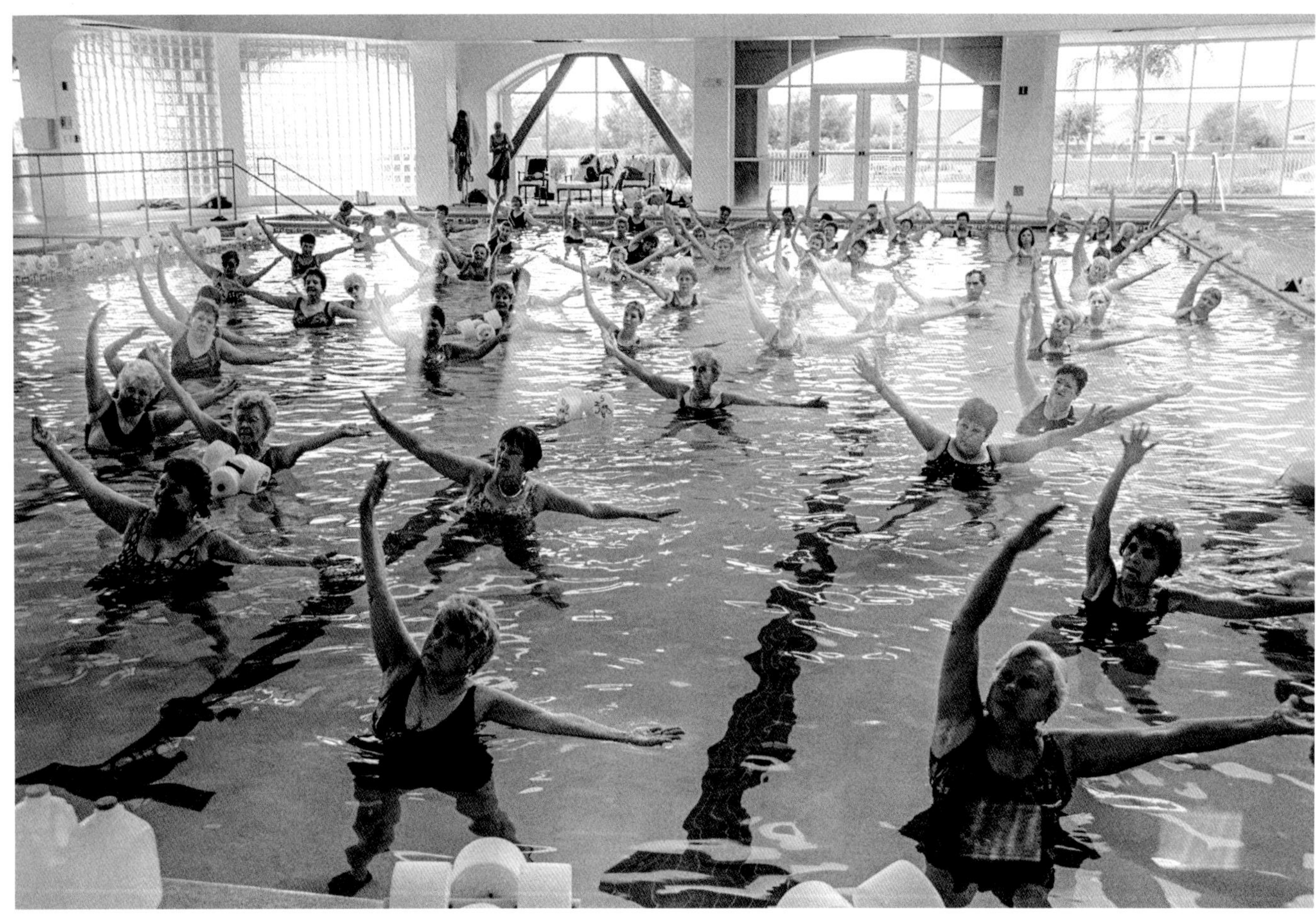

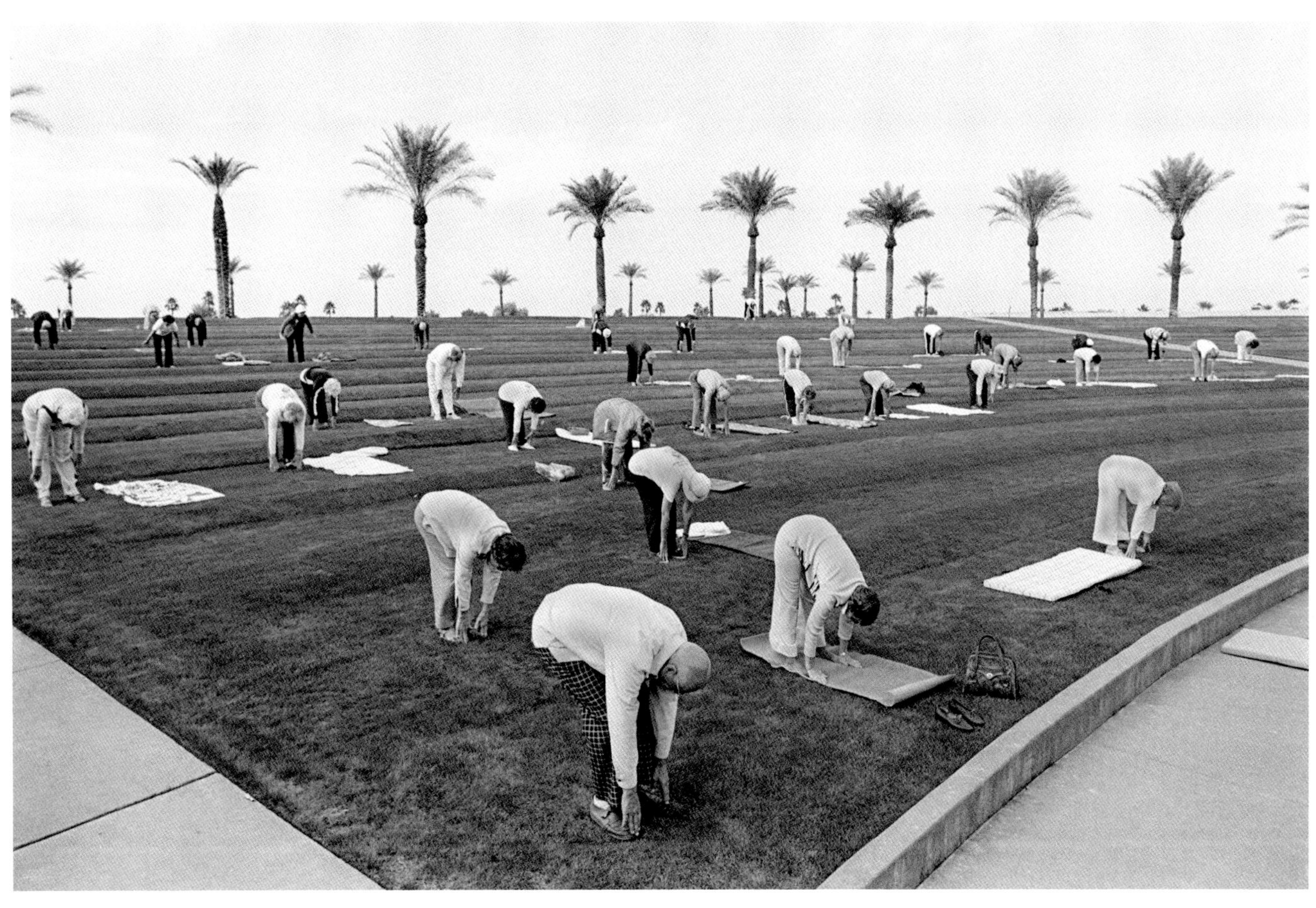

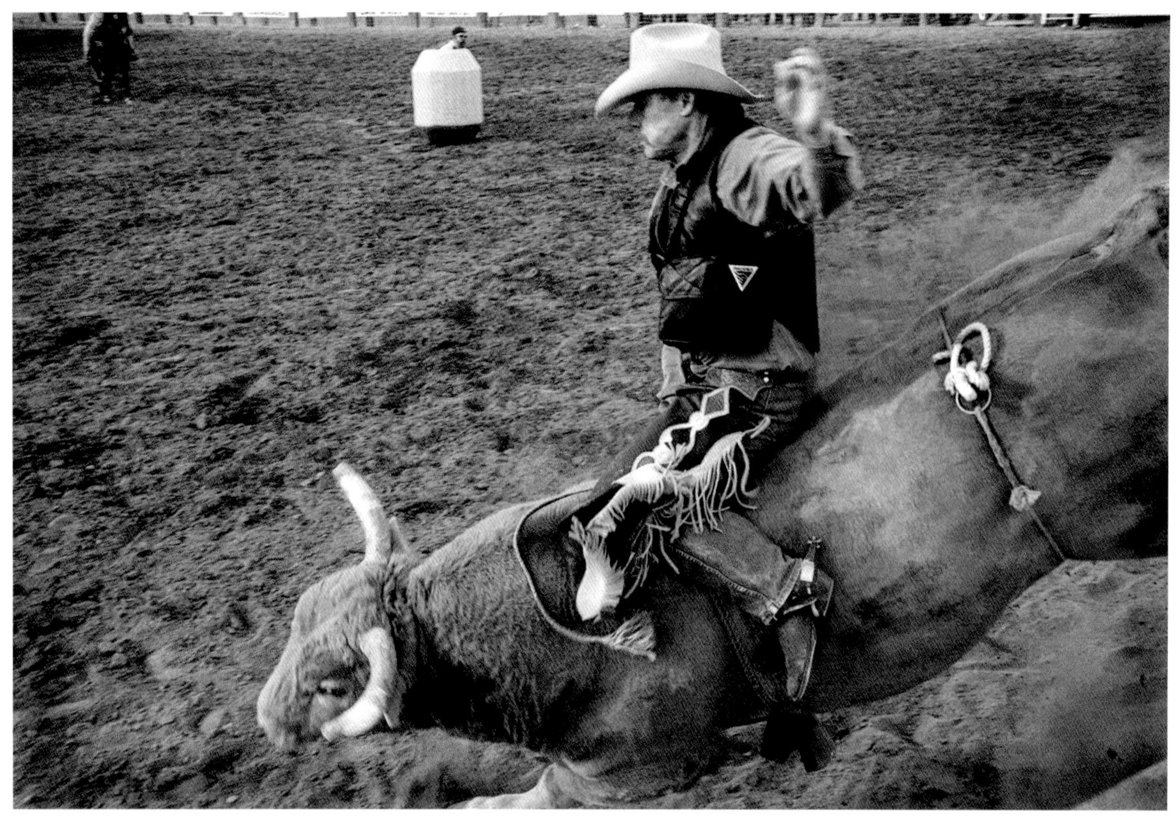

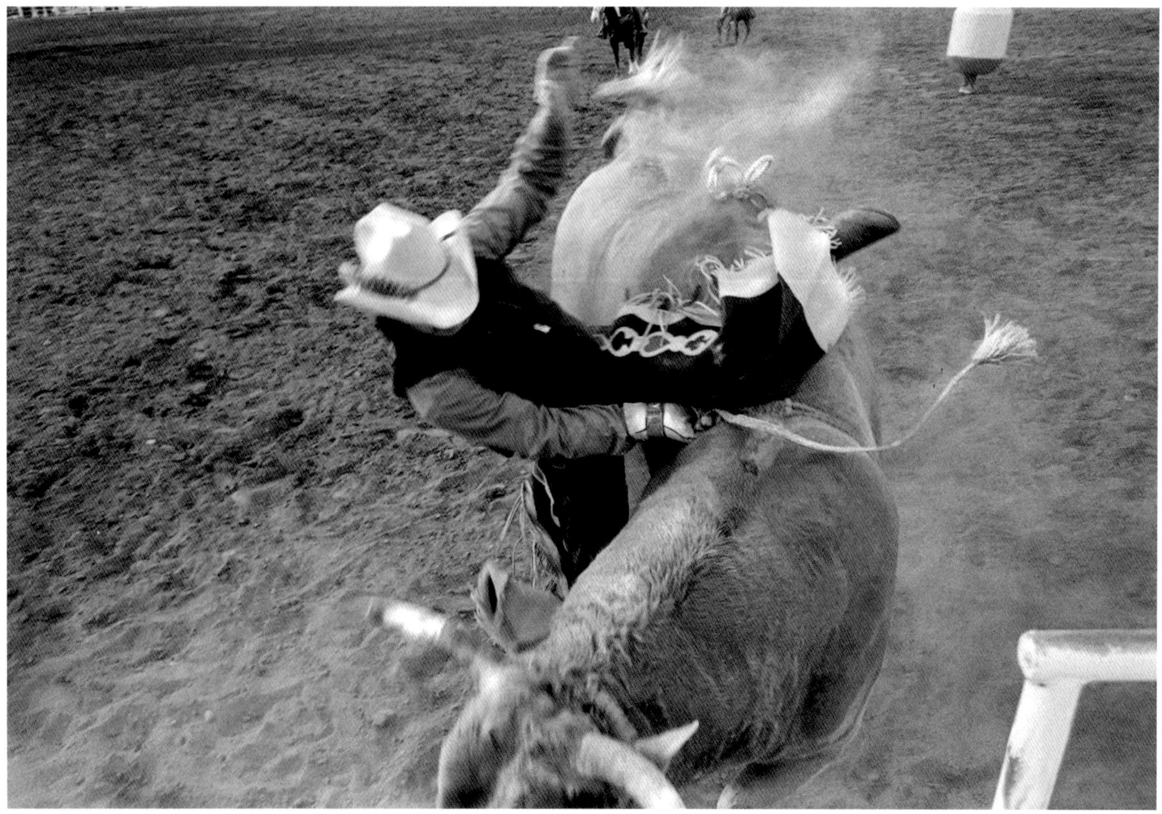

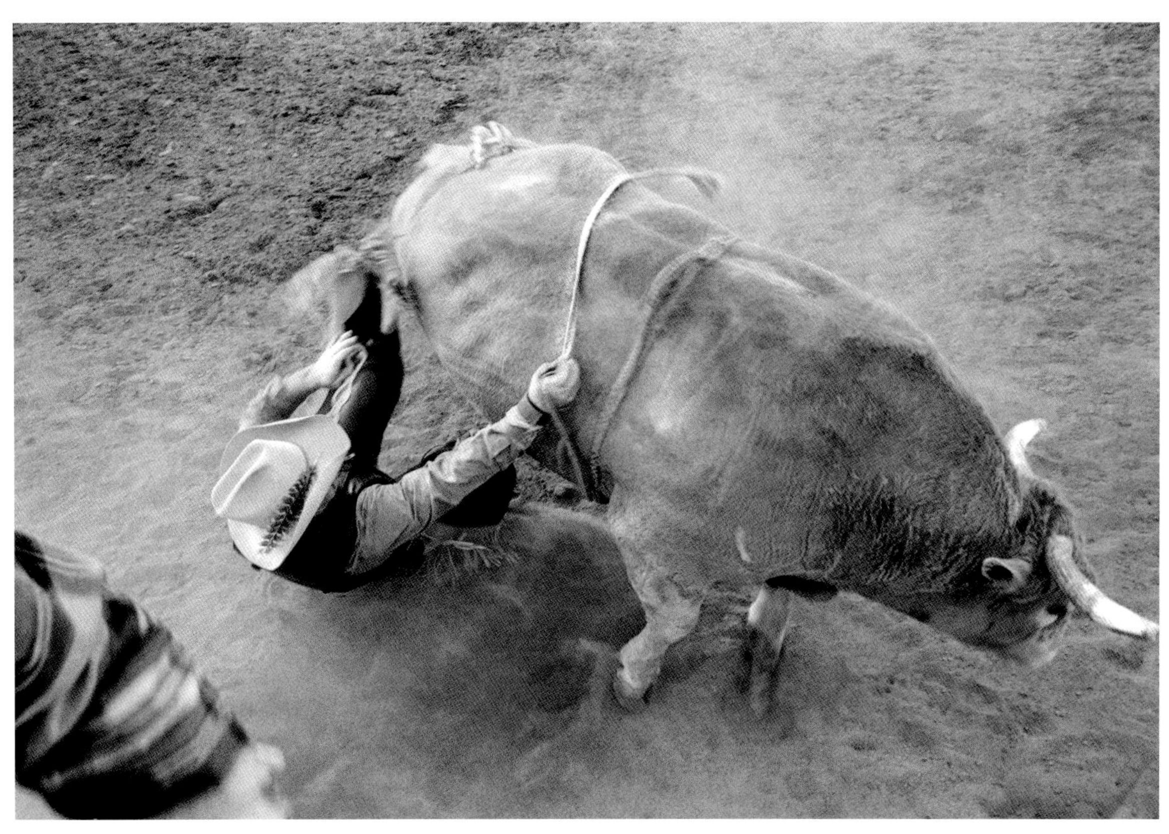

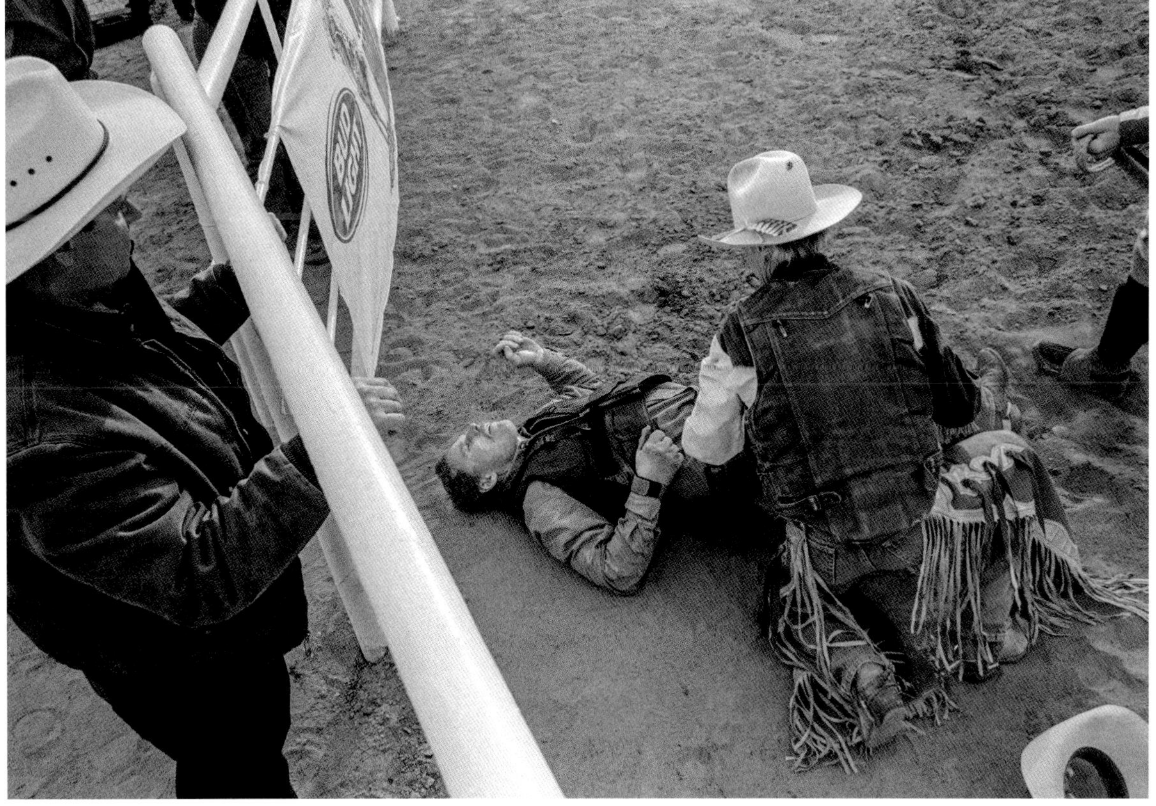

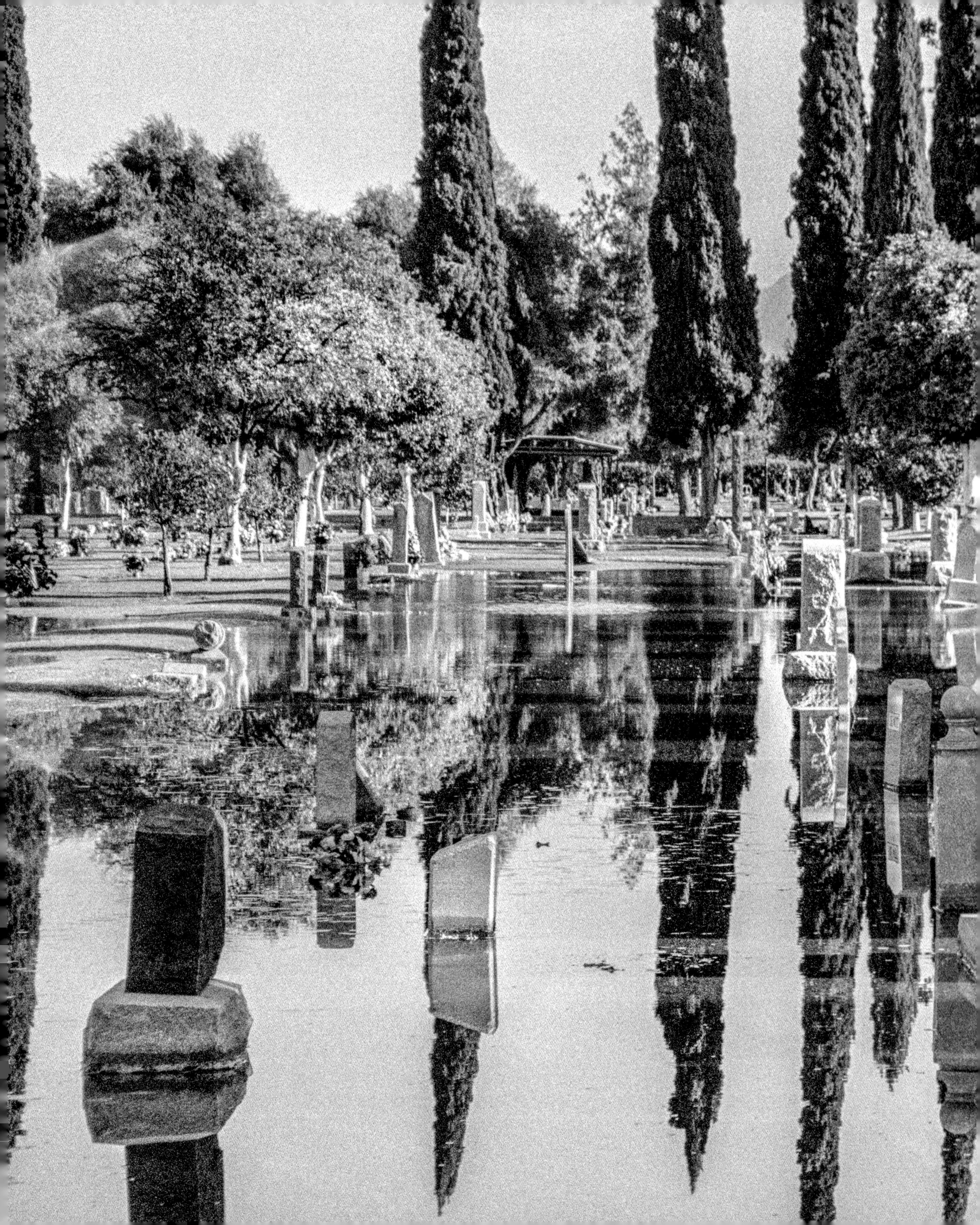

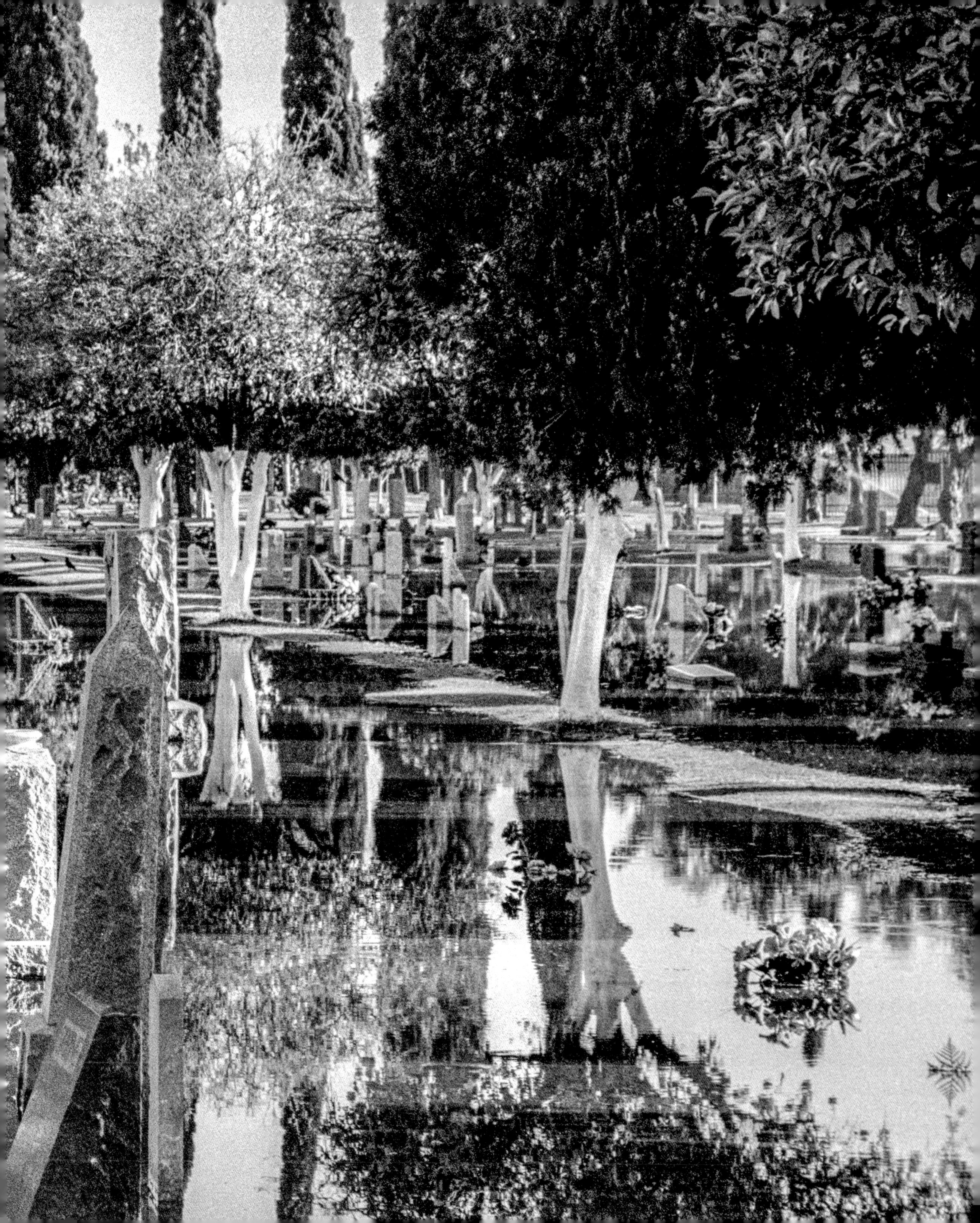

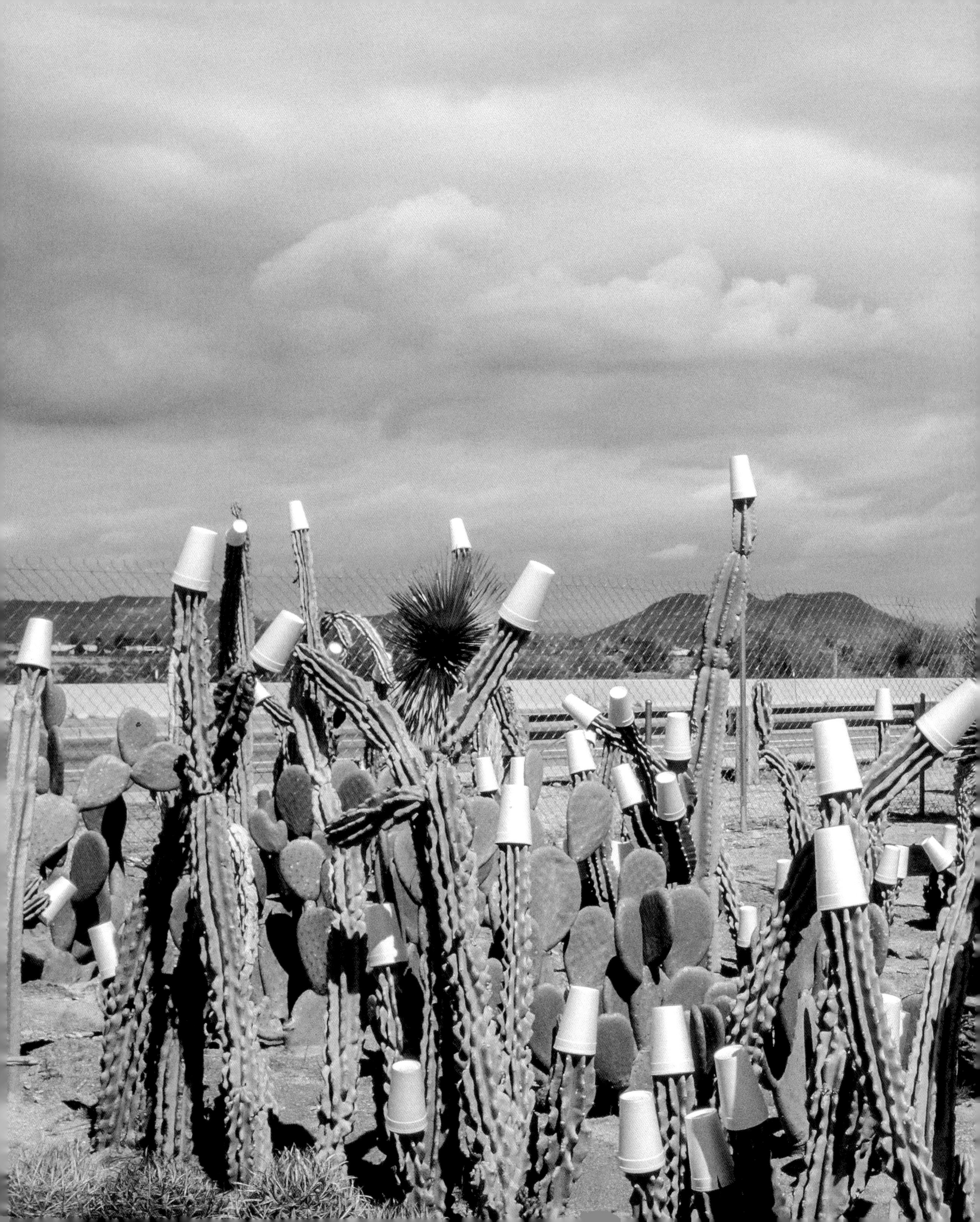

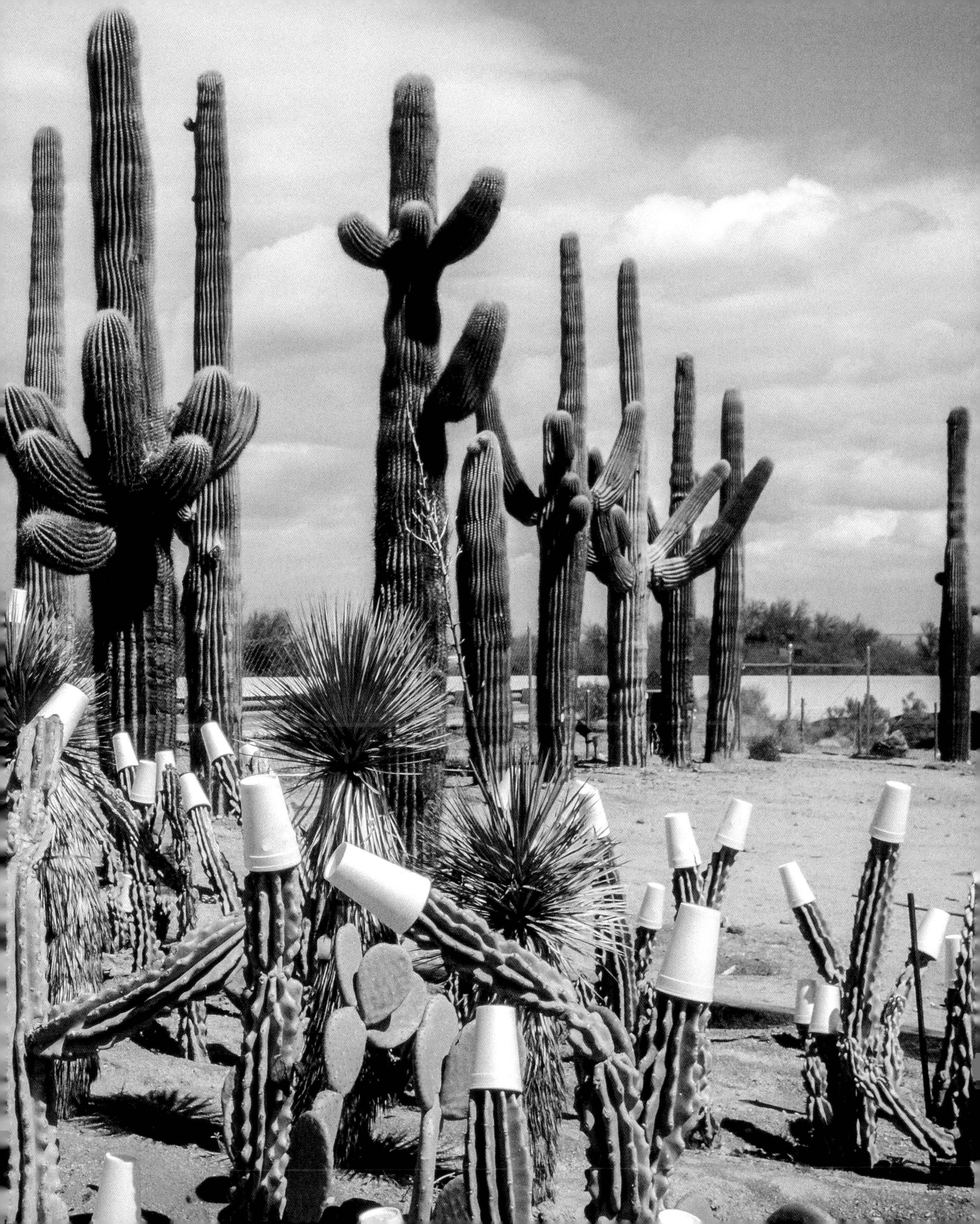

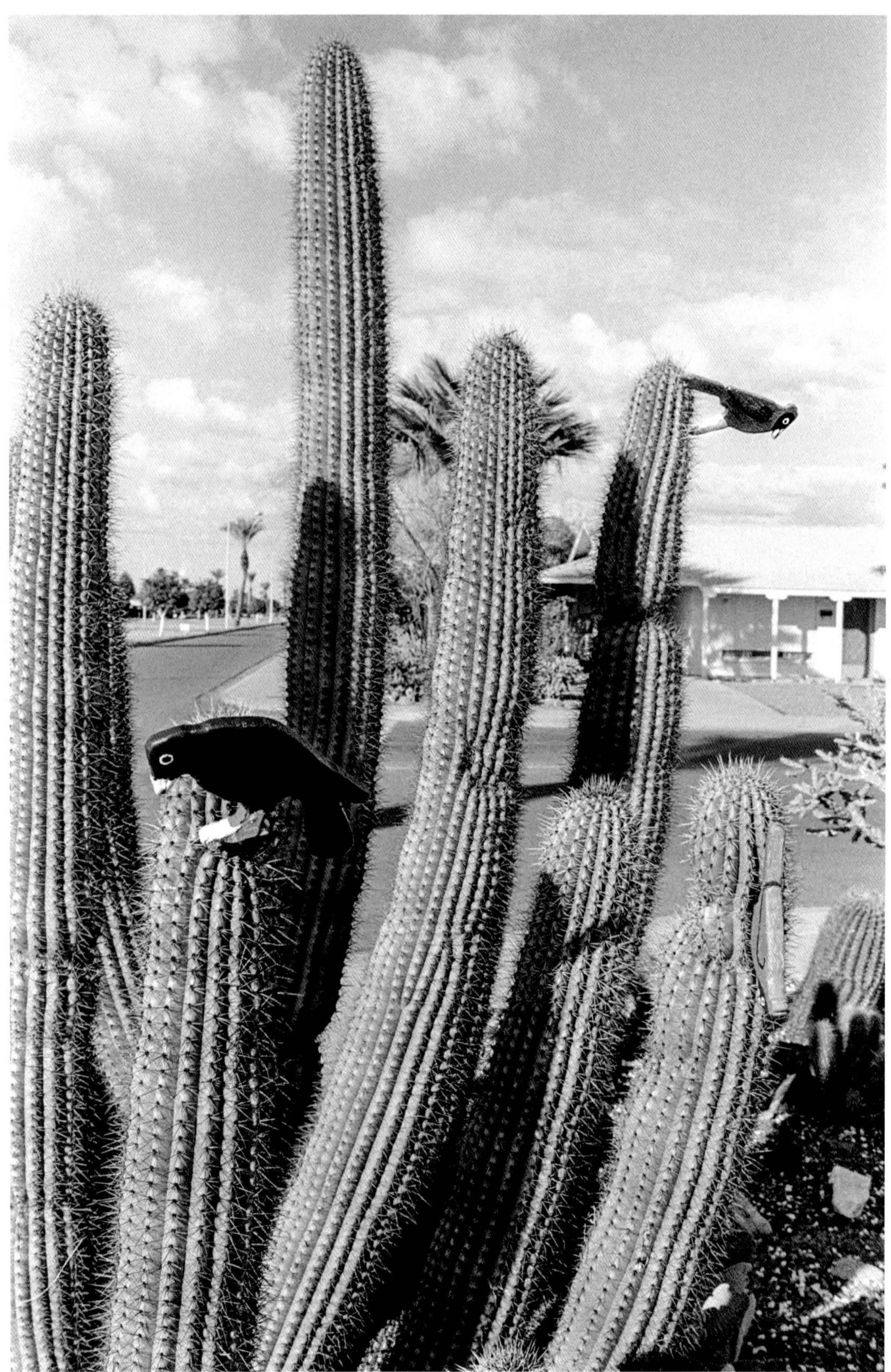

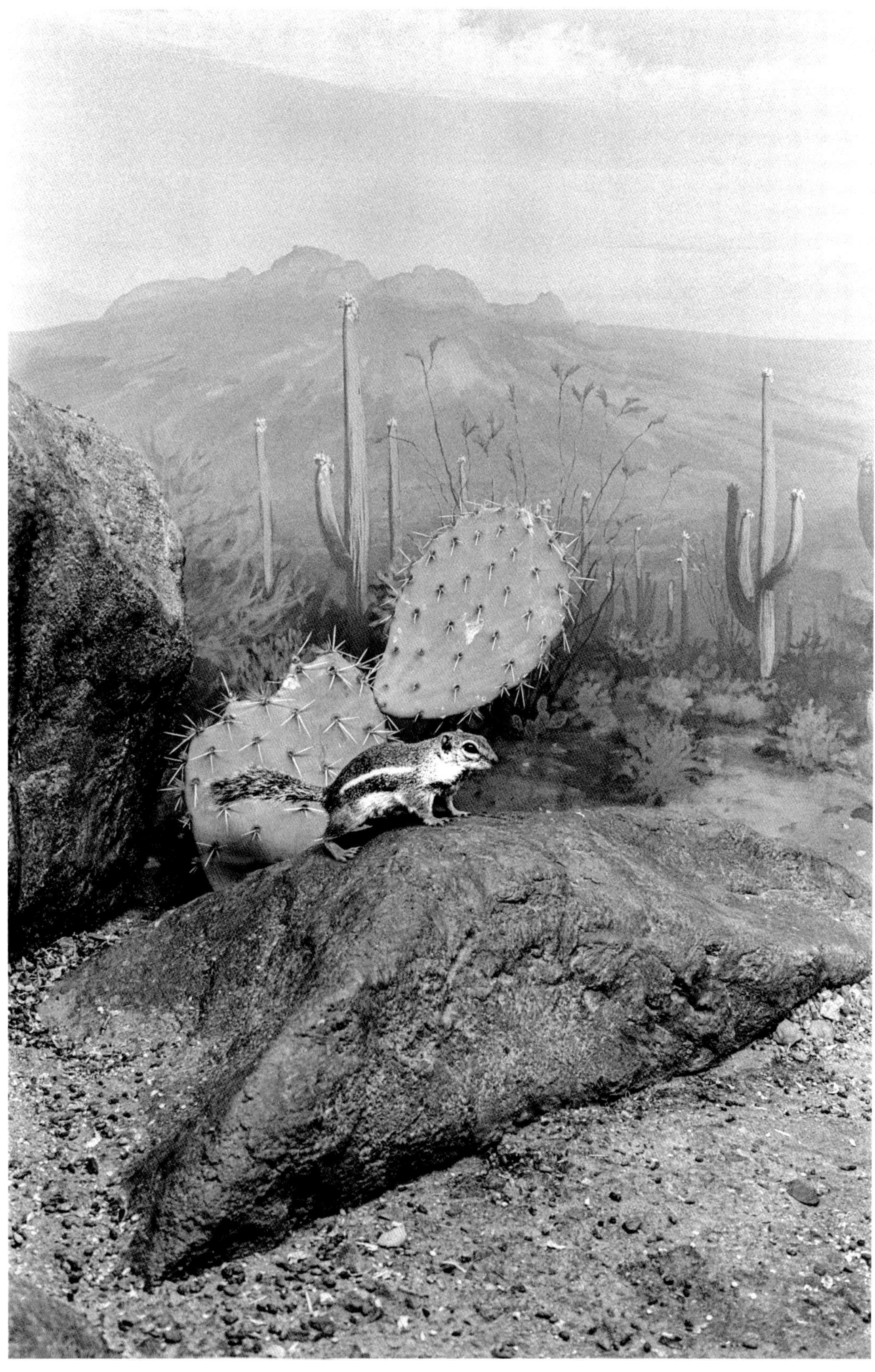

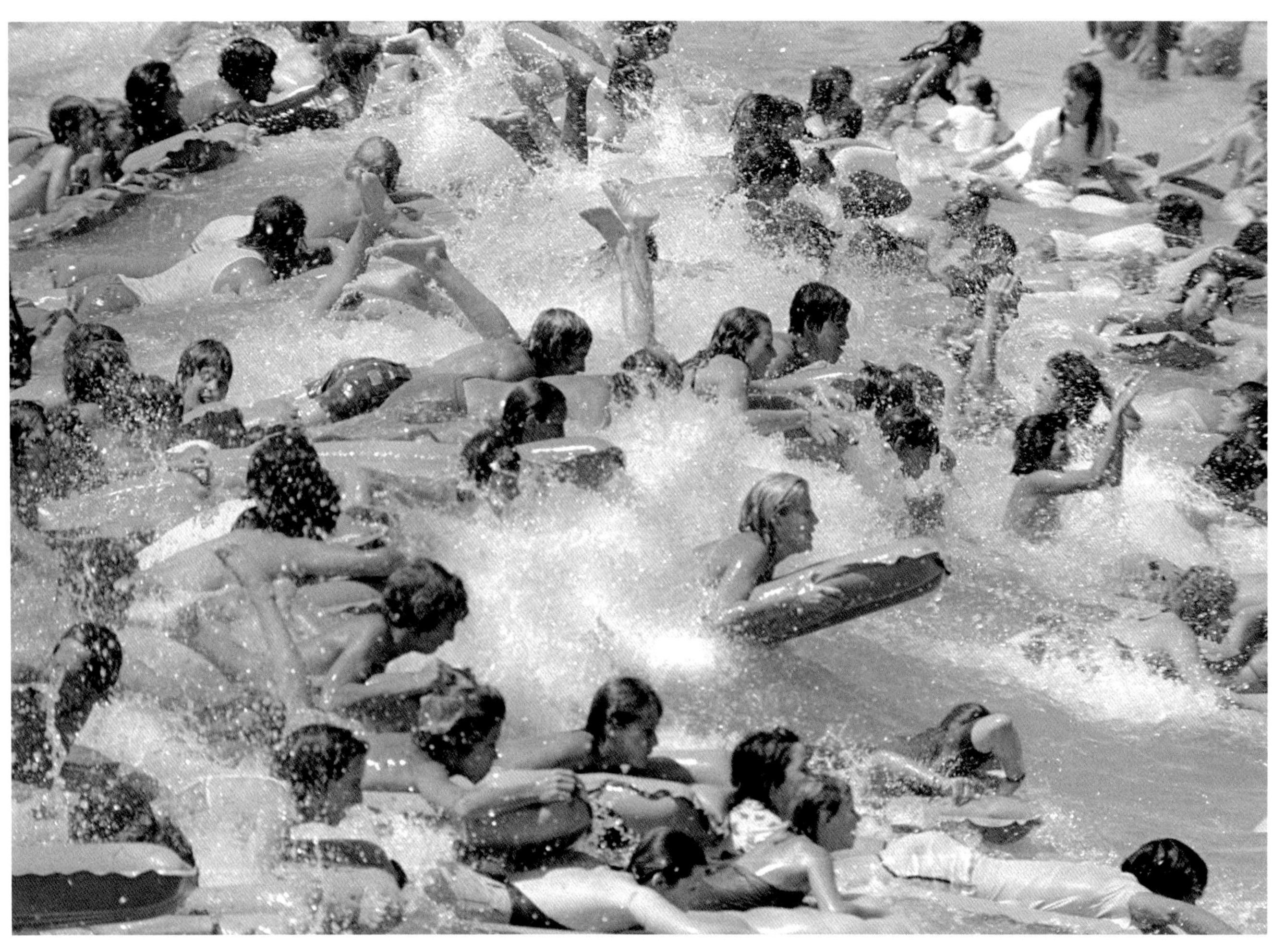

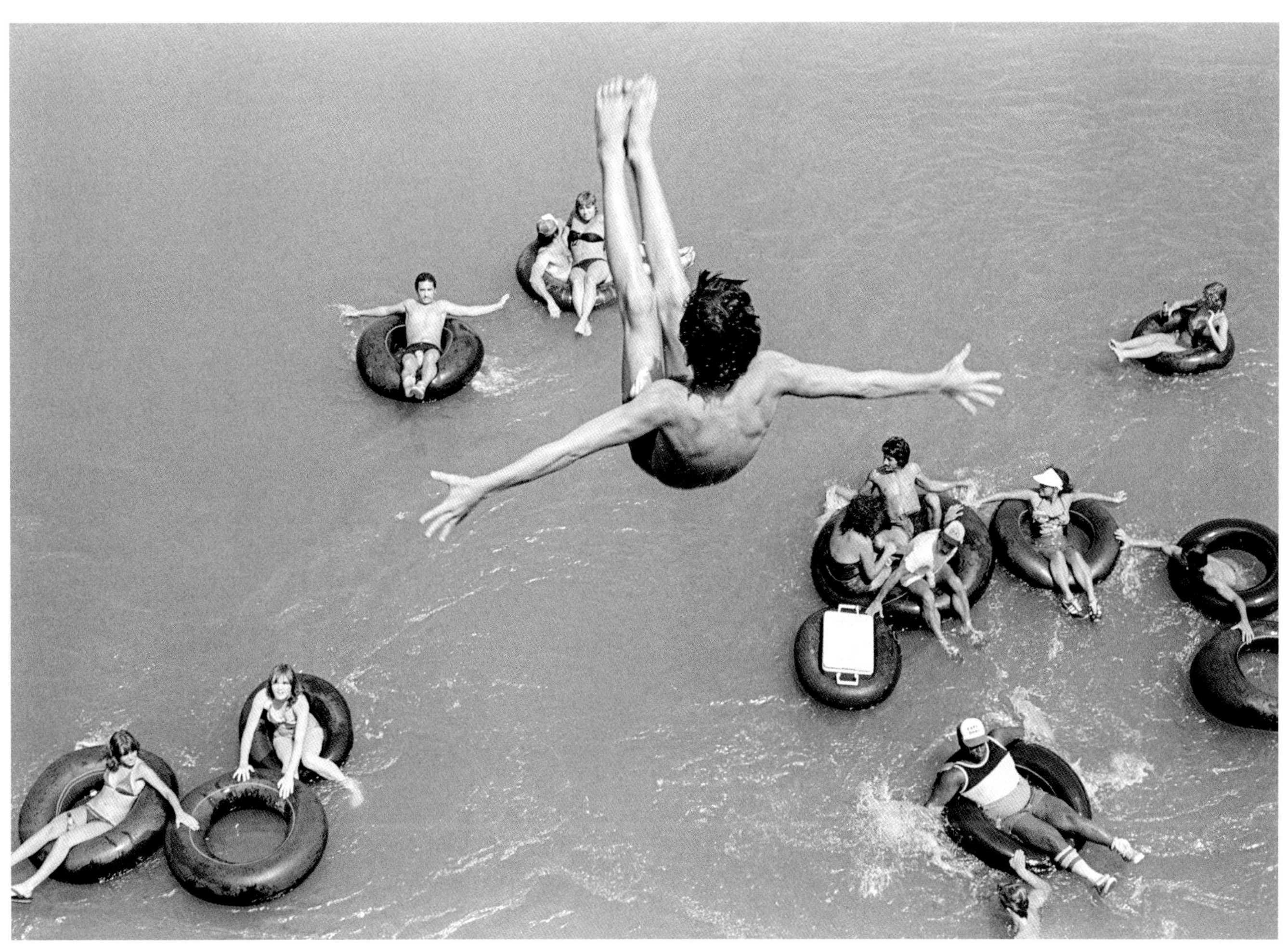

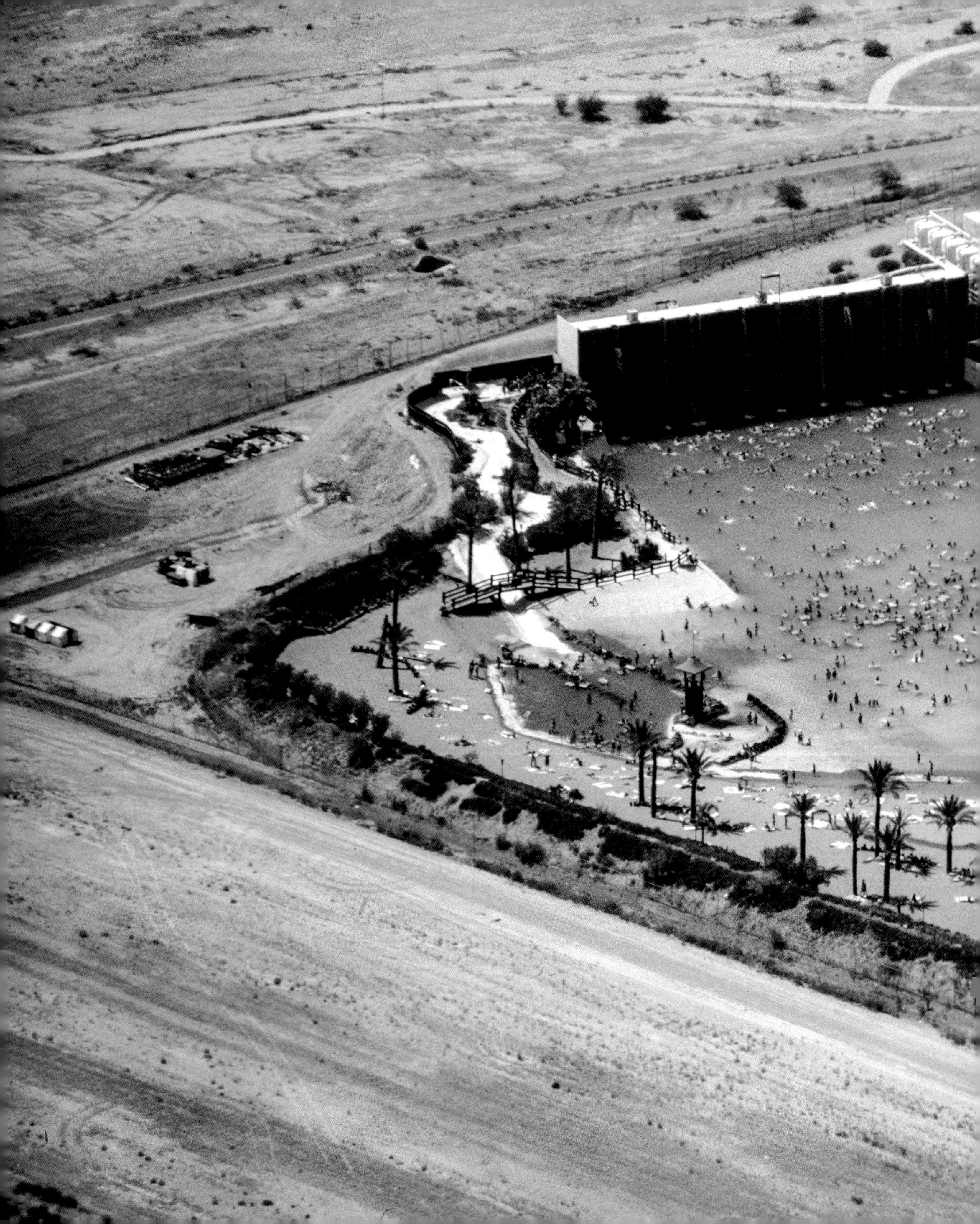

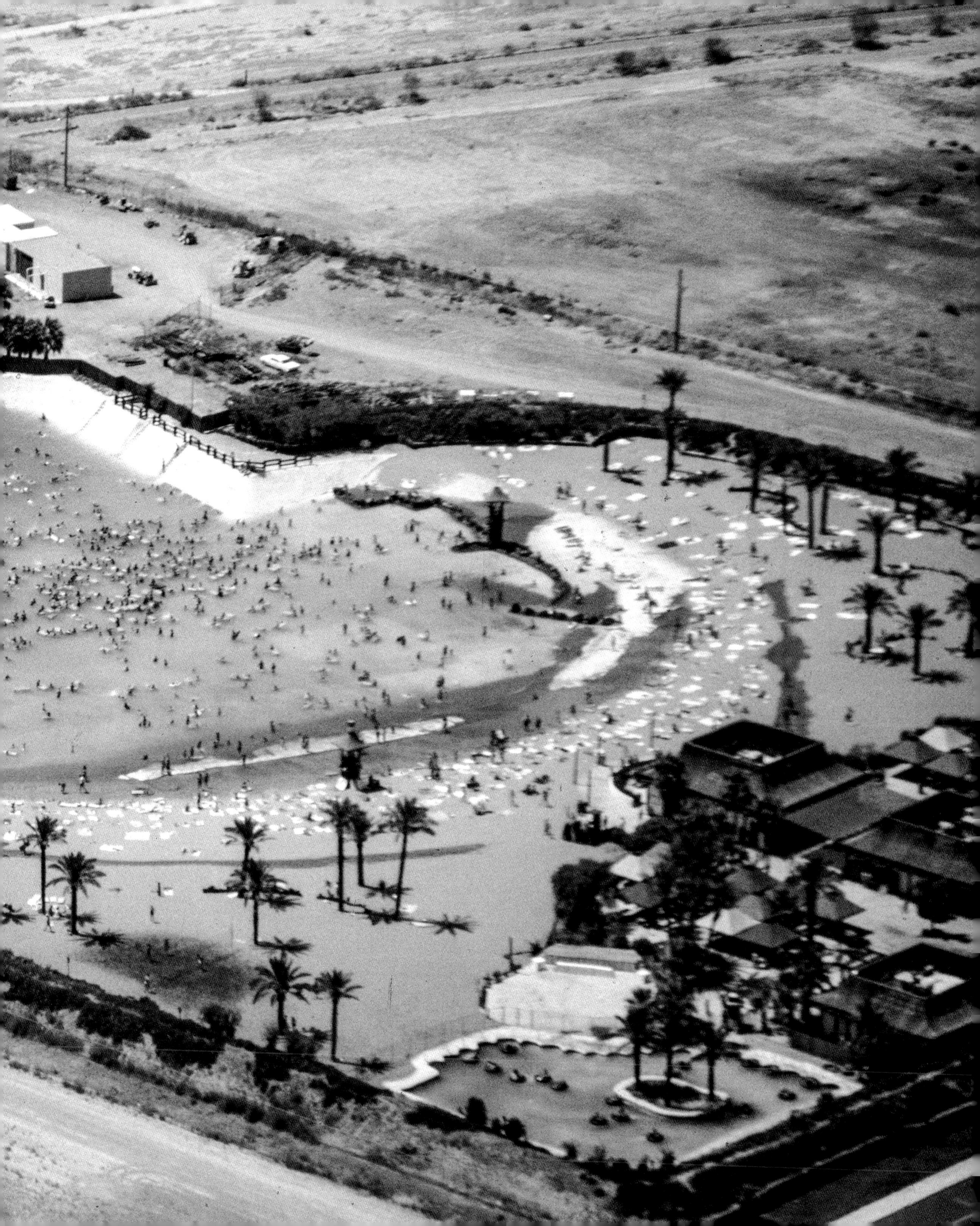

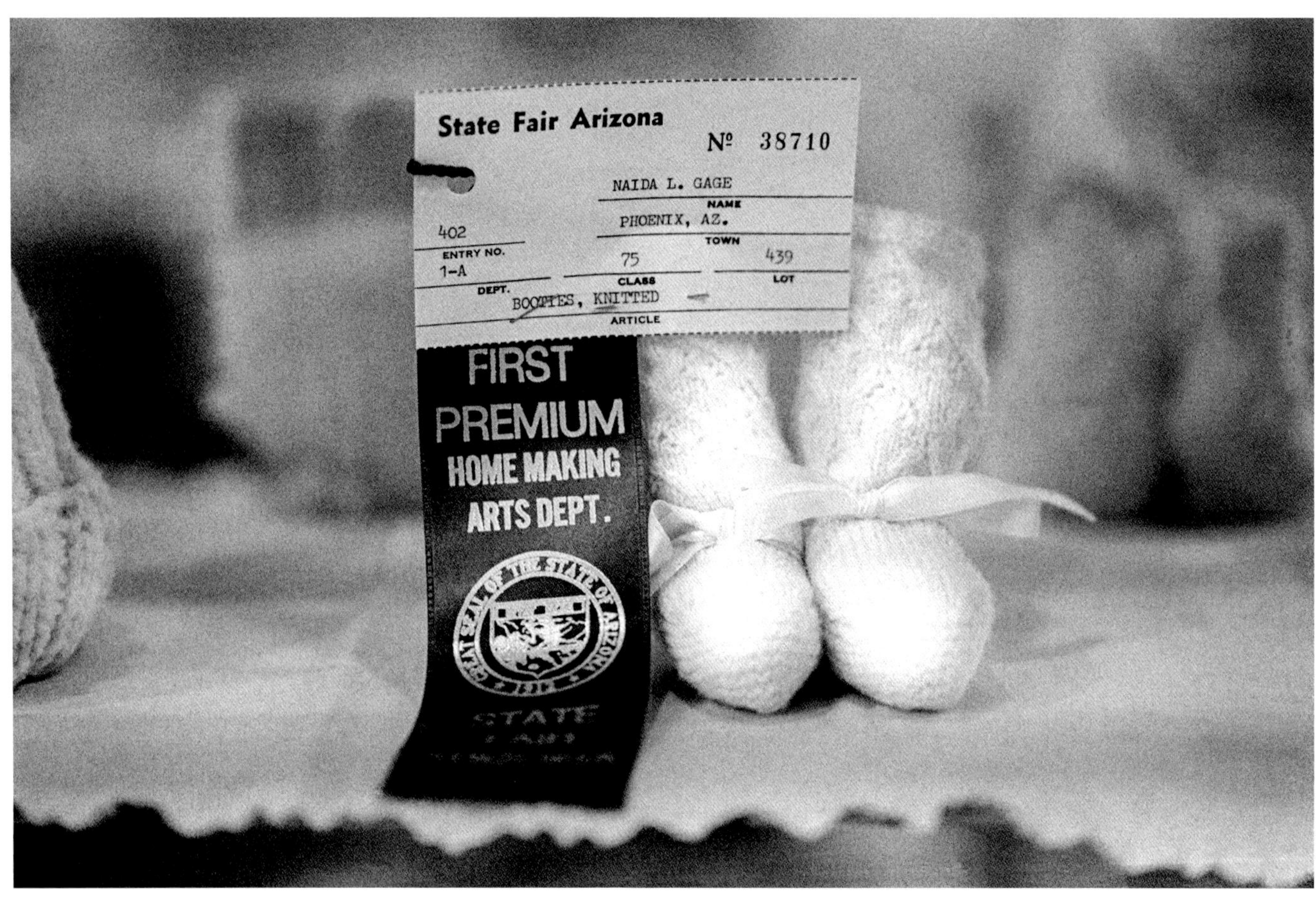
State Fair Arizona
Nº 38710
NAIDA L. GAGE
NAME
402
PHOENIX, AZ.
ENTRY NO.
TOWN
1-A
75
439
DEPT.
CLASS
LOT
BOOTIES, KNITTED
ARTICLE
FIRST
PREMIUM
HOME MAKING
ARTS DEPT.
STATE

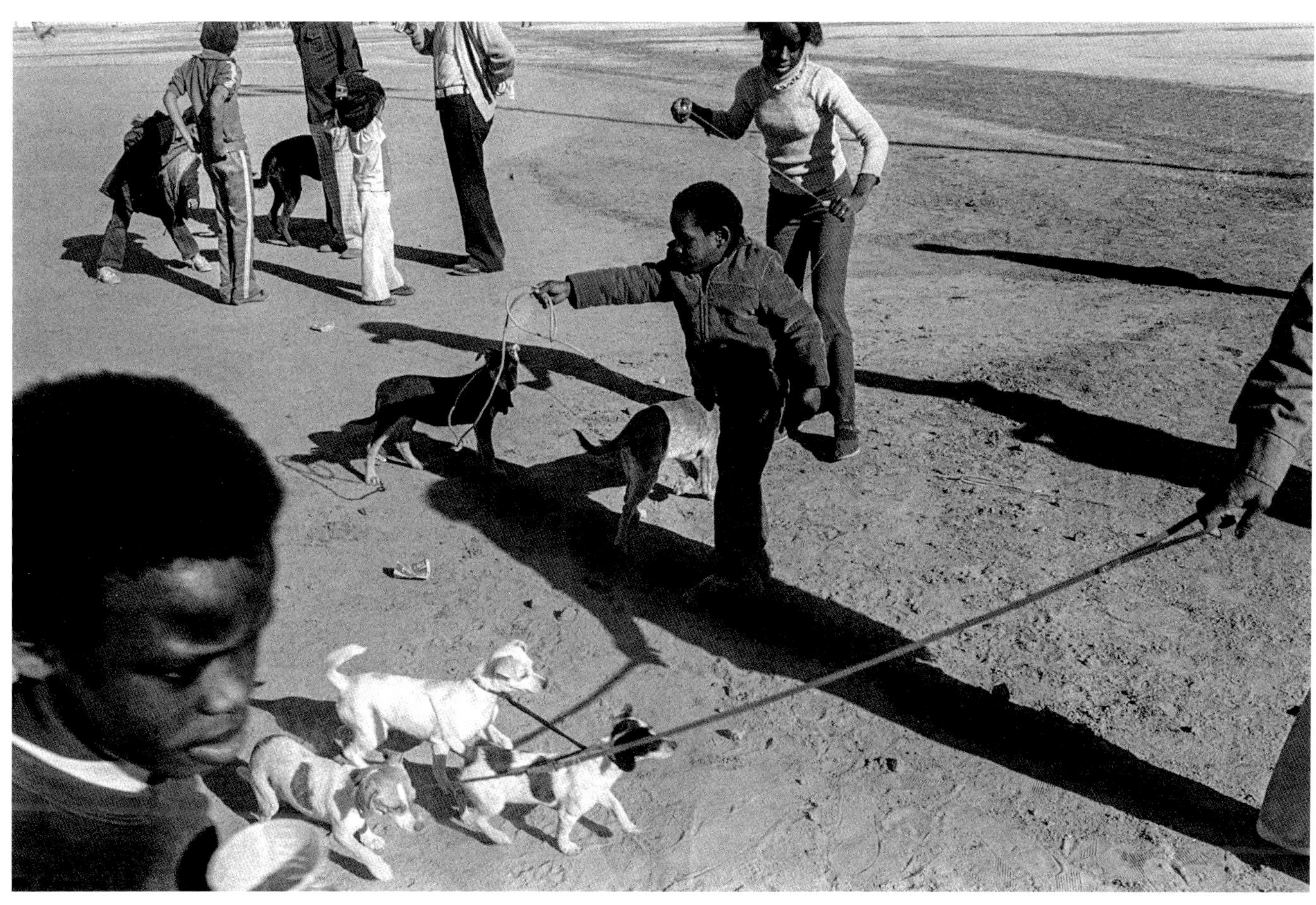

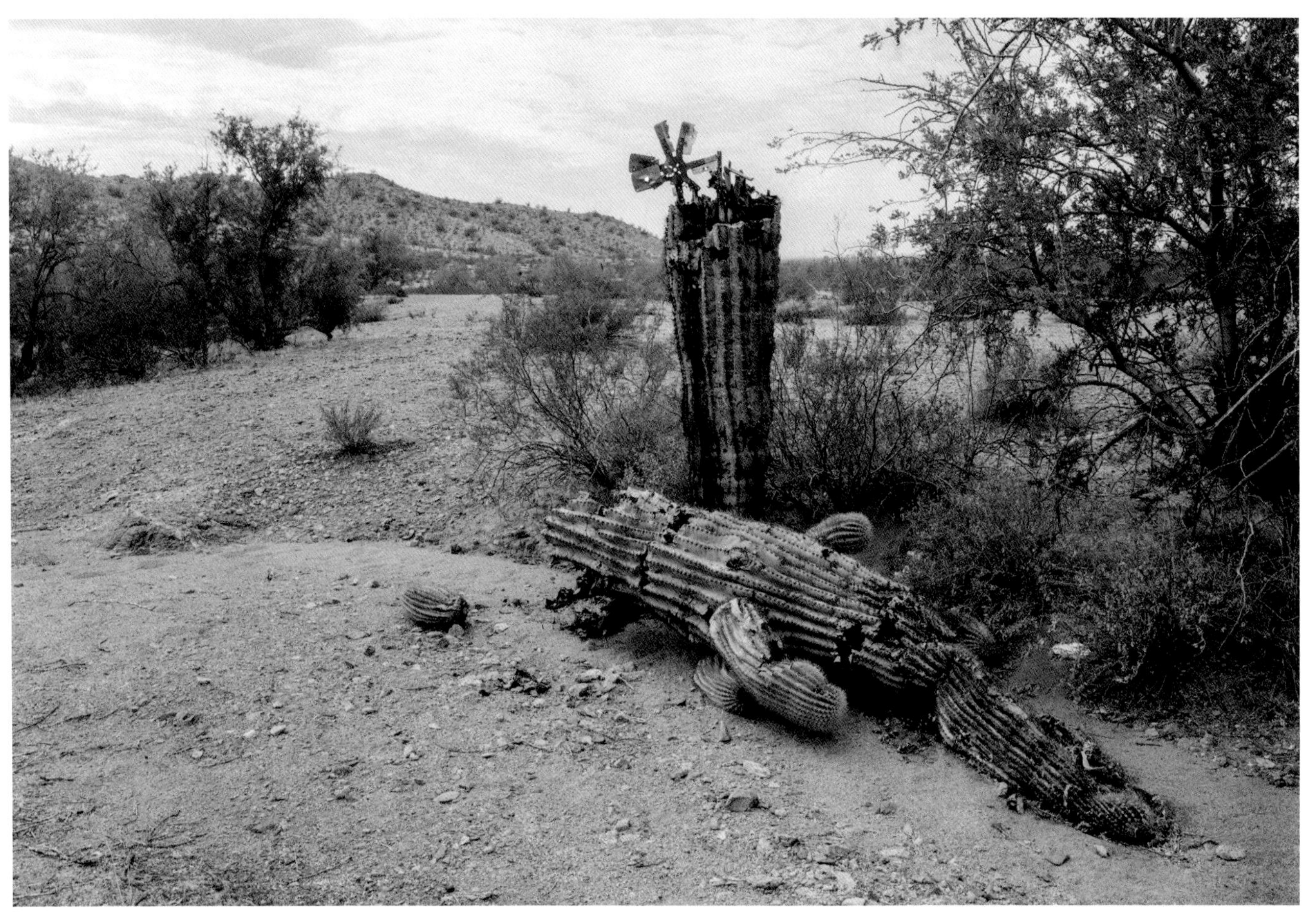

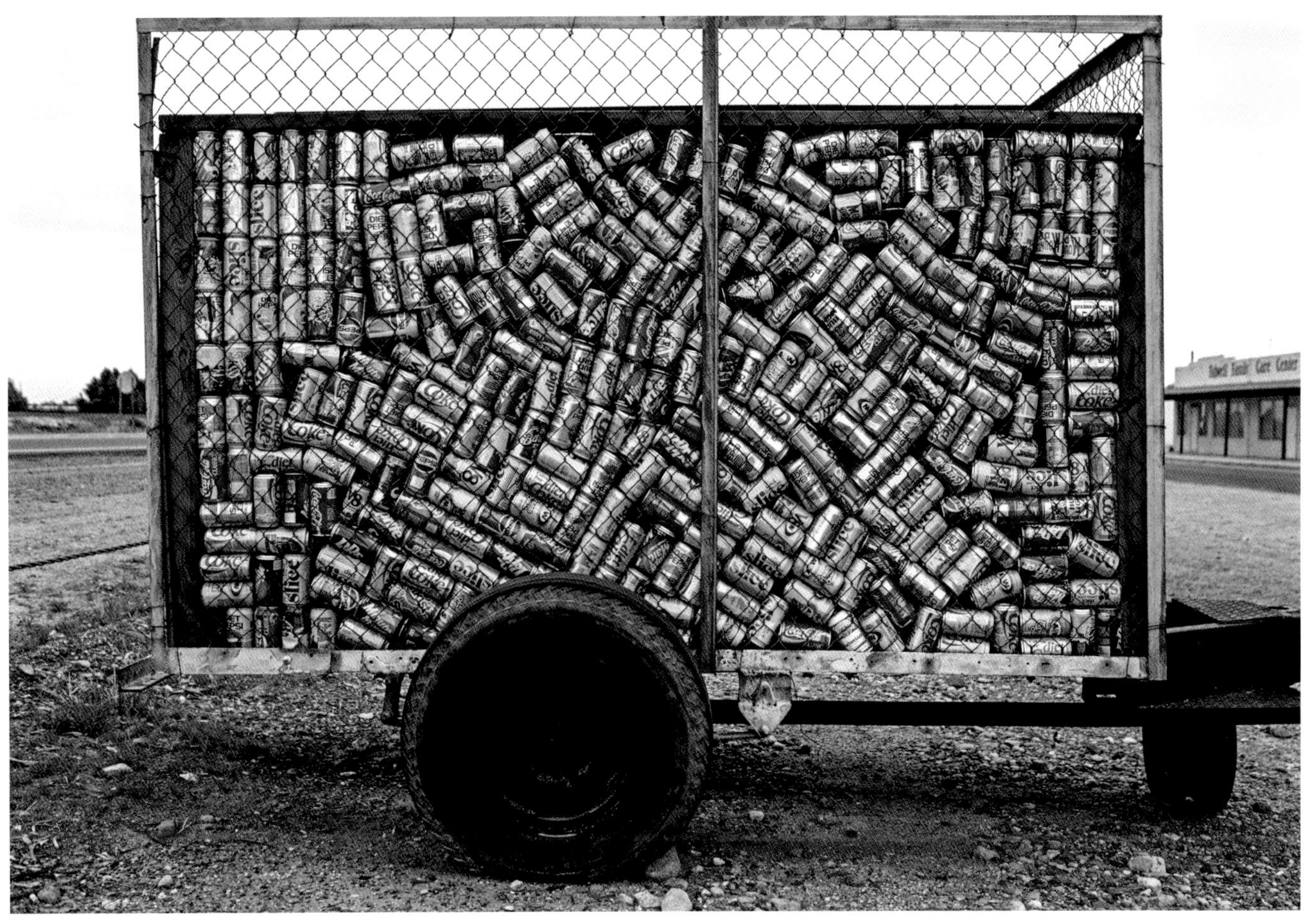

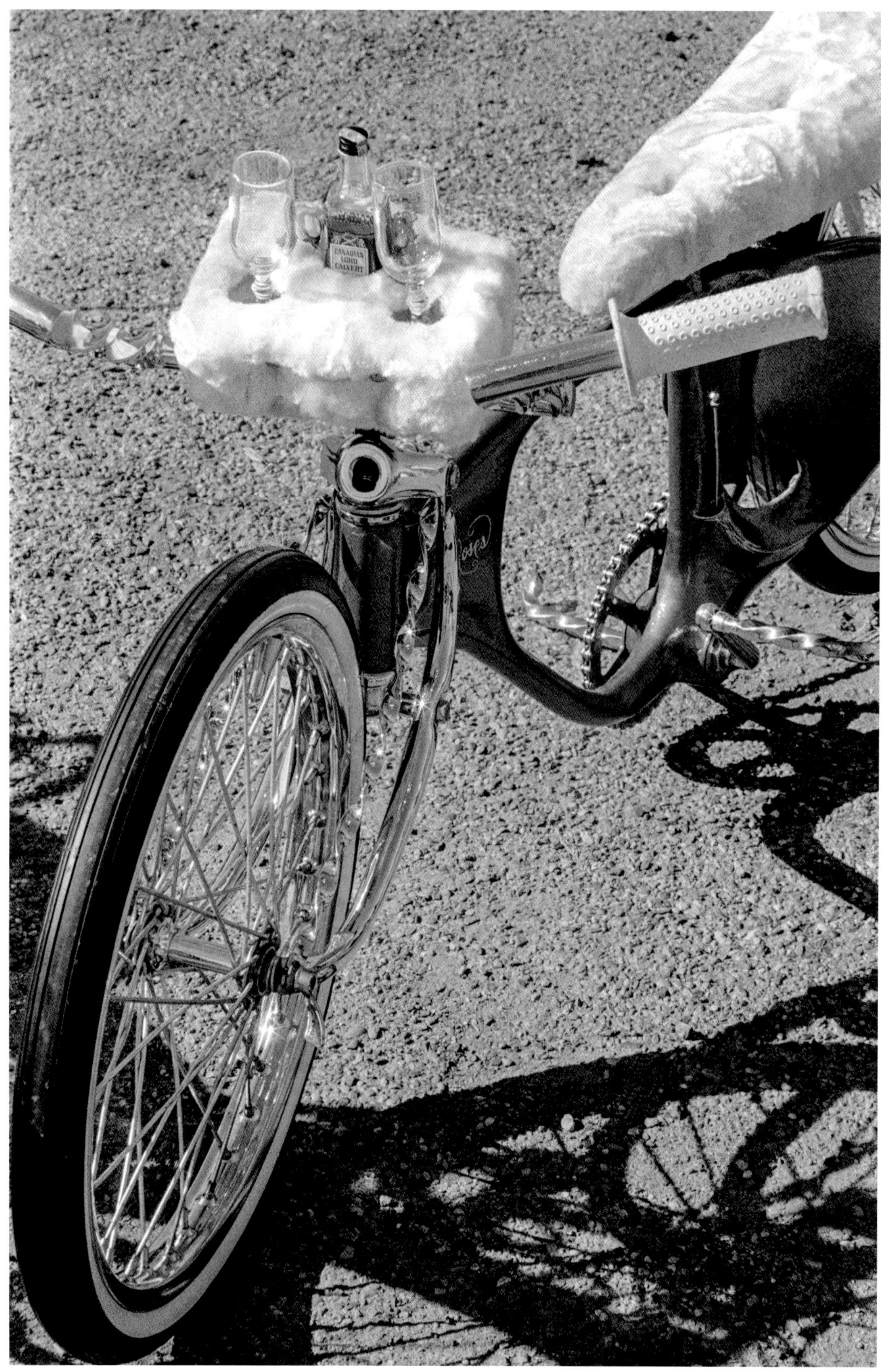

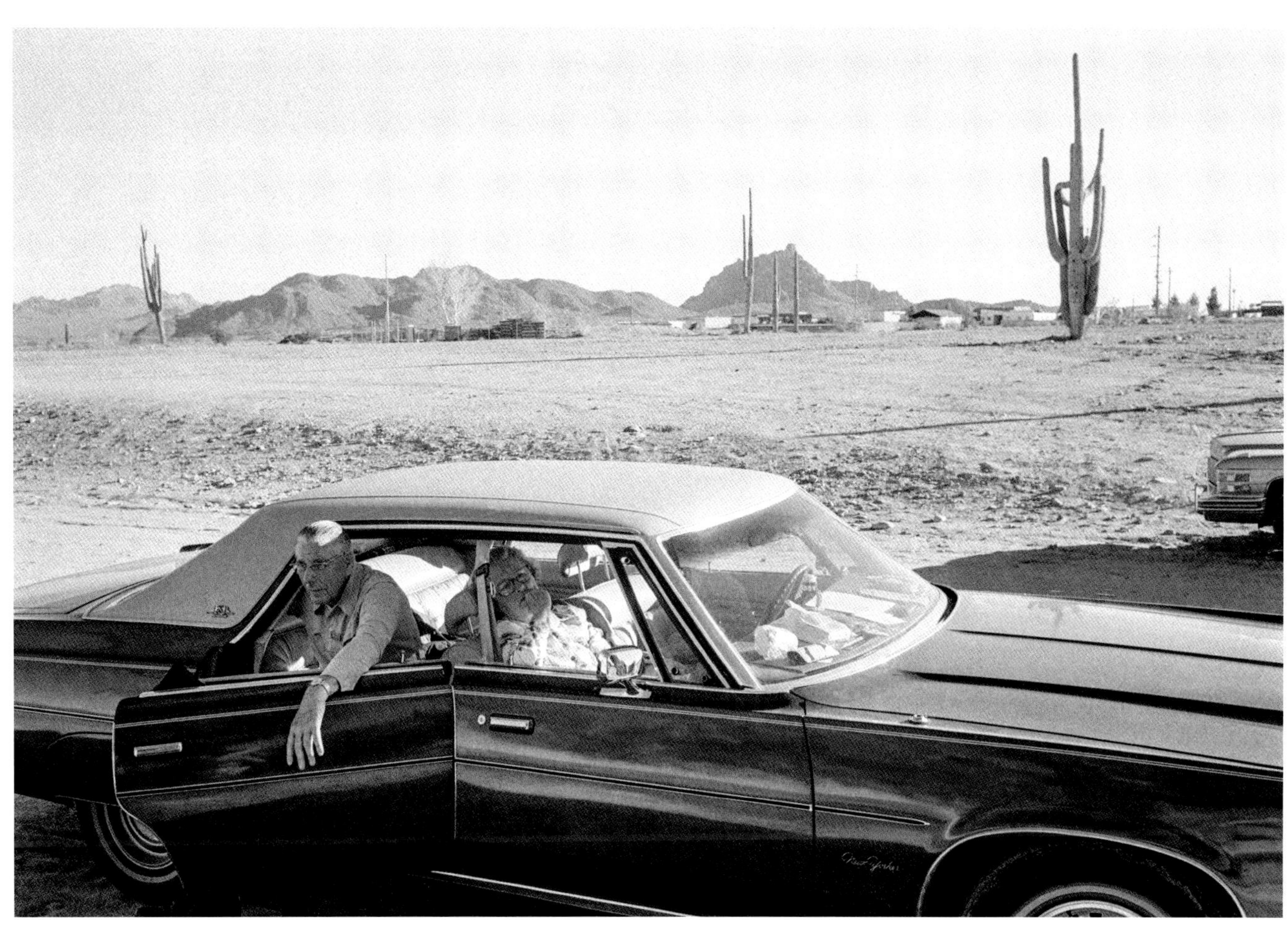

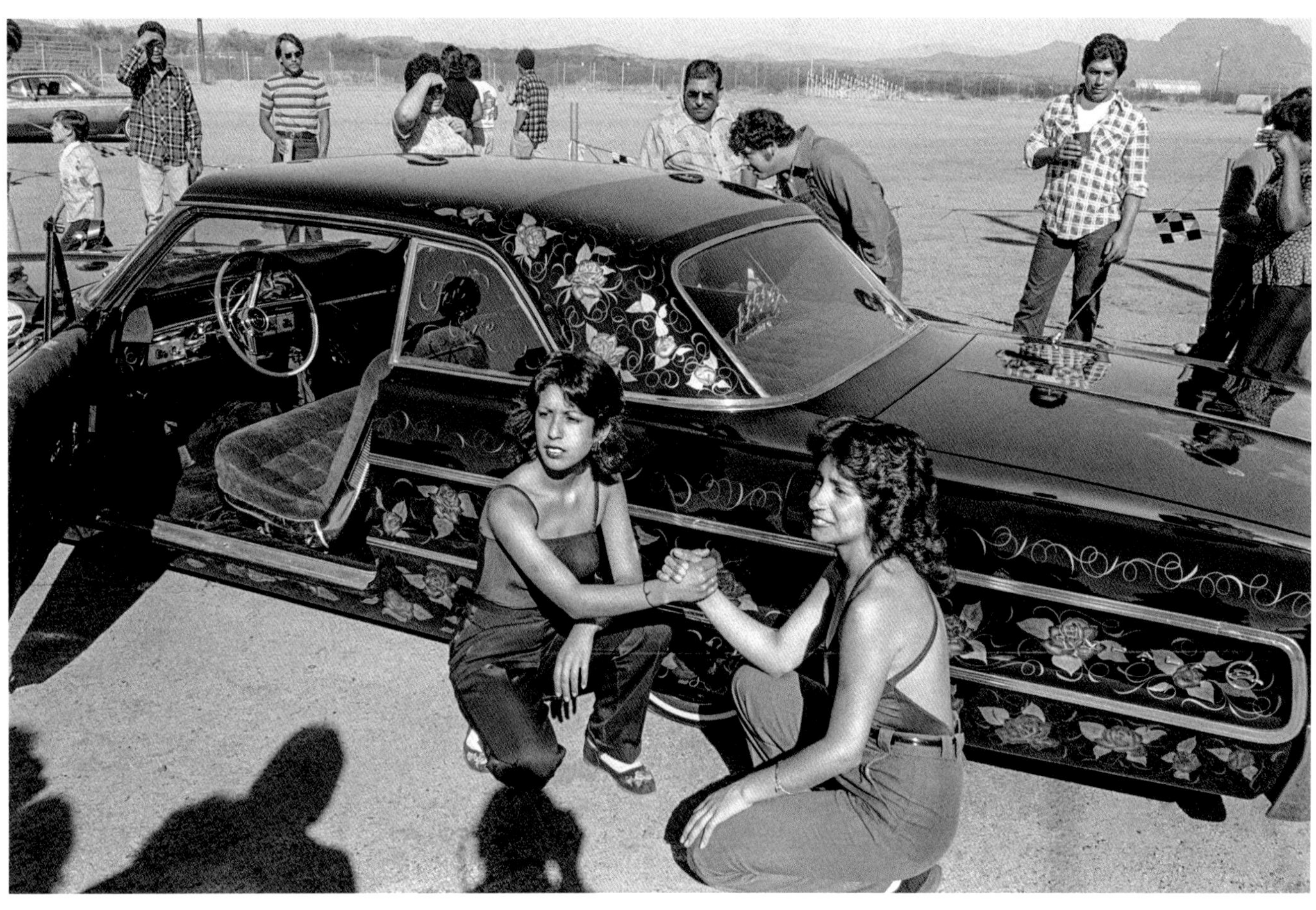

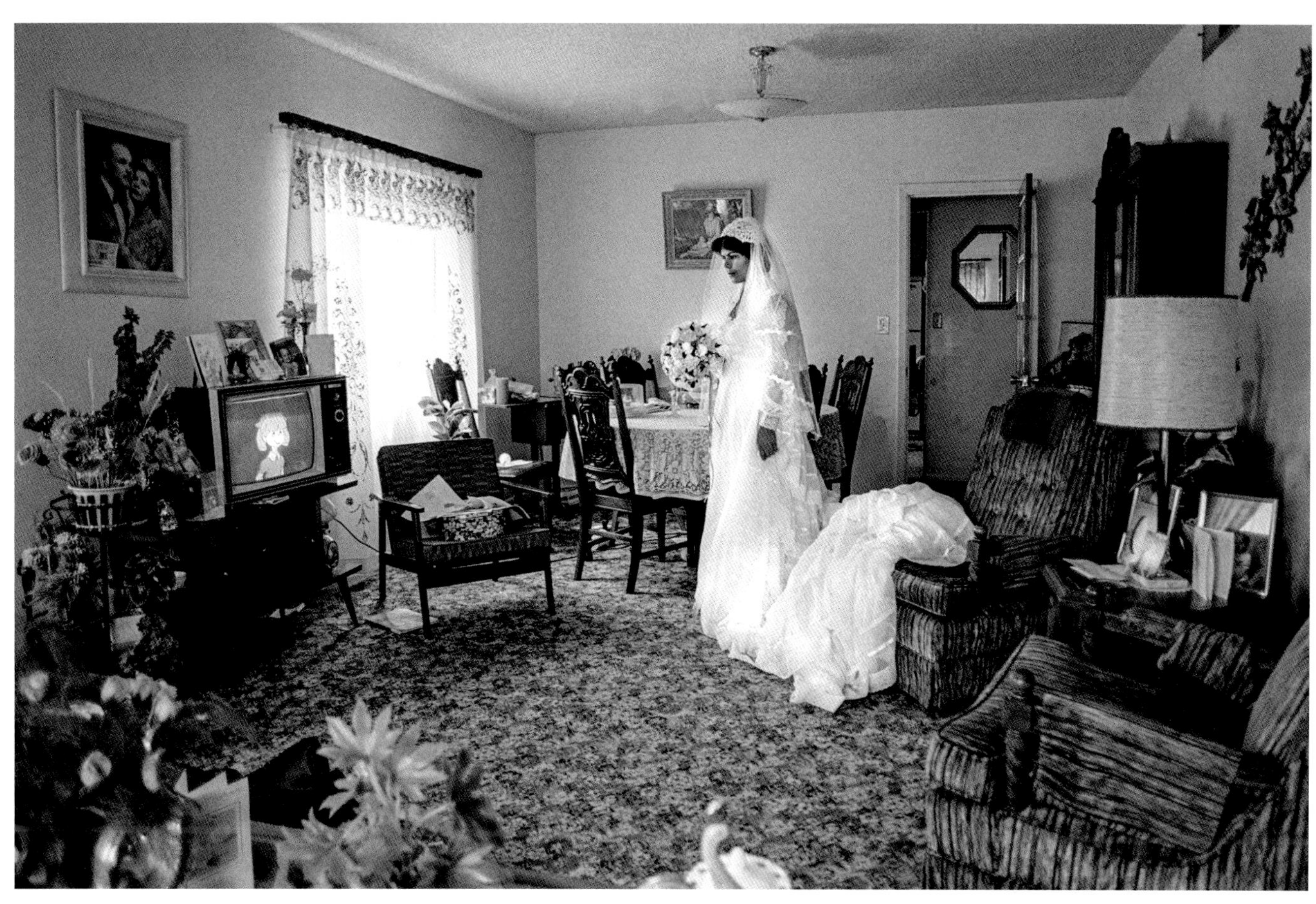

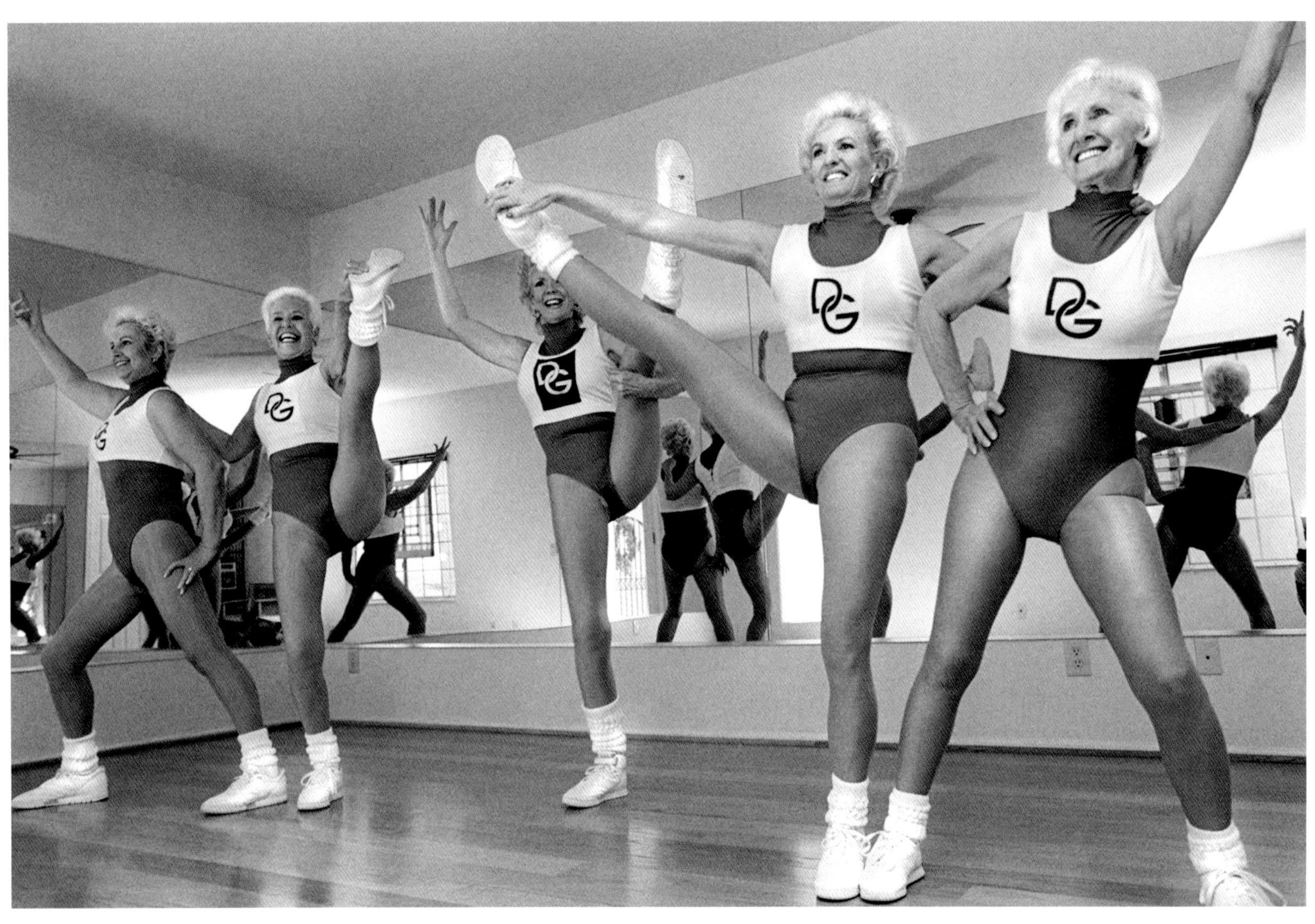

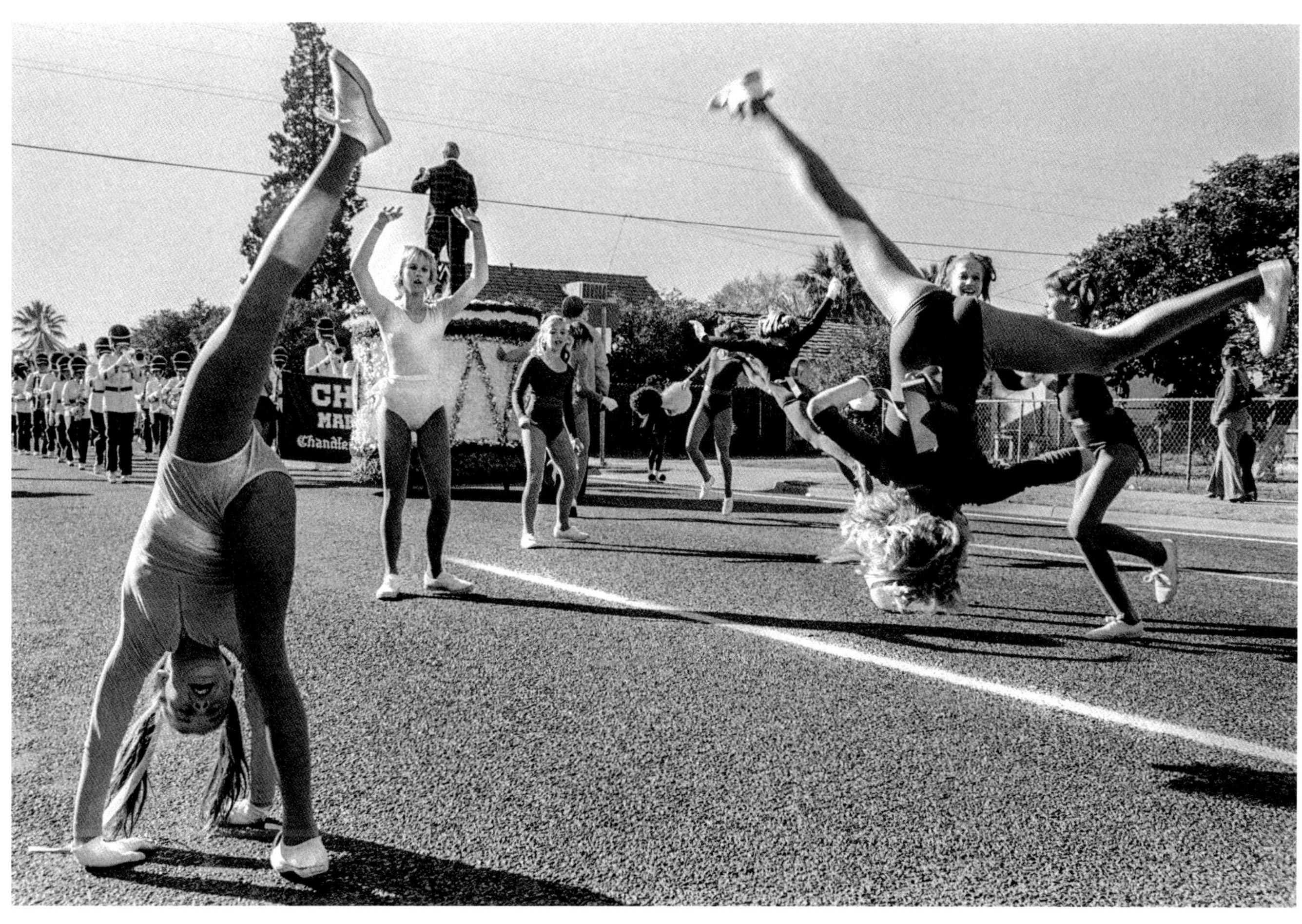

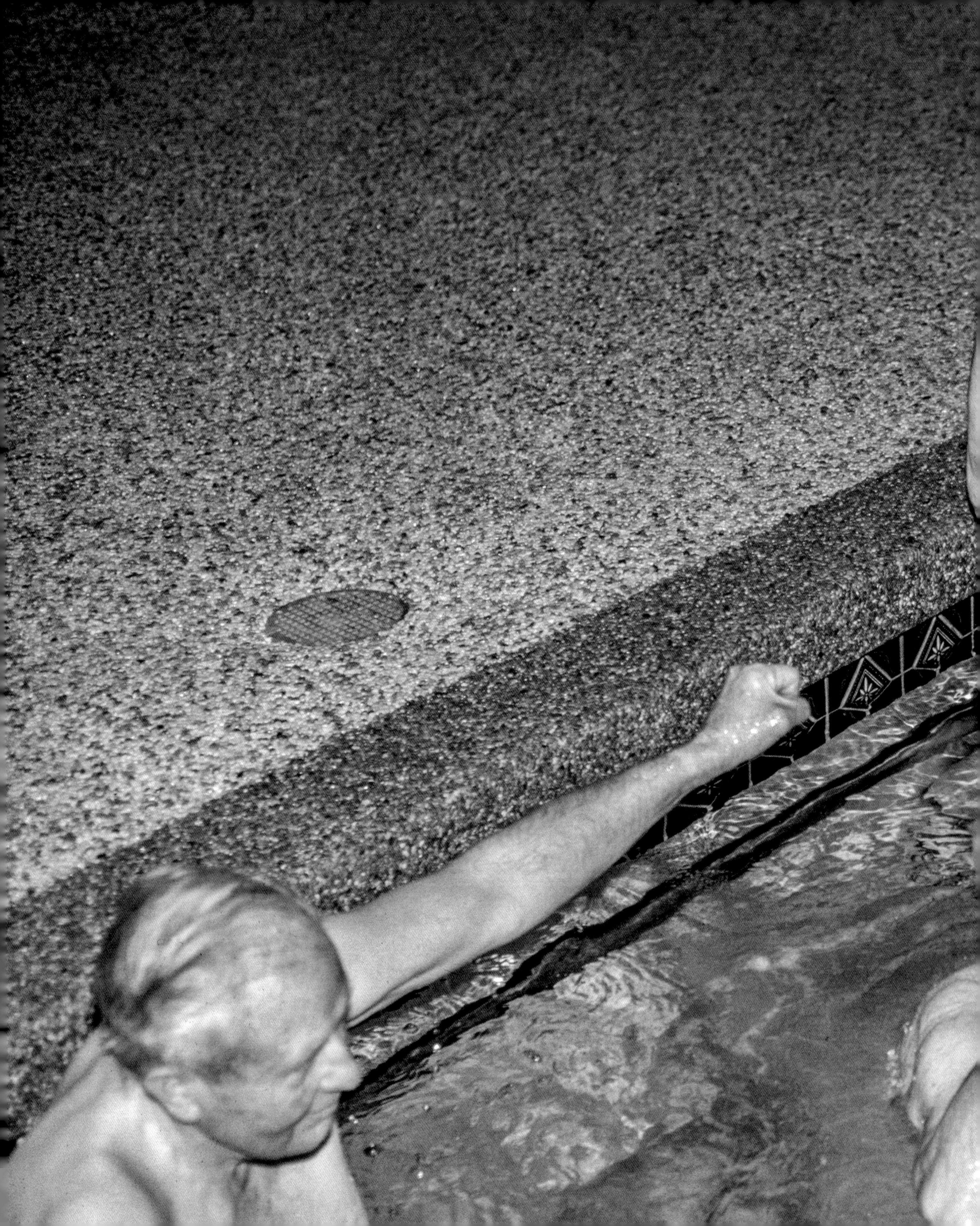

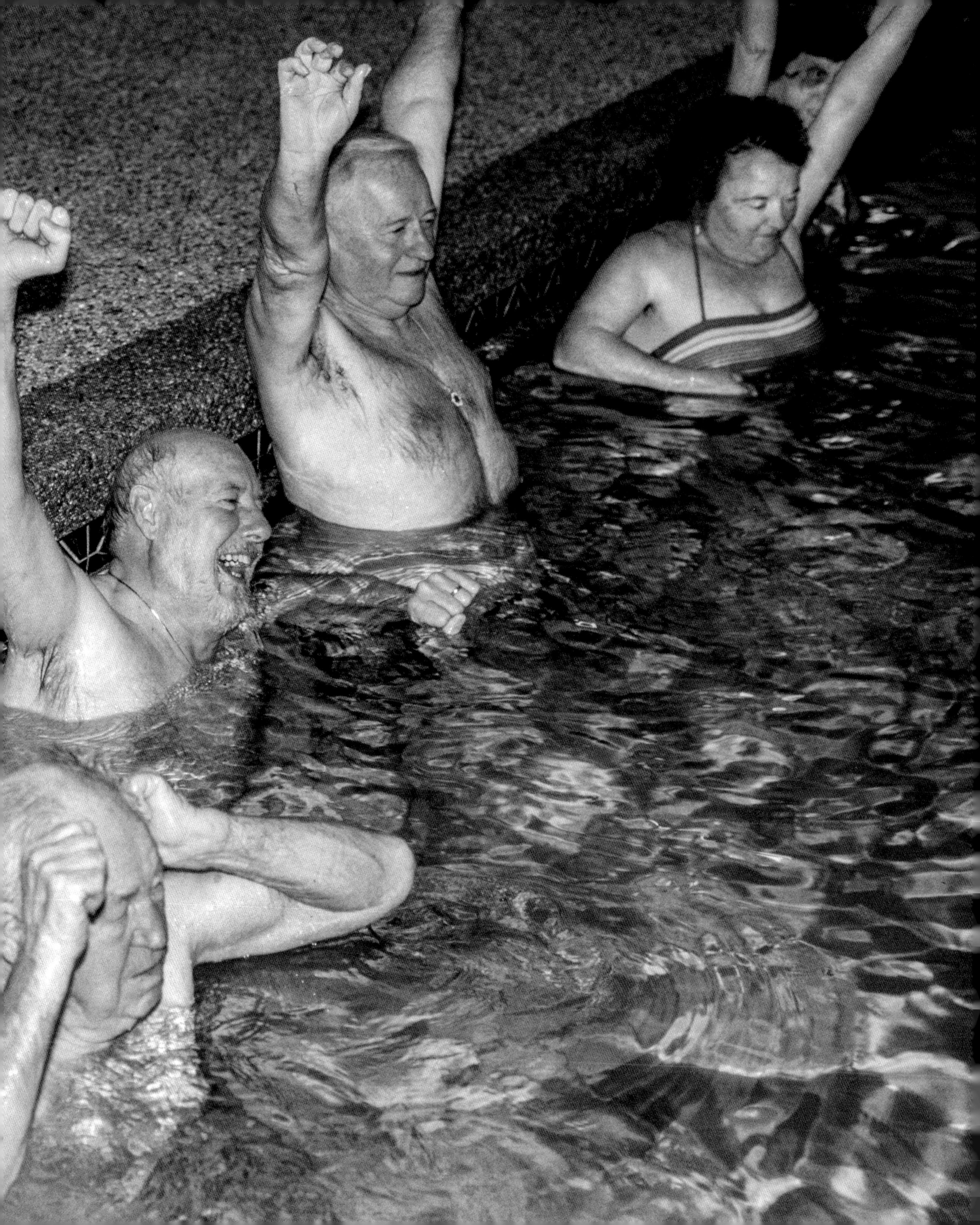

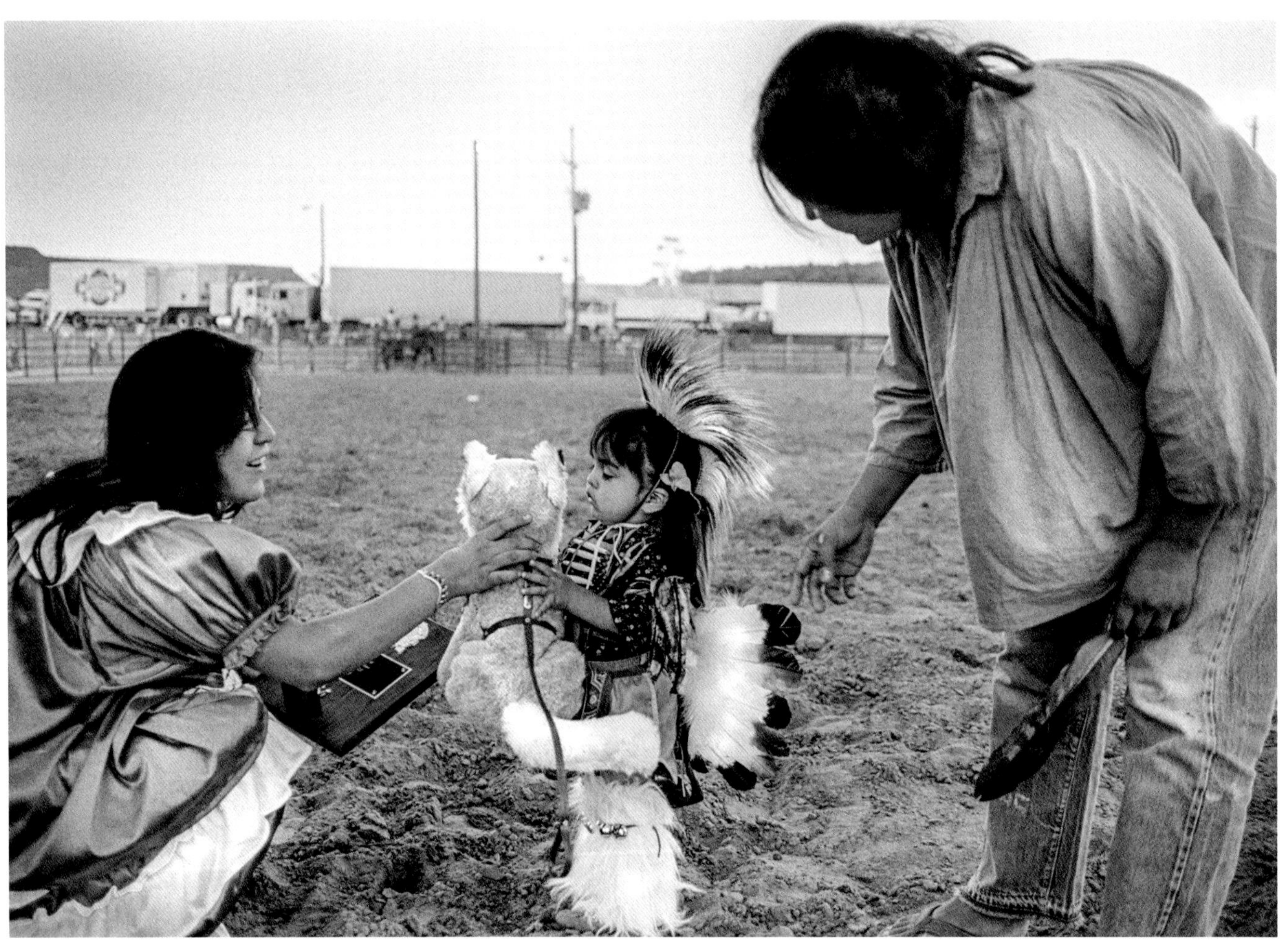

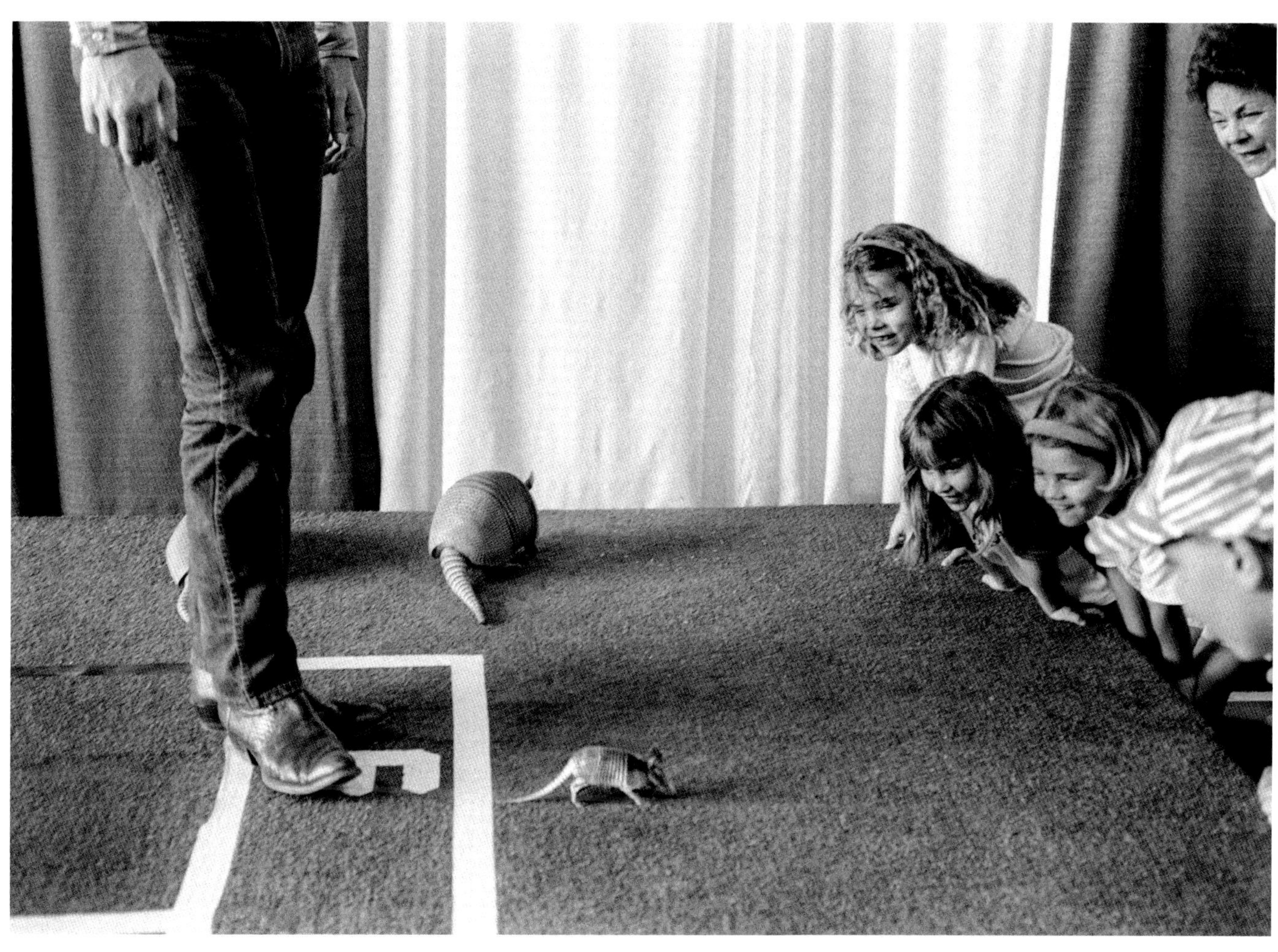

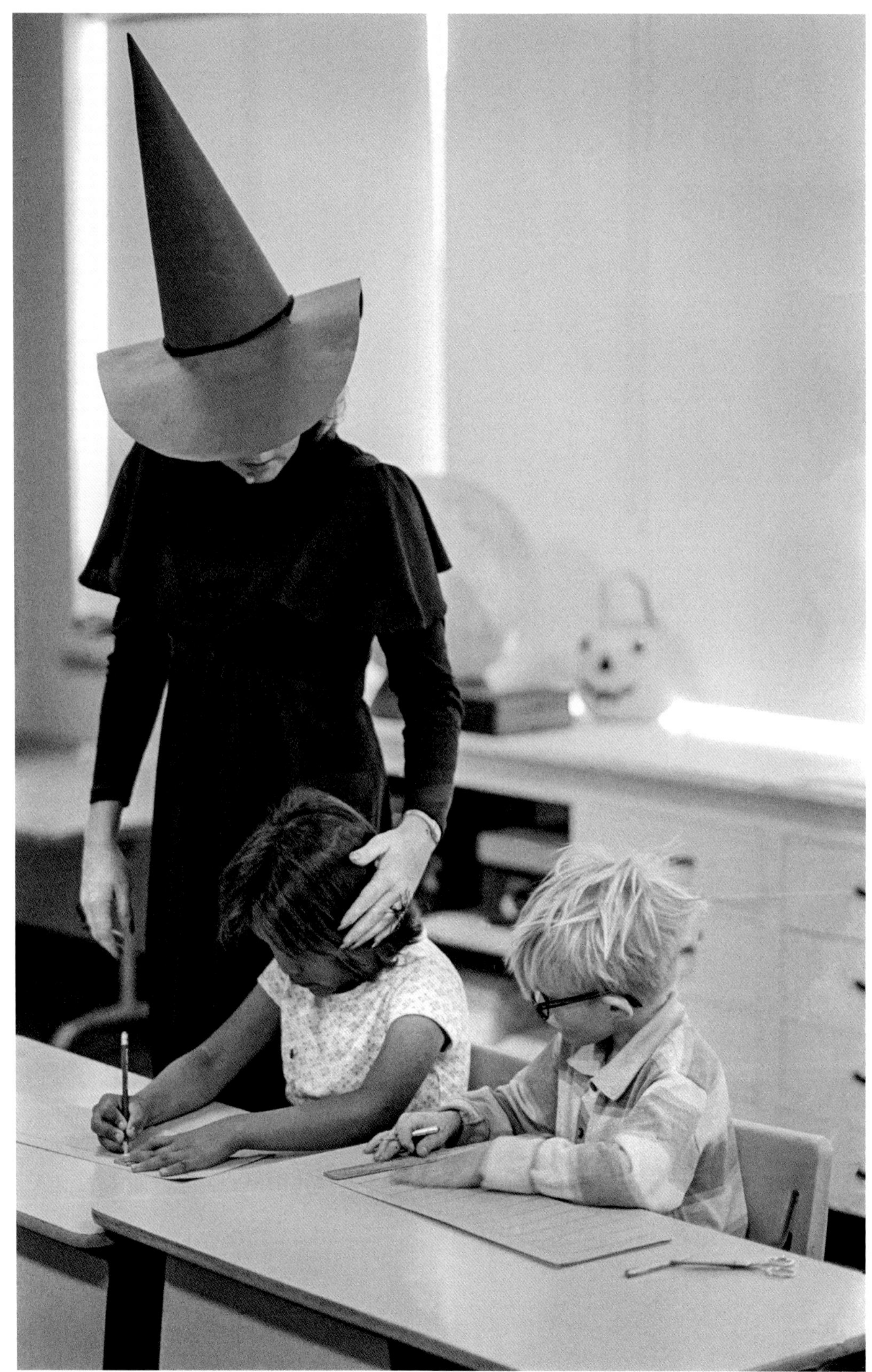

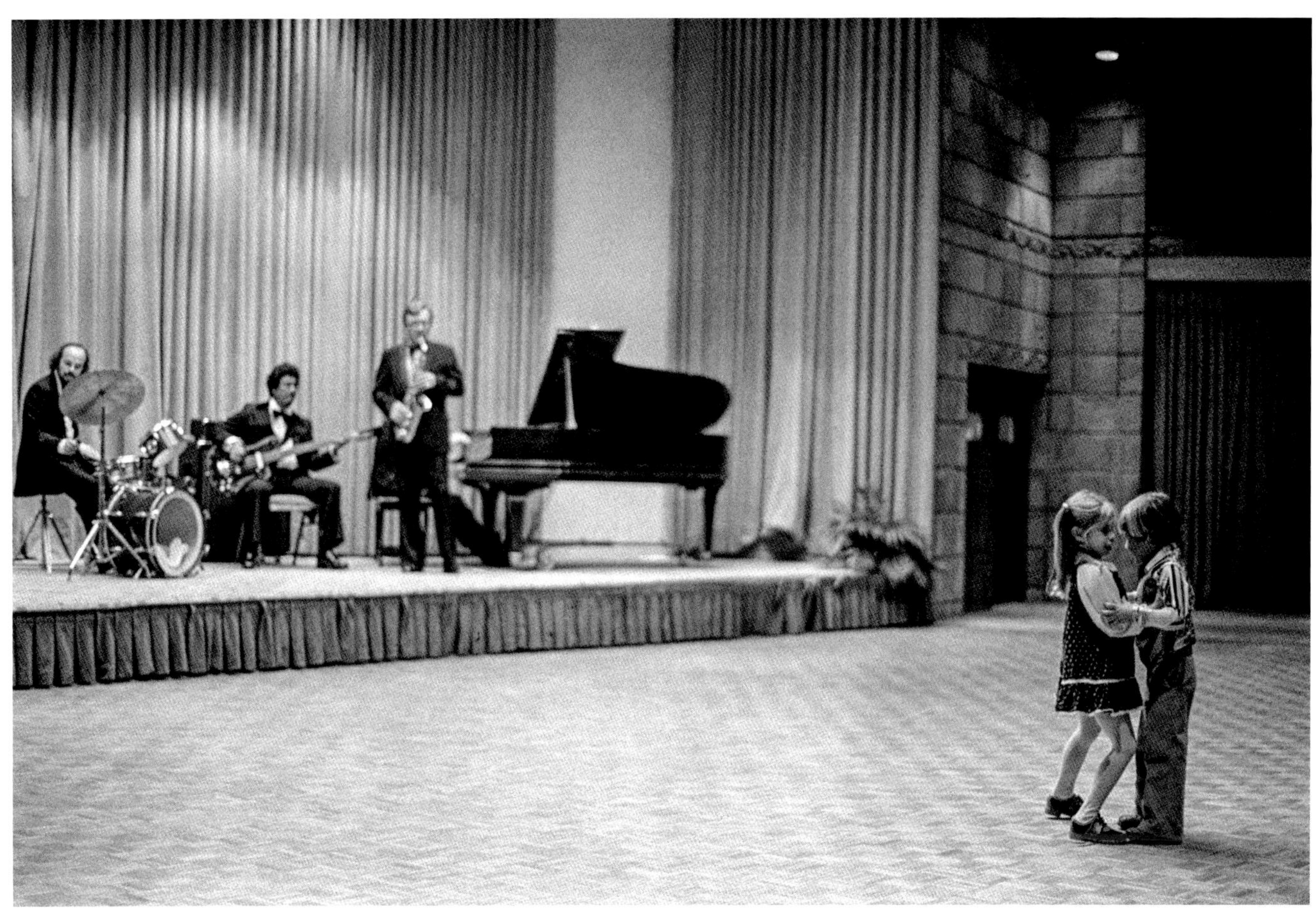

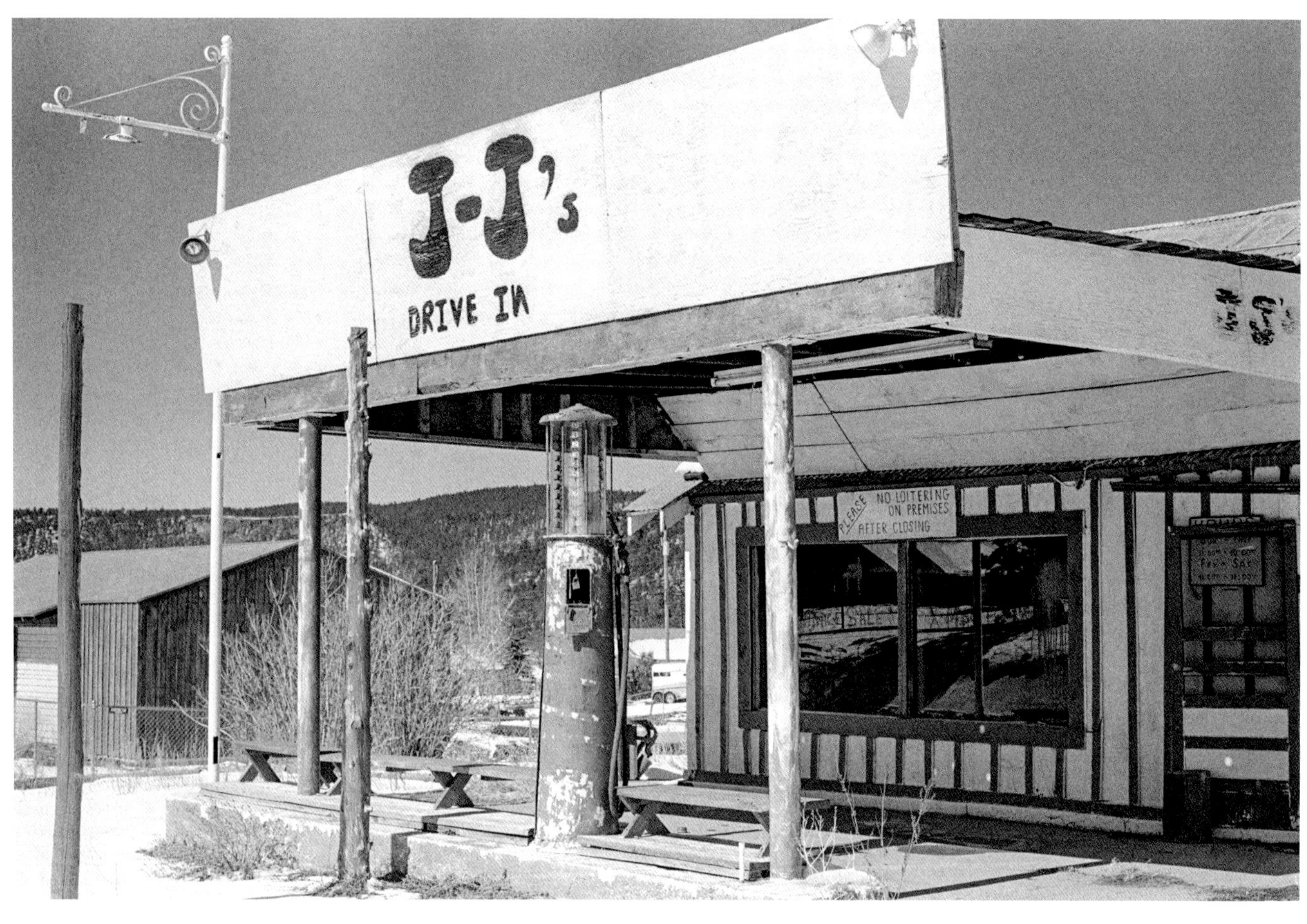
J-J's
DRIVE IN
PLEASE NO LOITERING
ON PREMISES
AFTER CLOSING

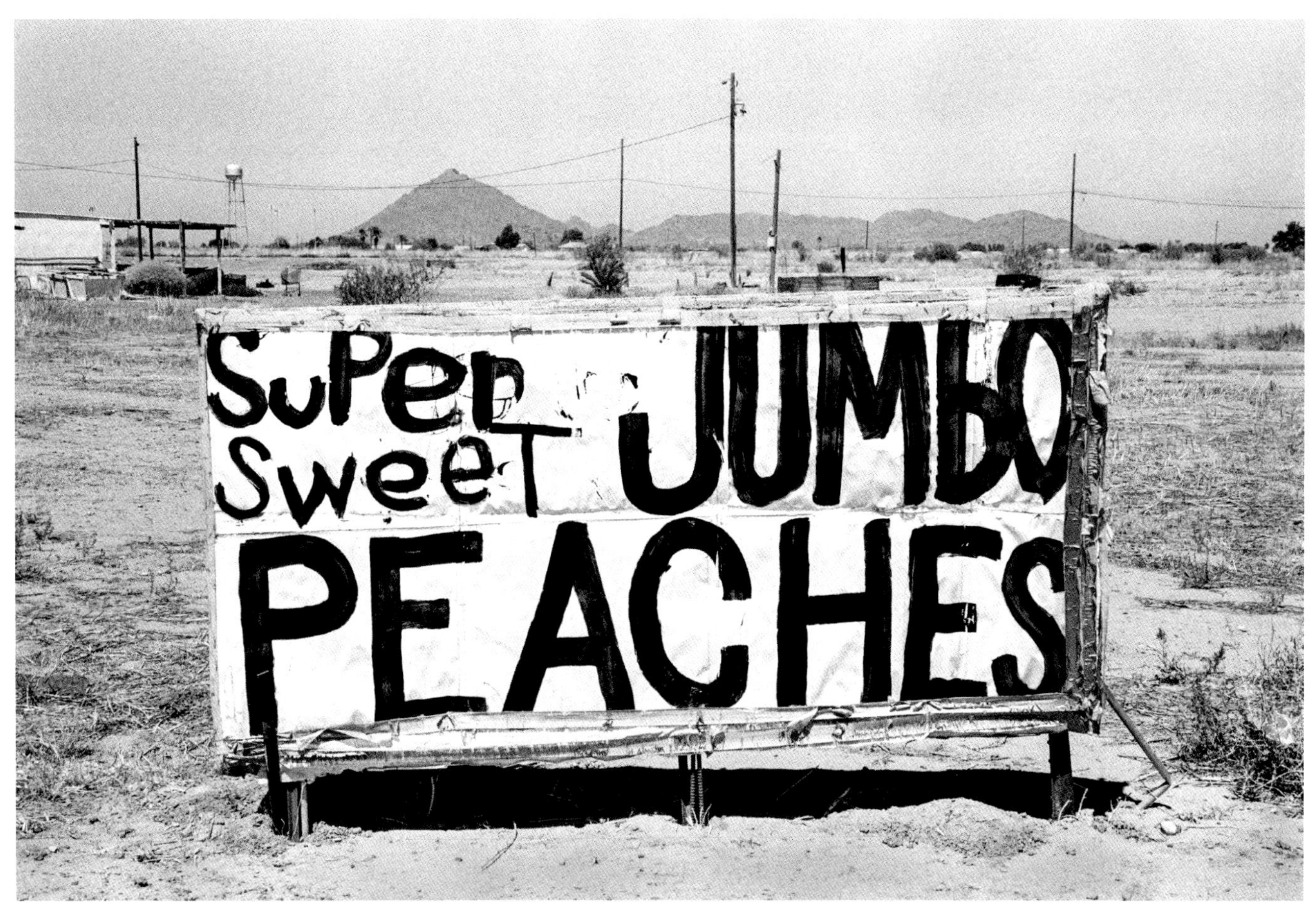

SuPer JUMbO
Sweet PEACHES

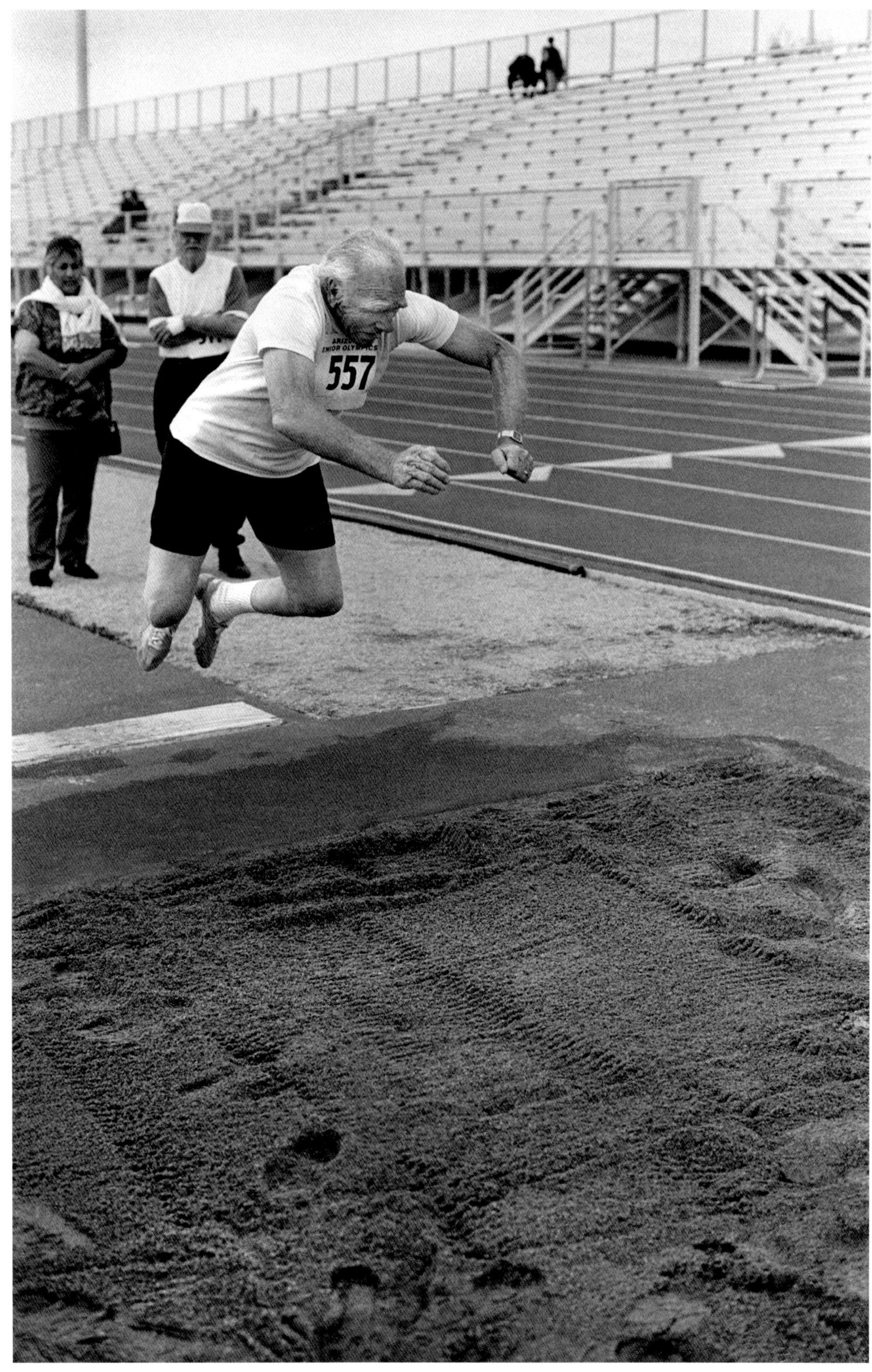

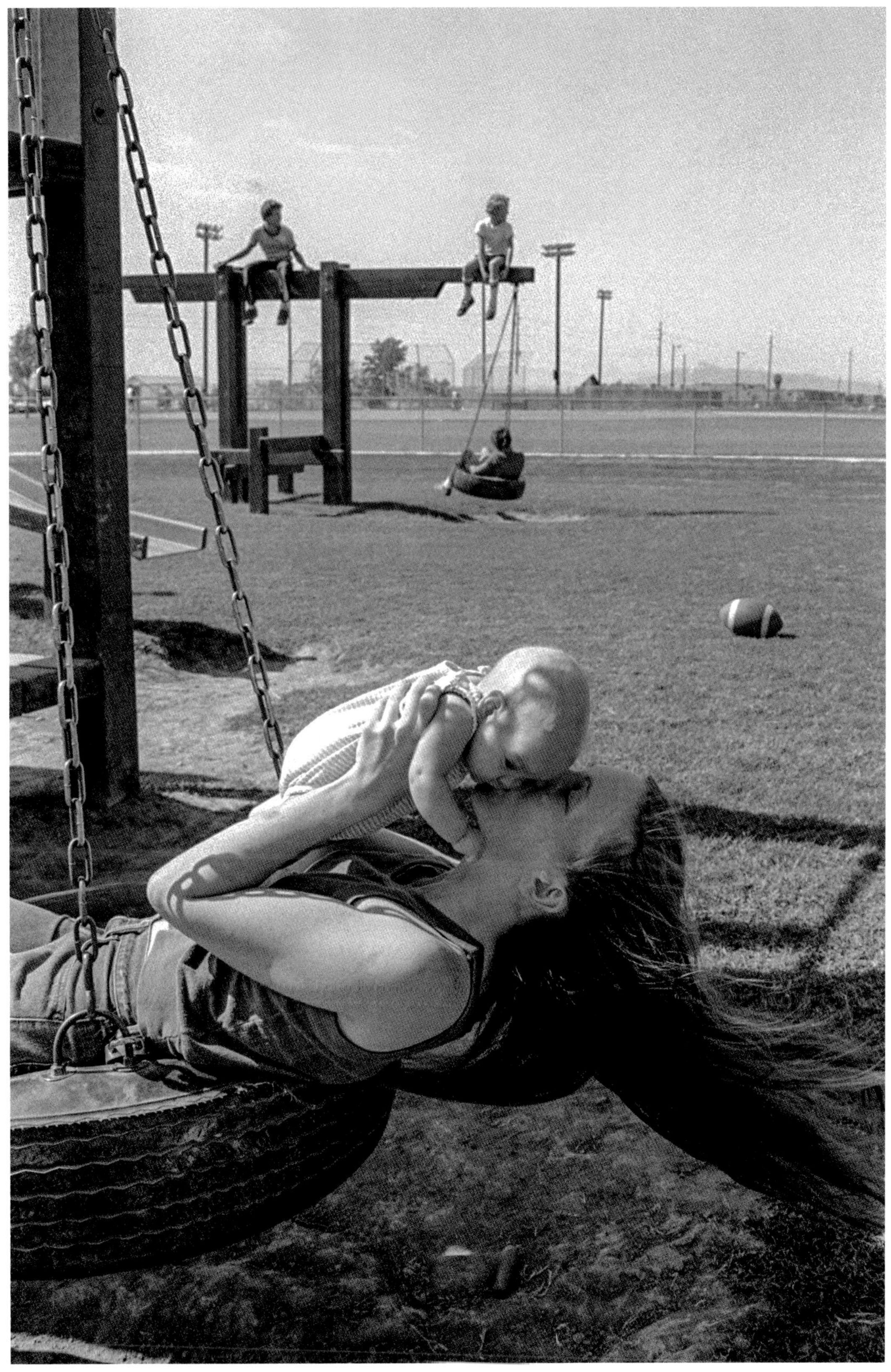

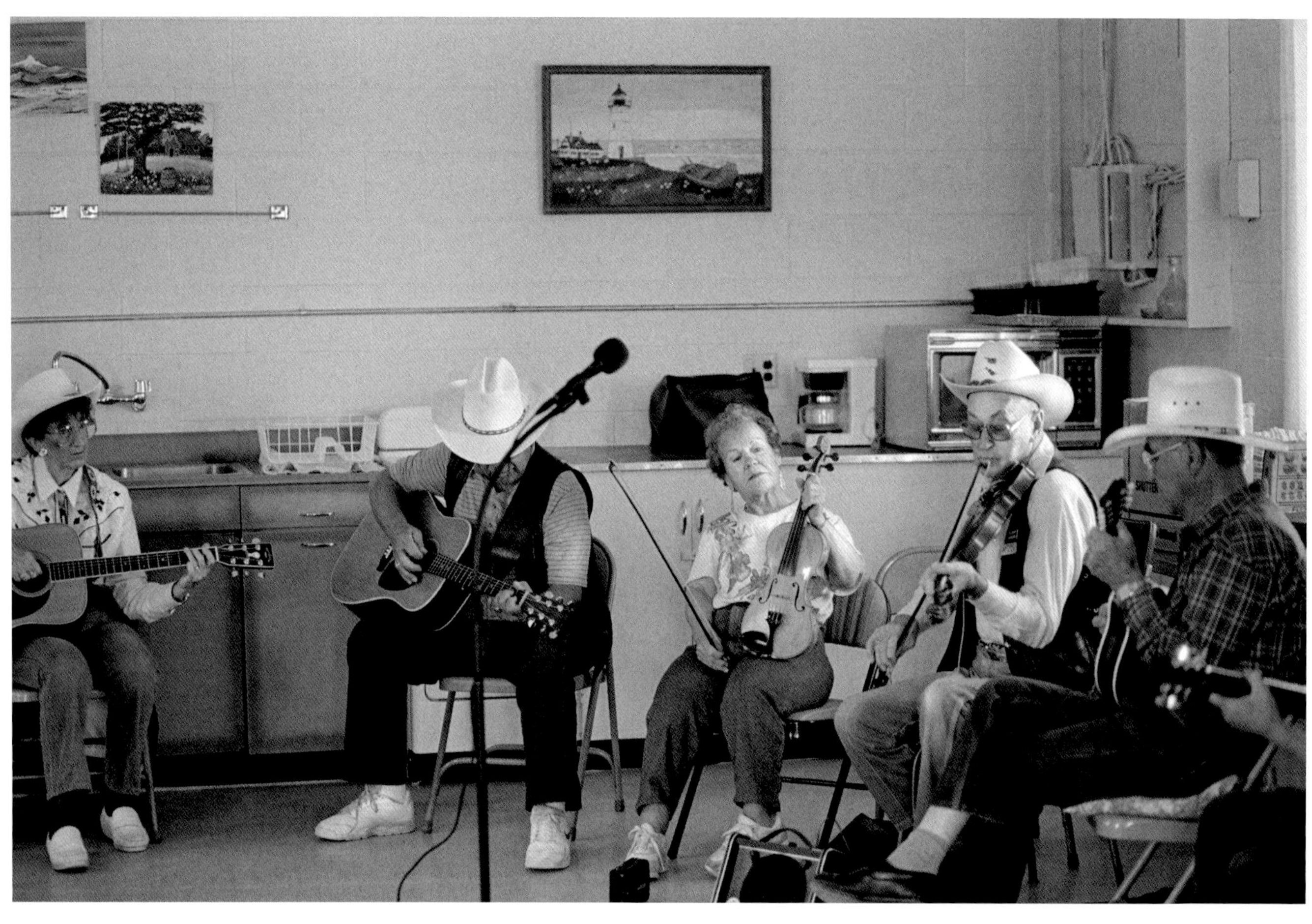

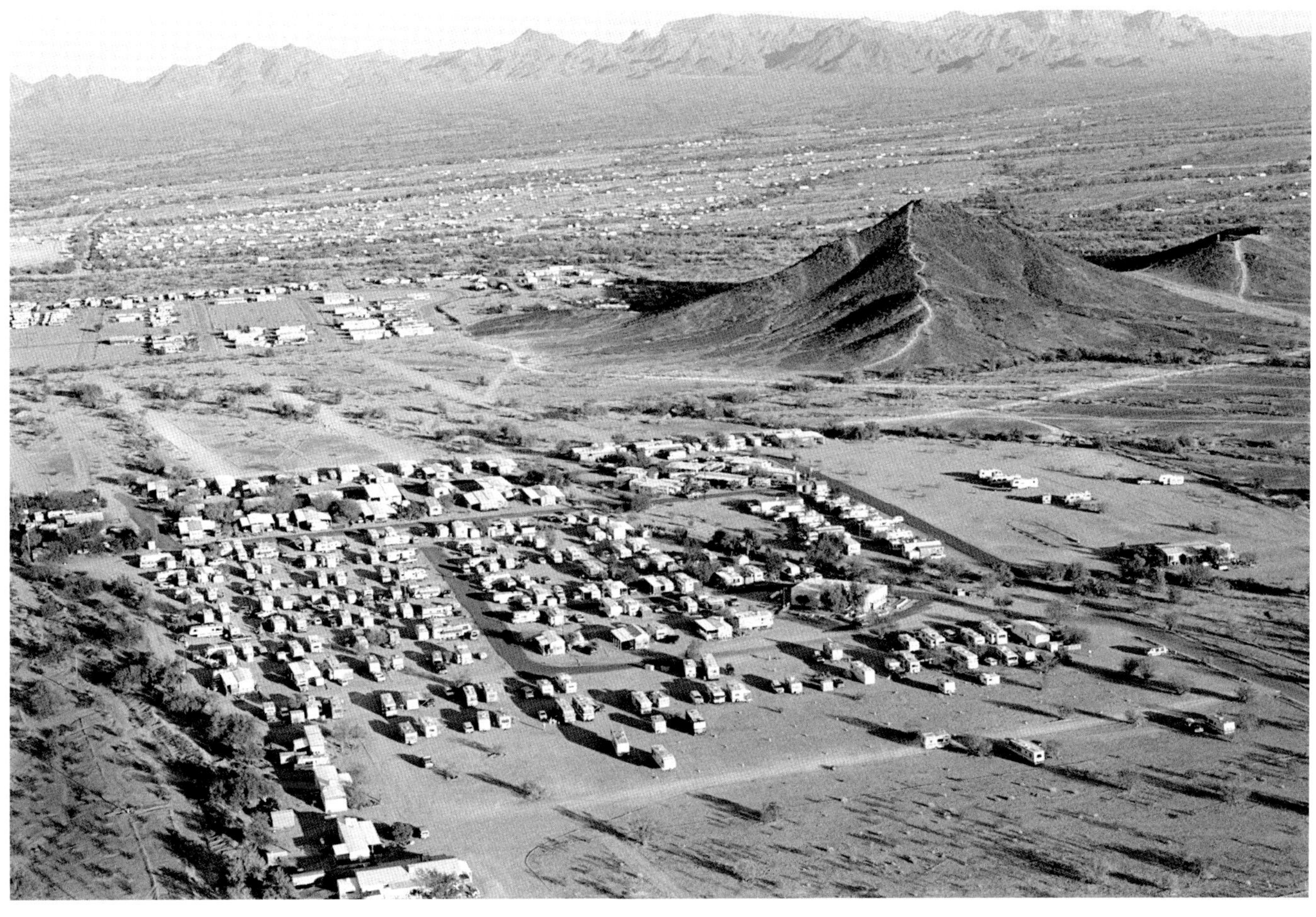

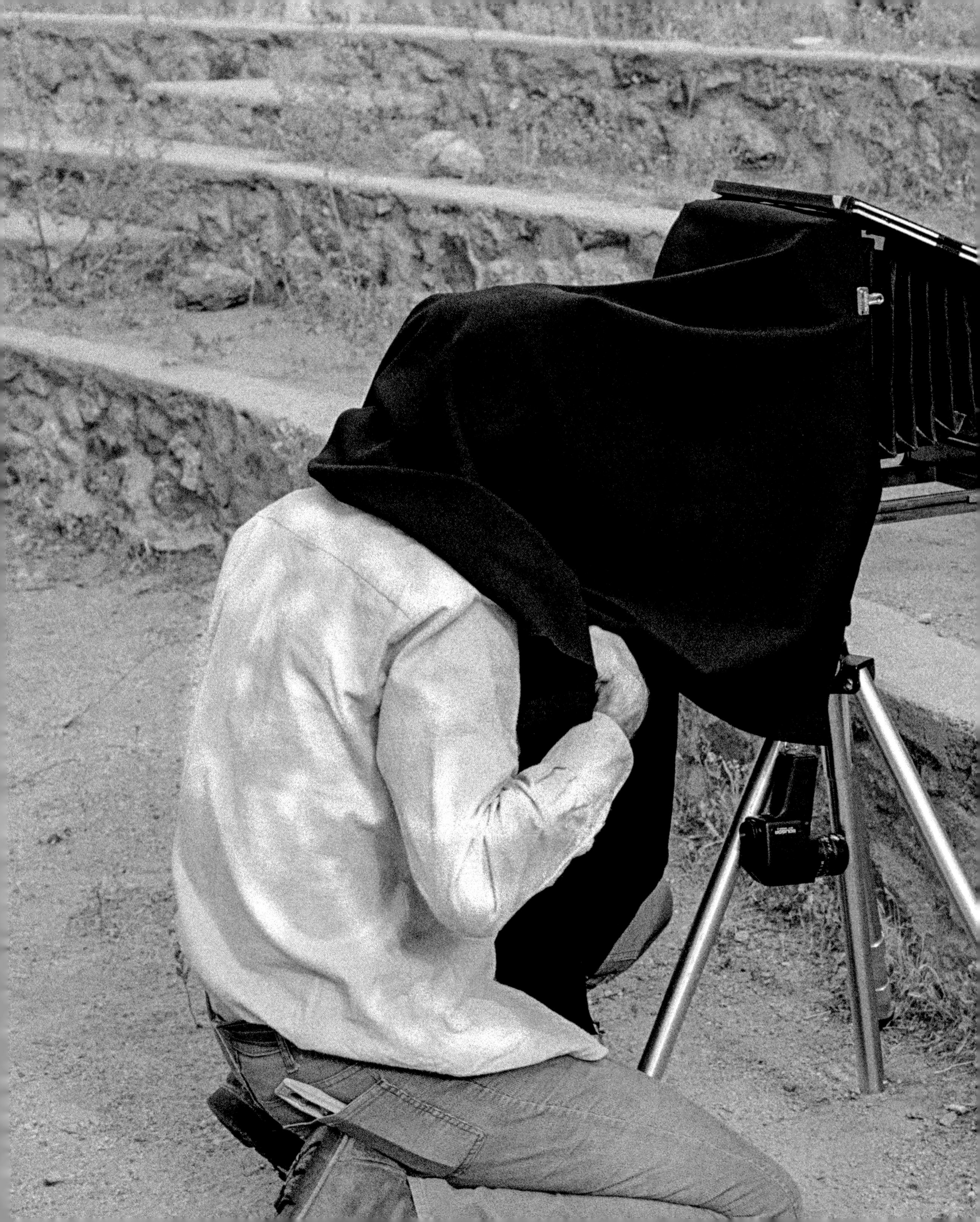

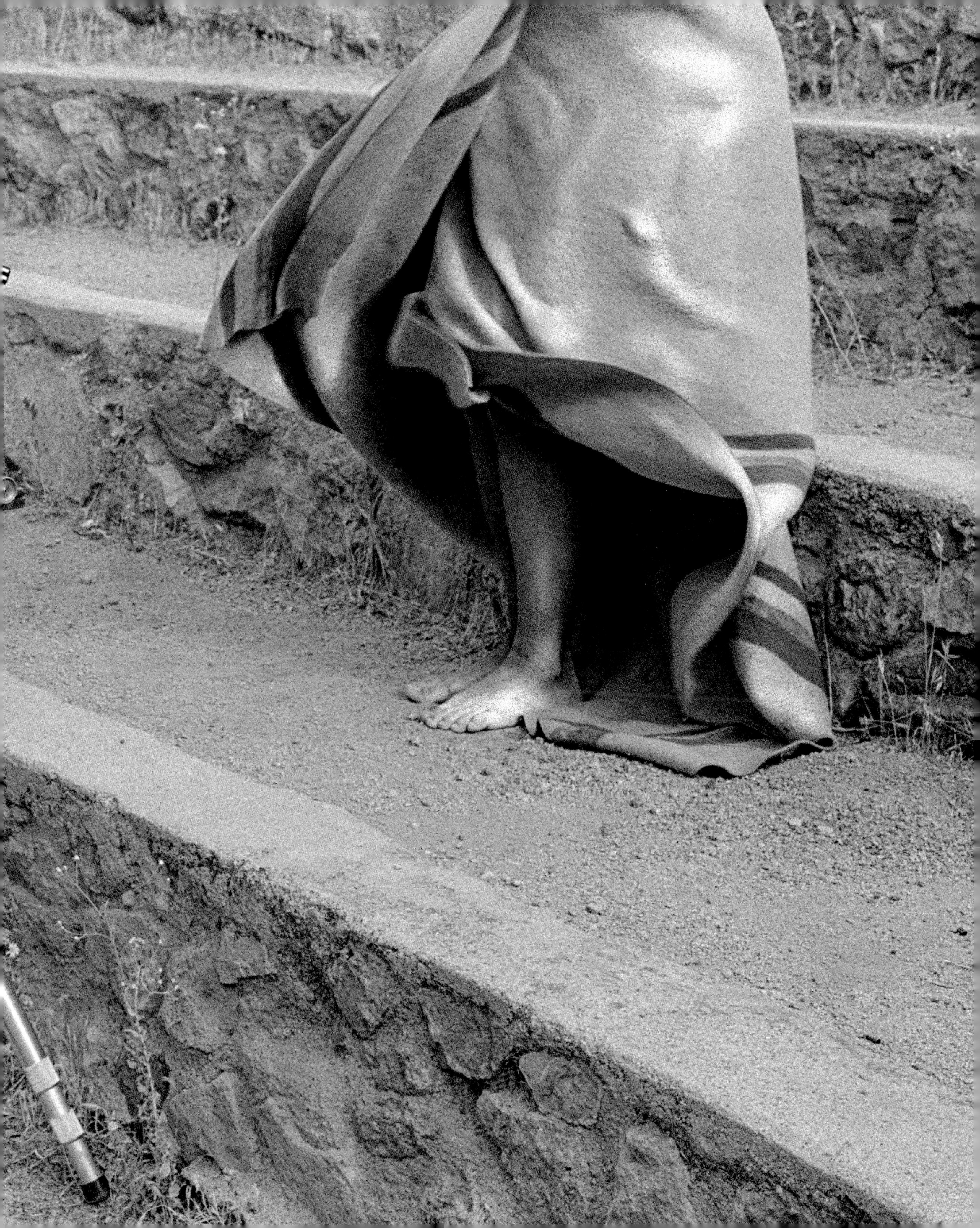

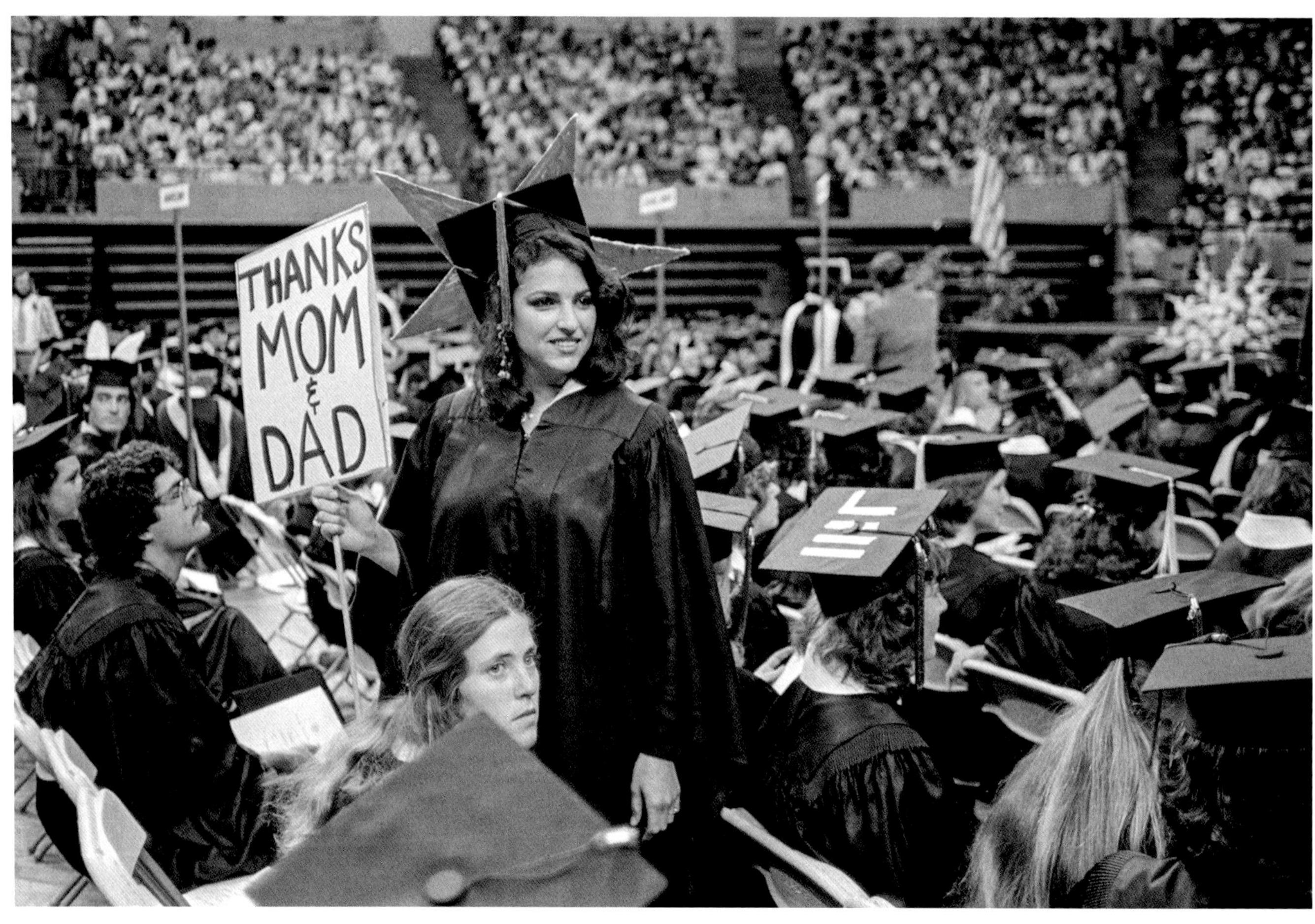
THANKS
MOM
&
DAD

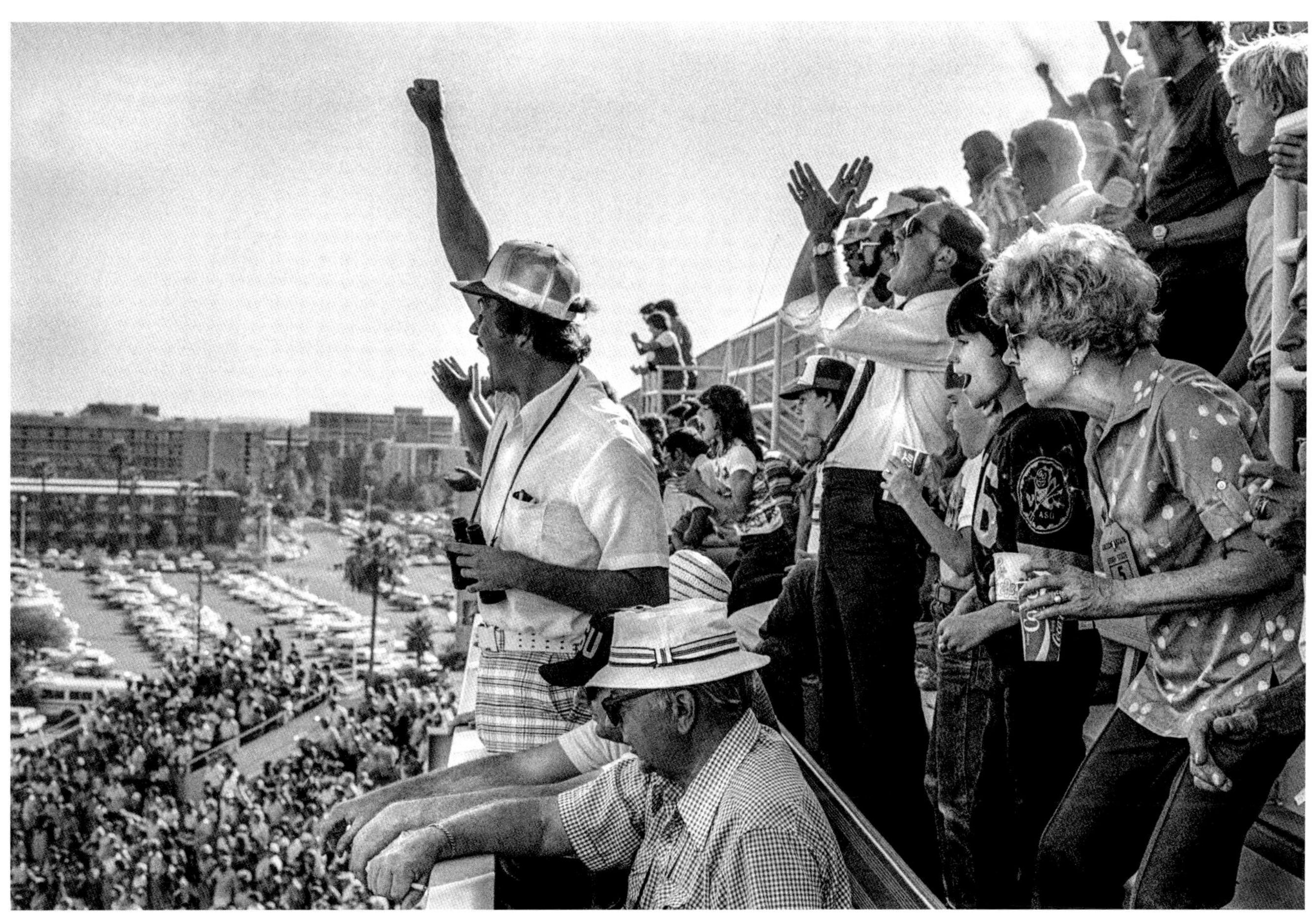

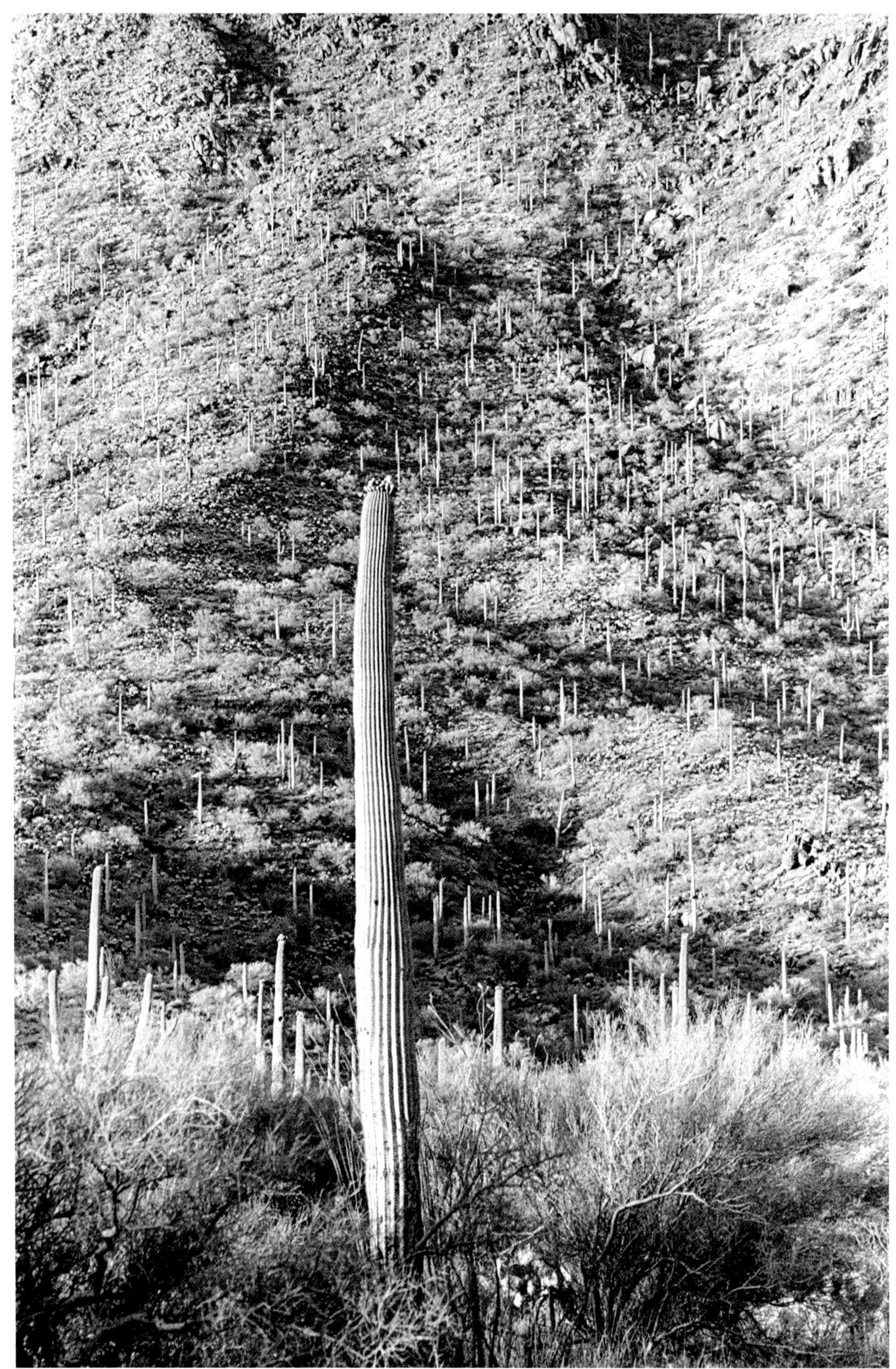

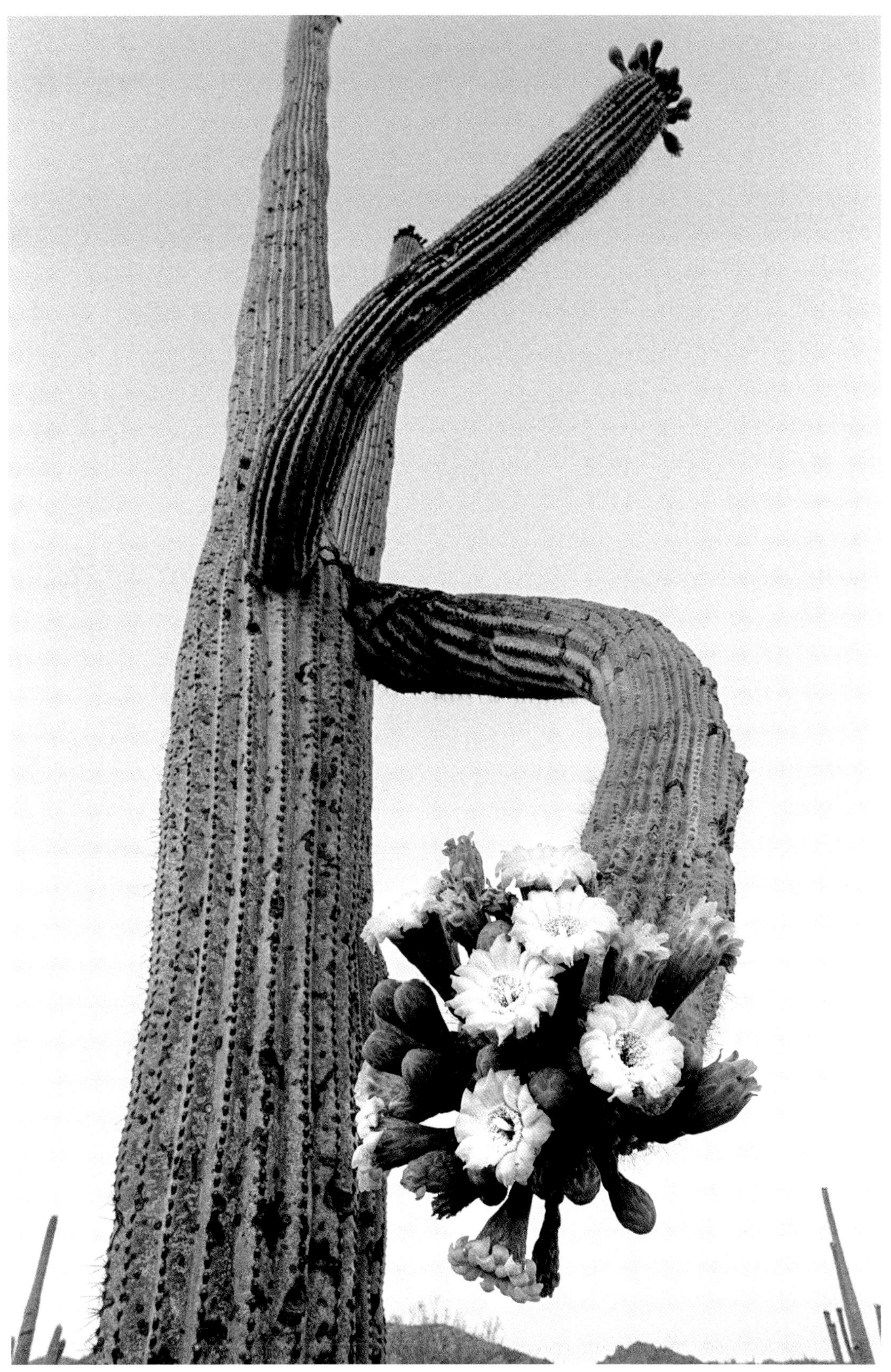

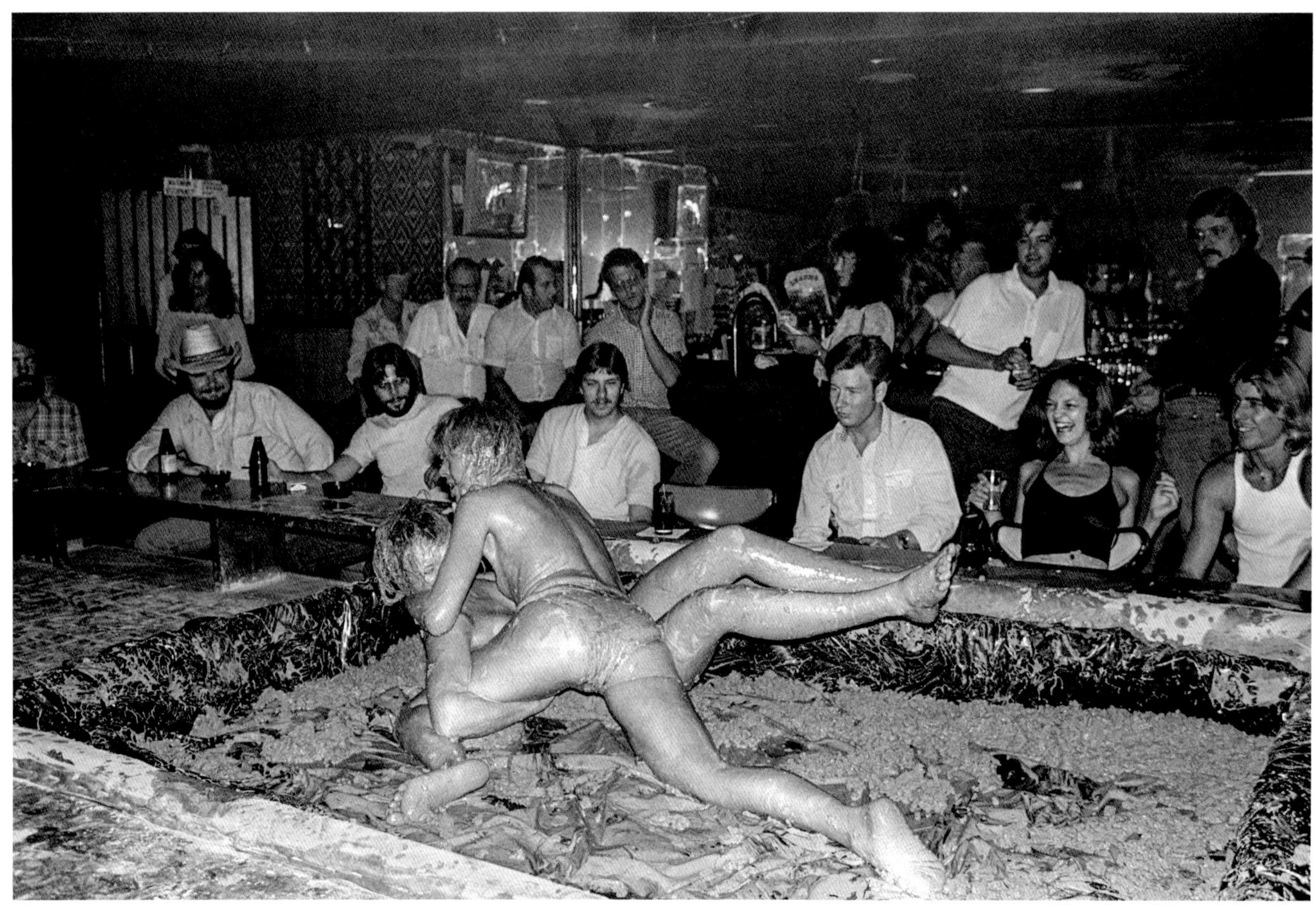

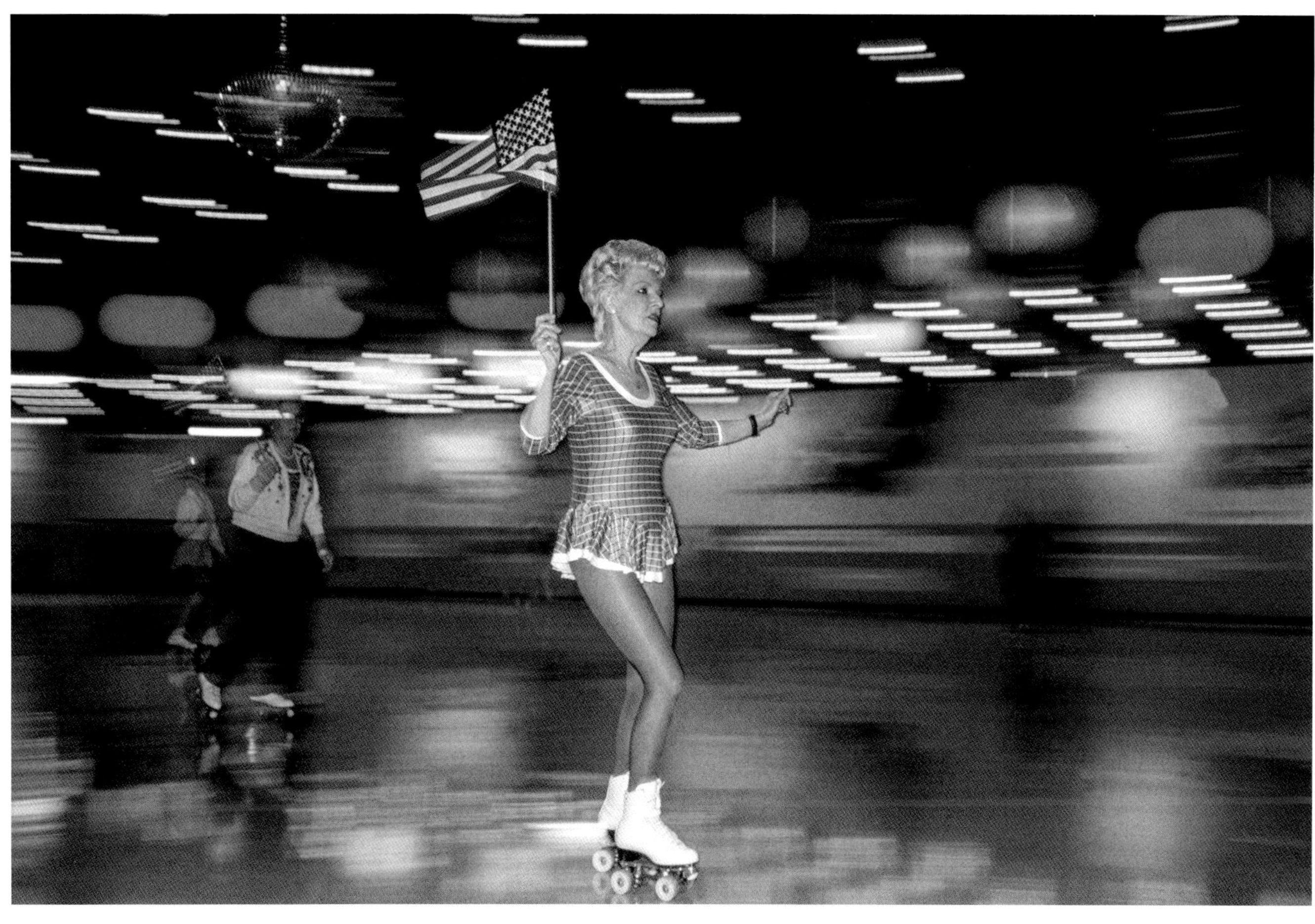

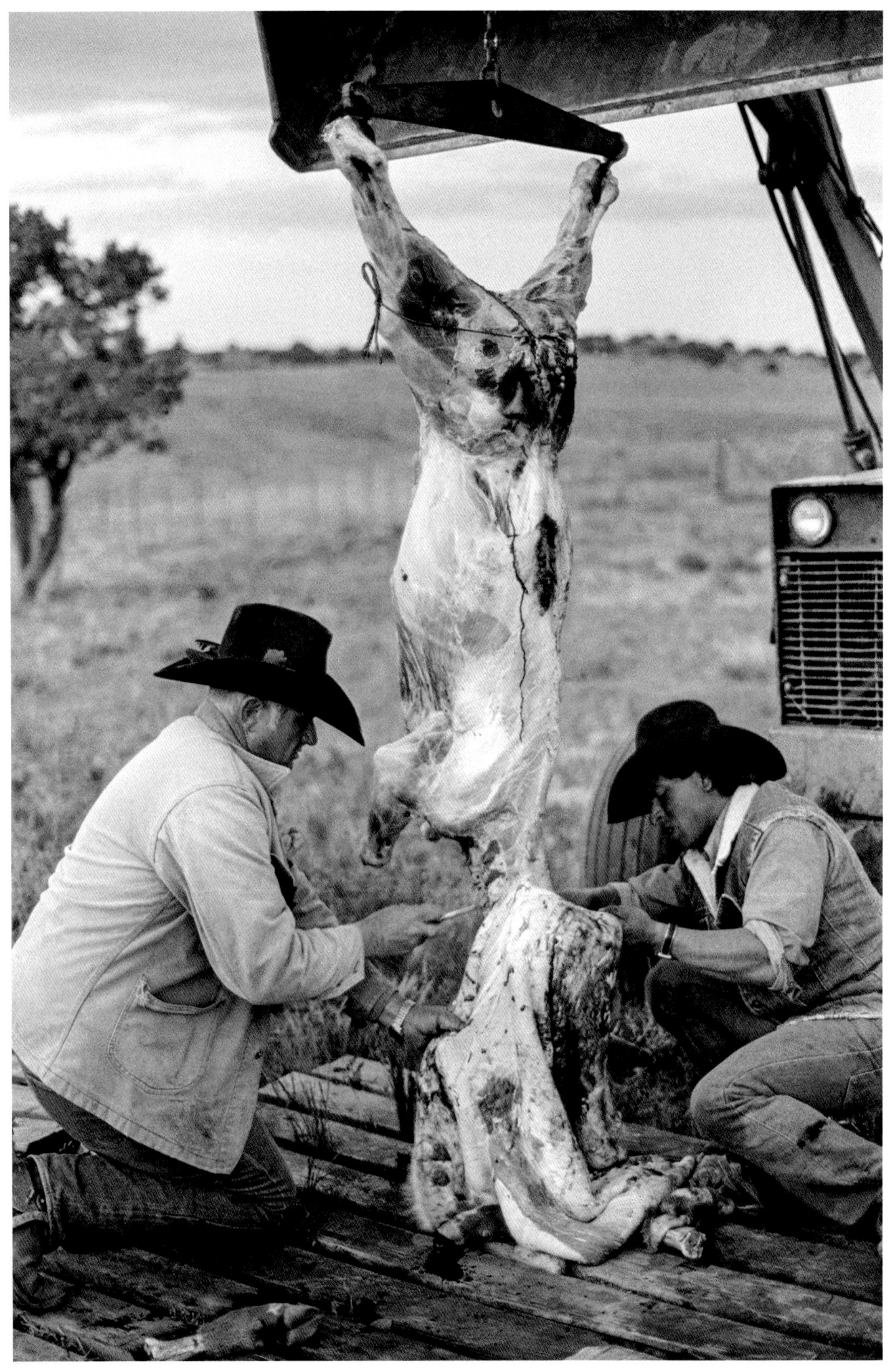

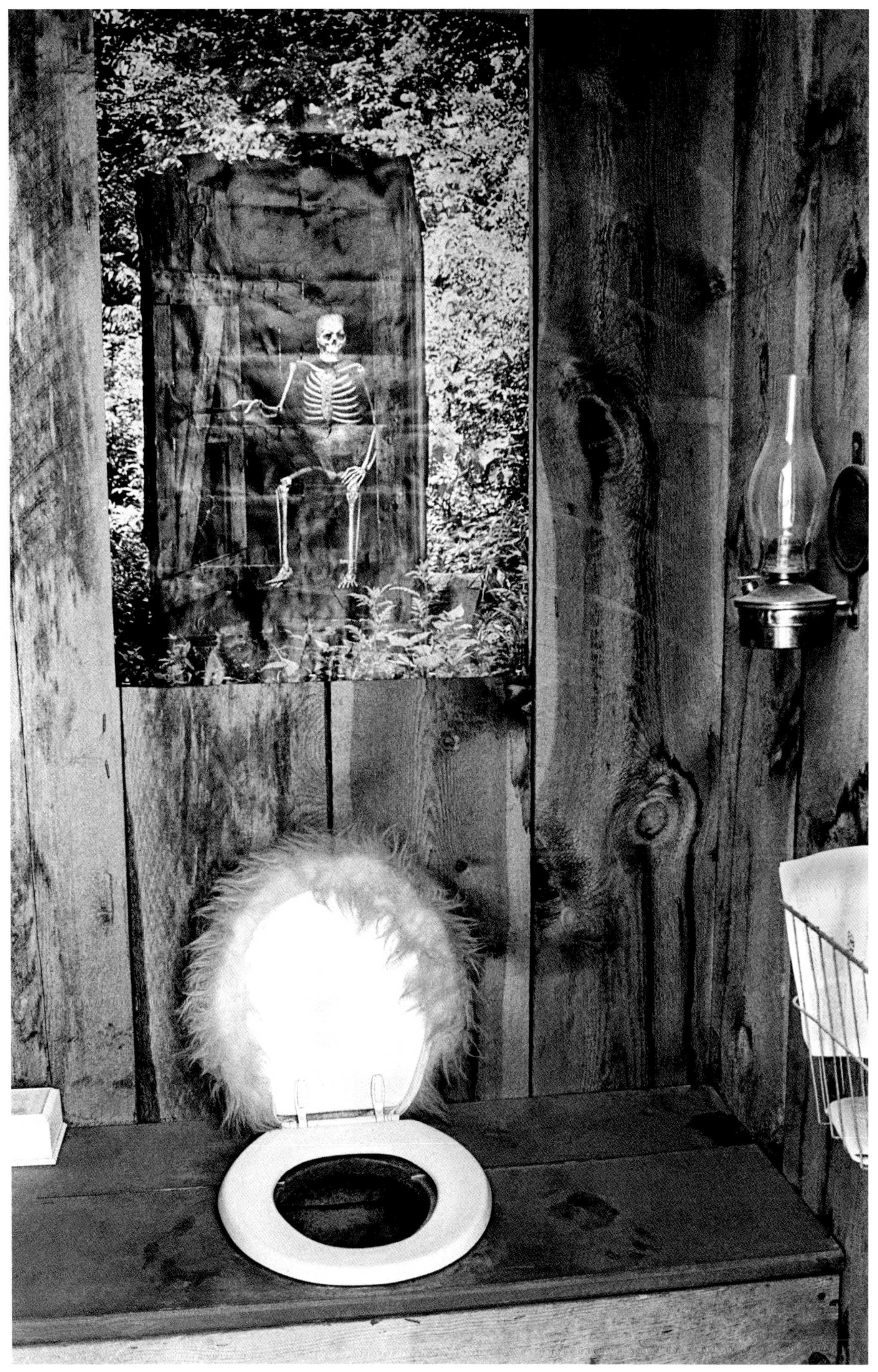

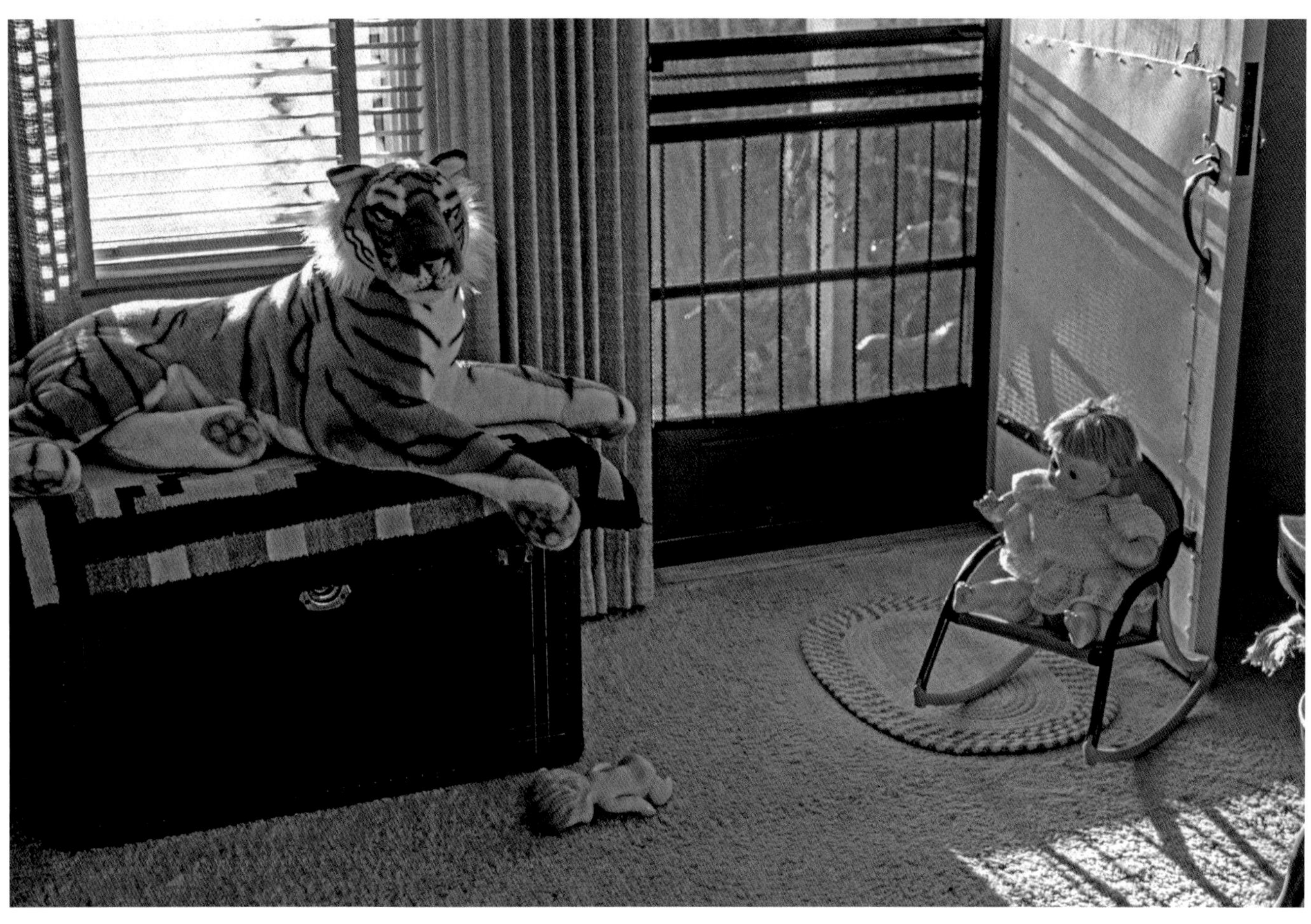

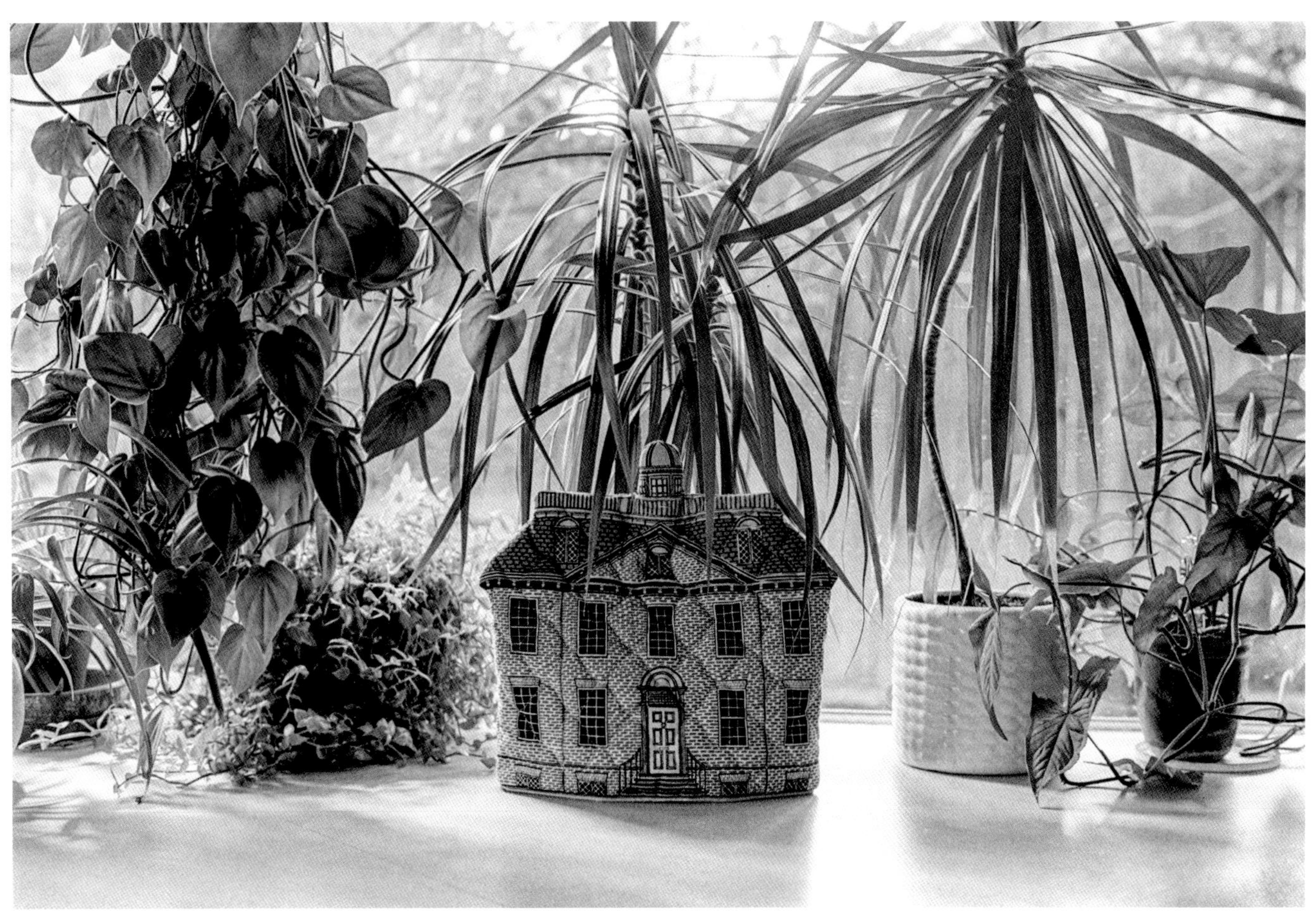

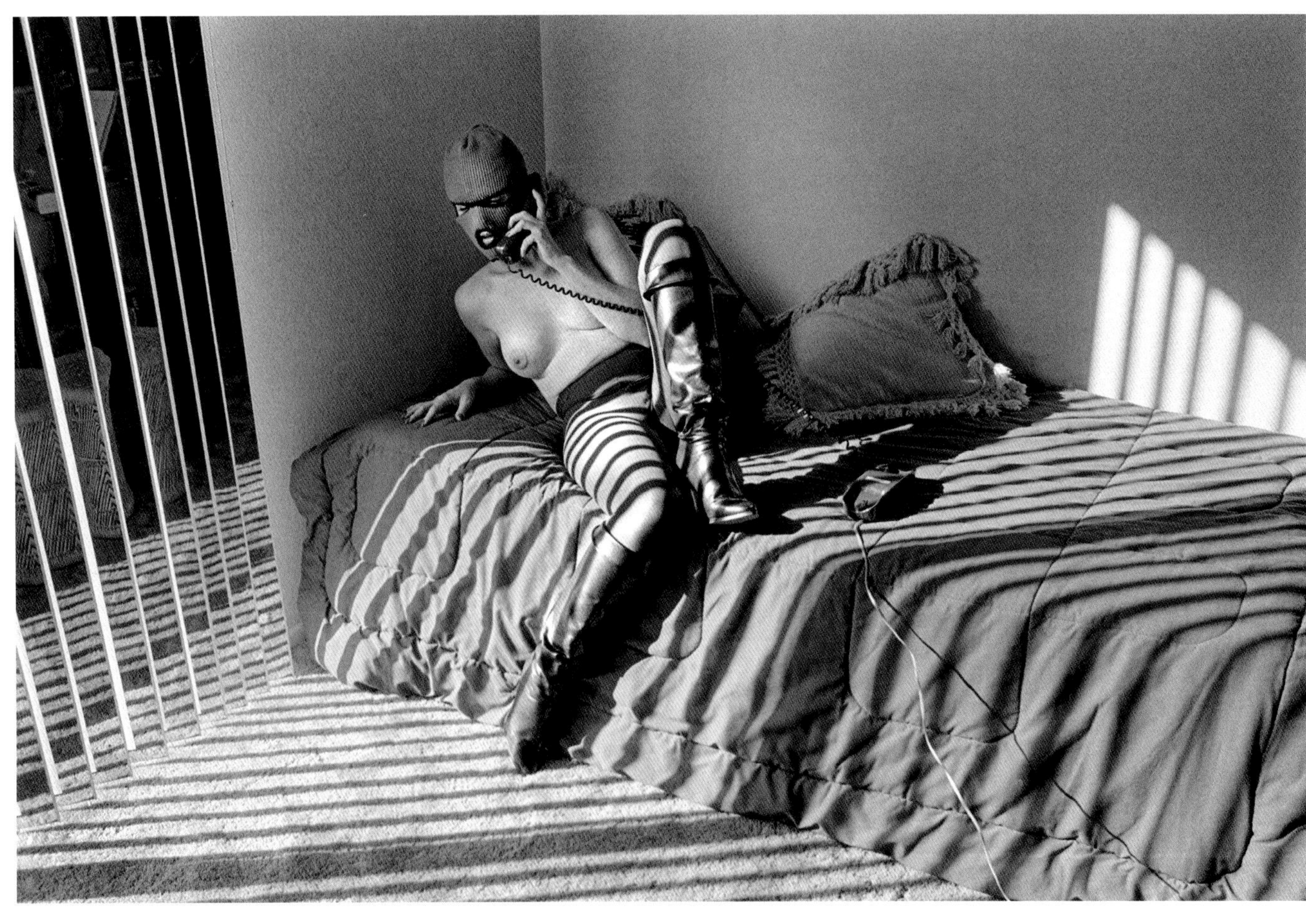

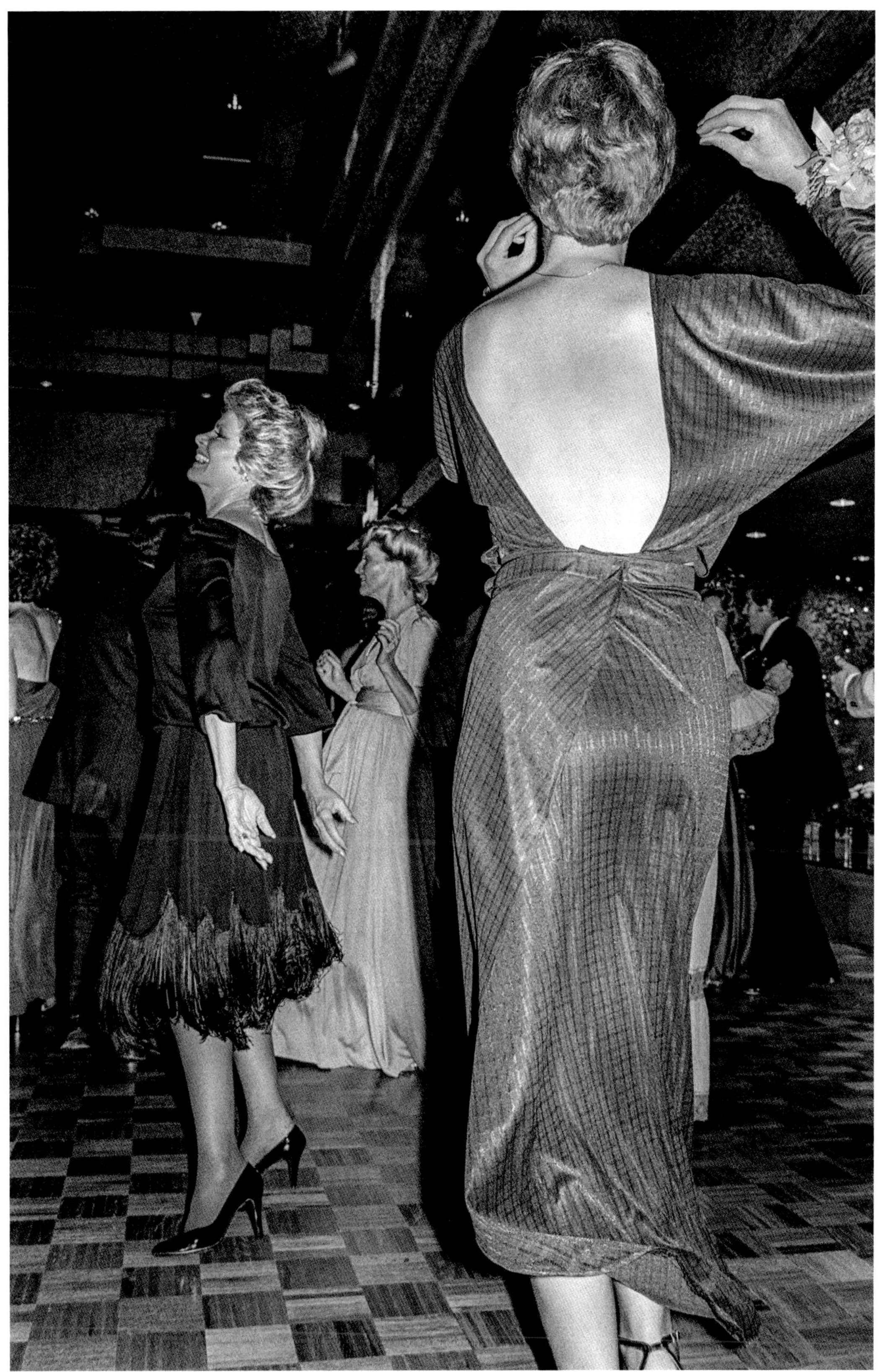

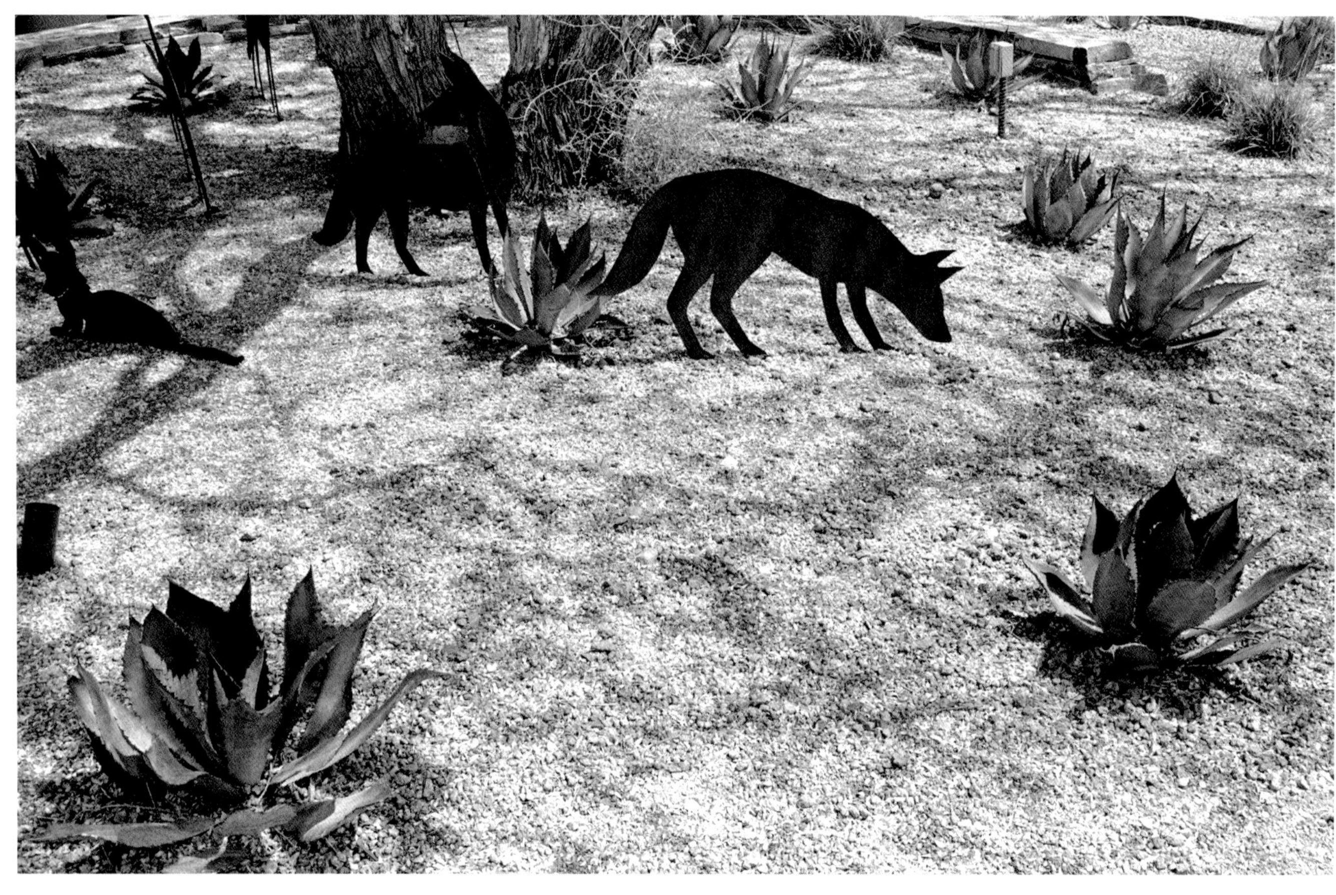

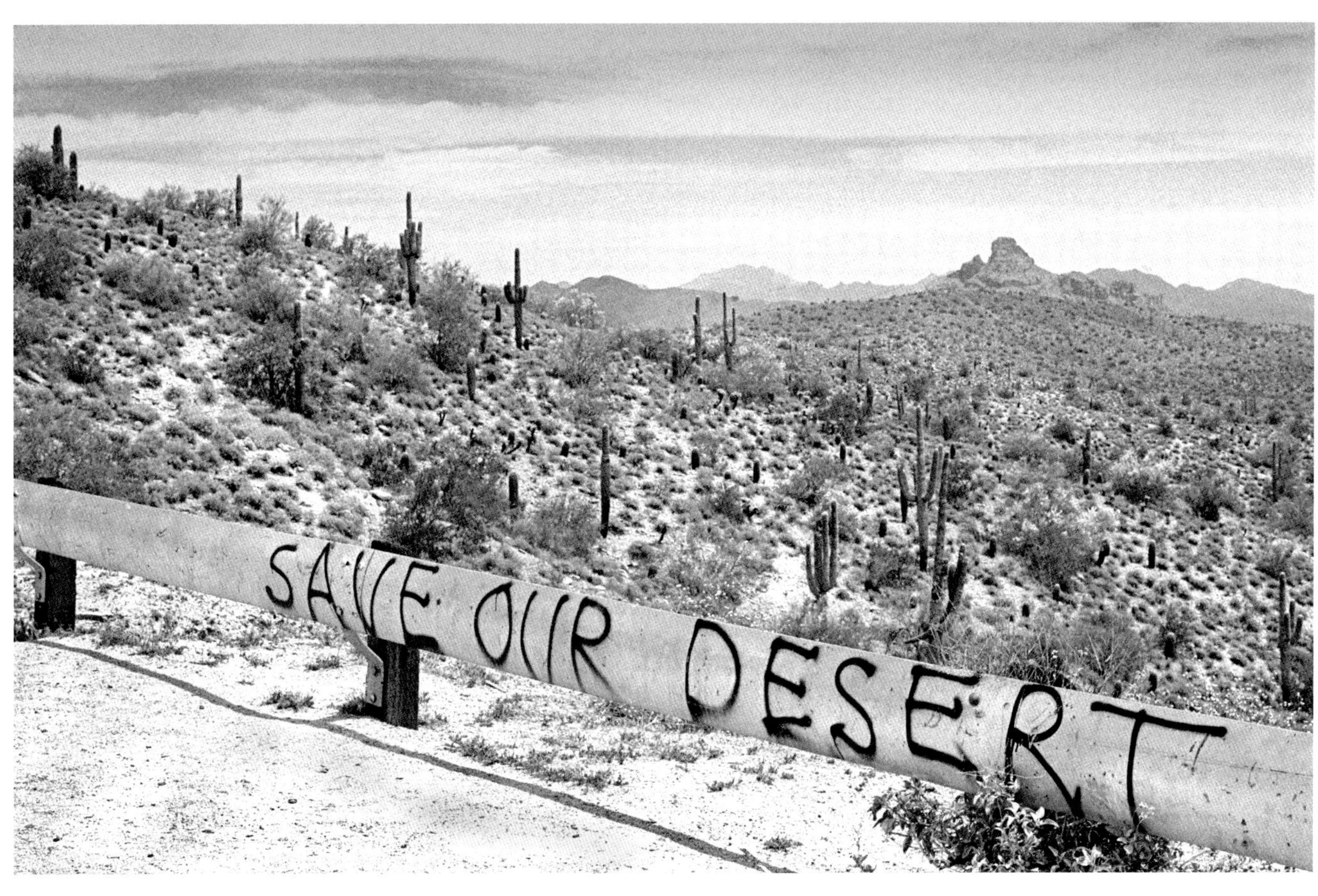

SAVE OUR DESERT

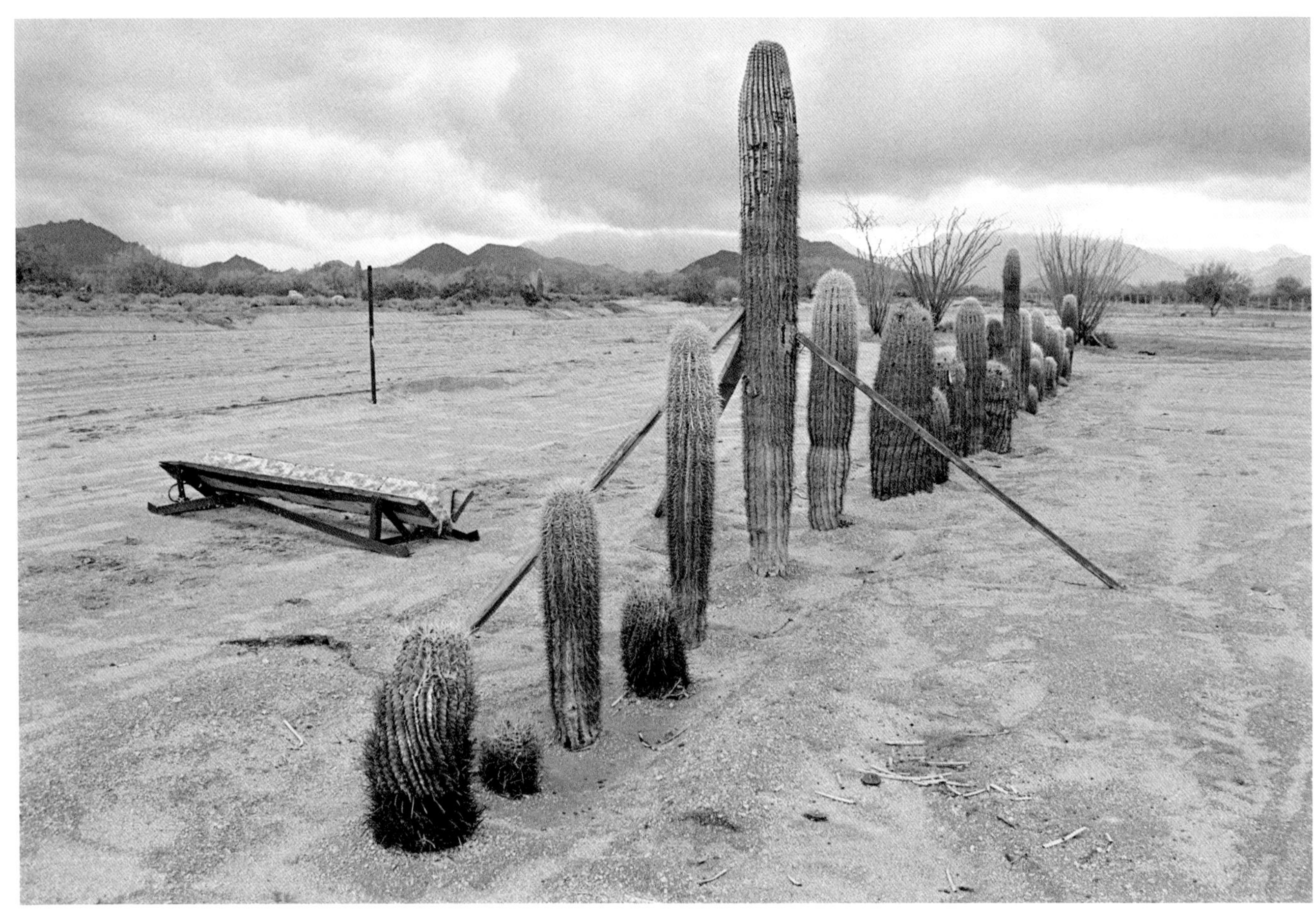

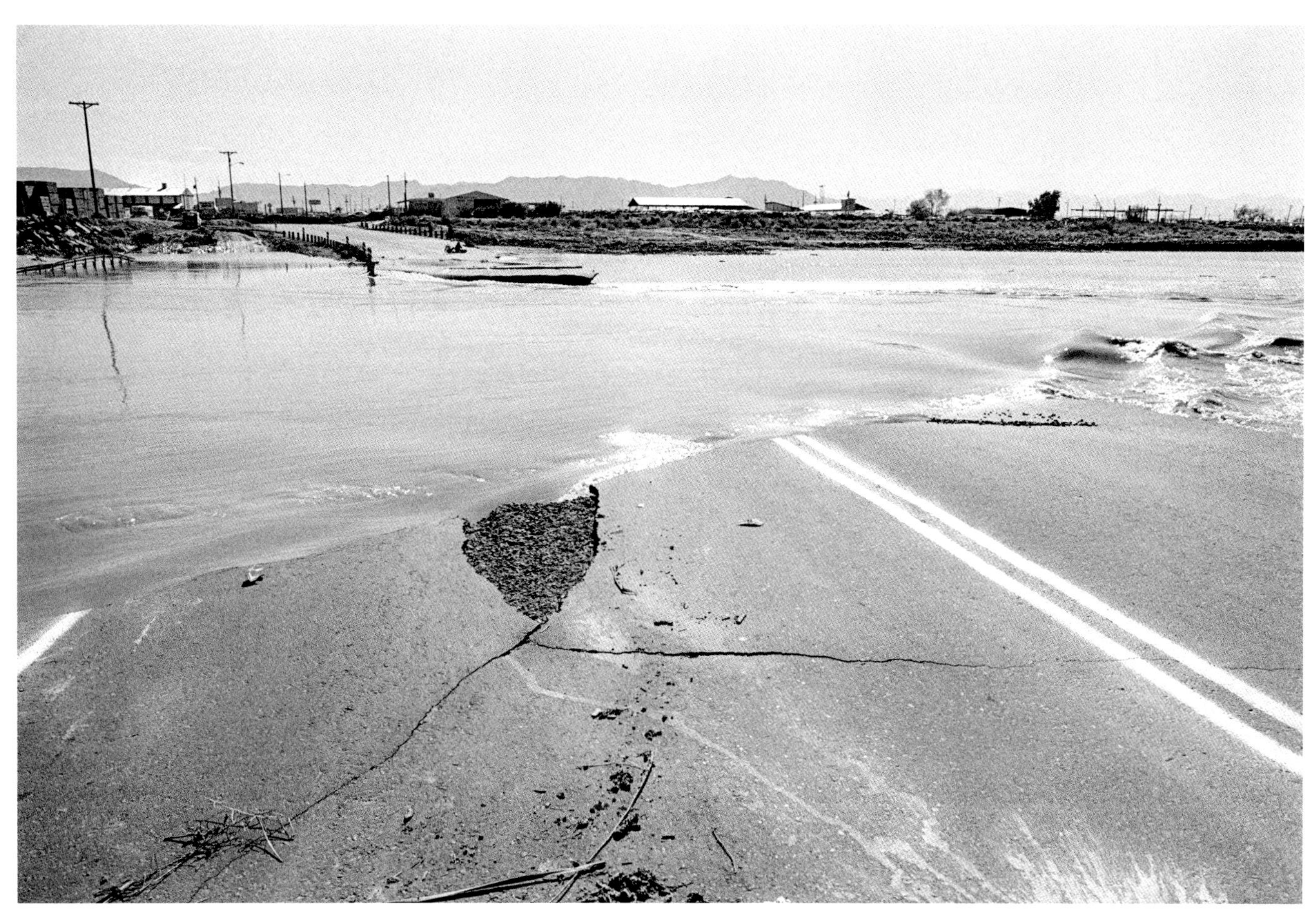

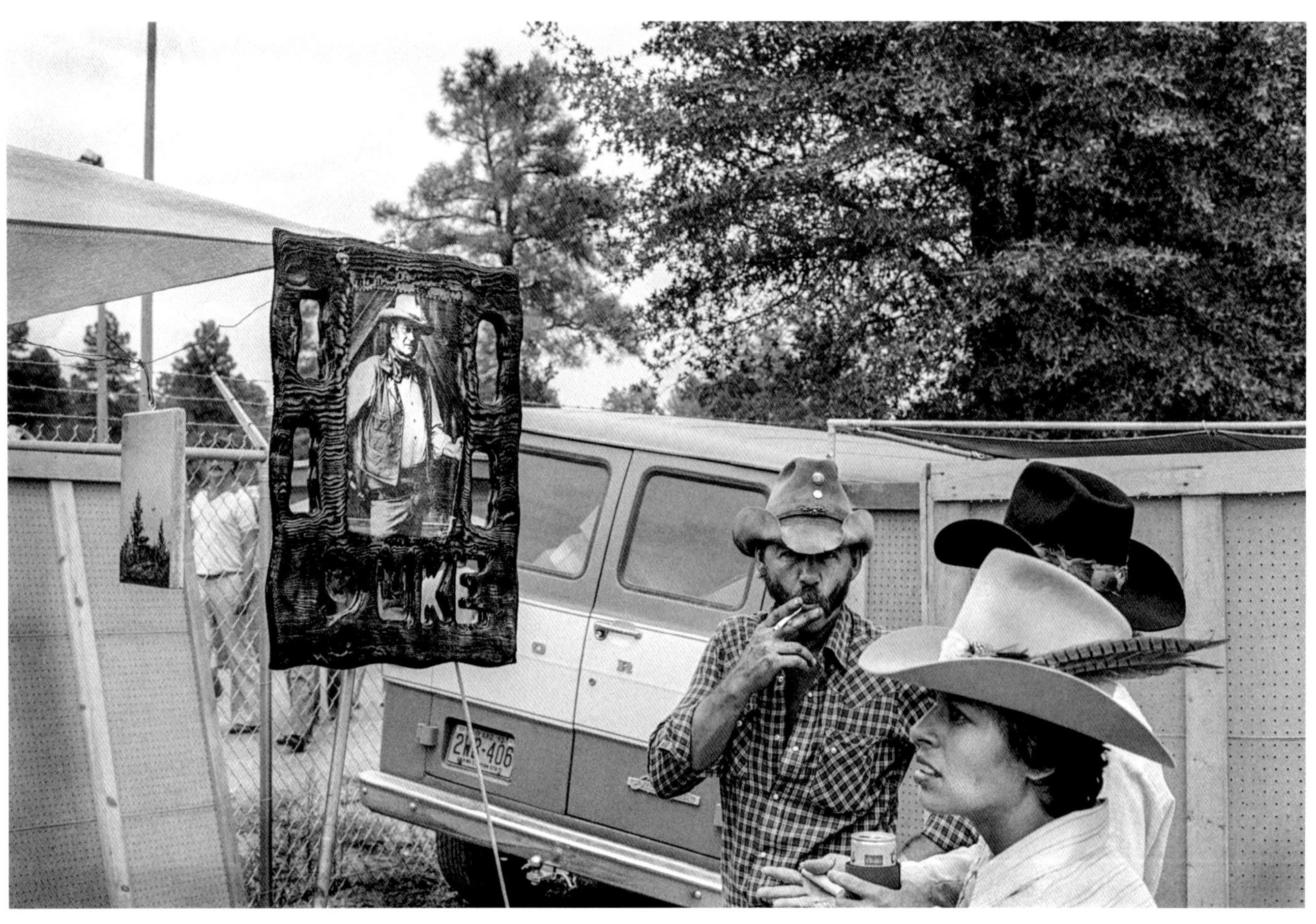
DUKE

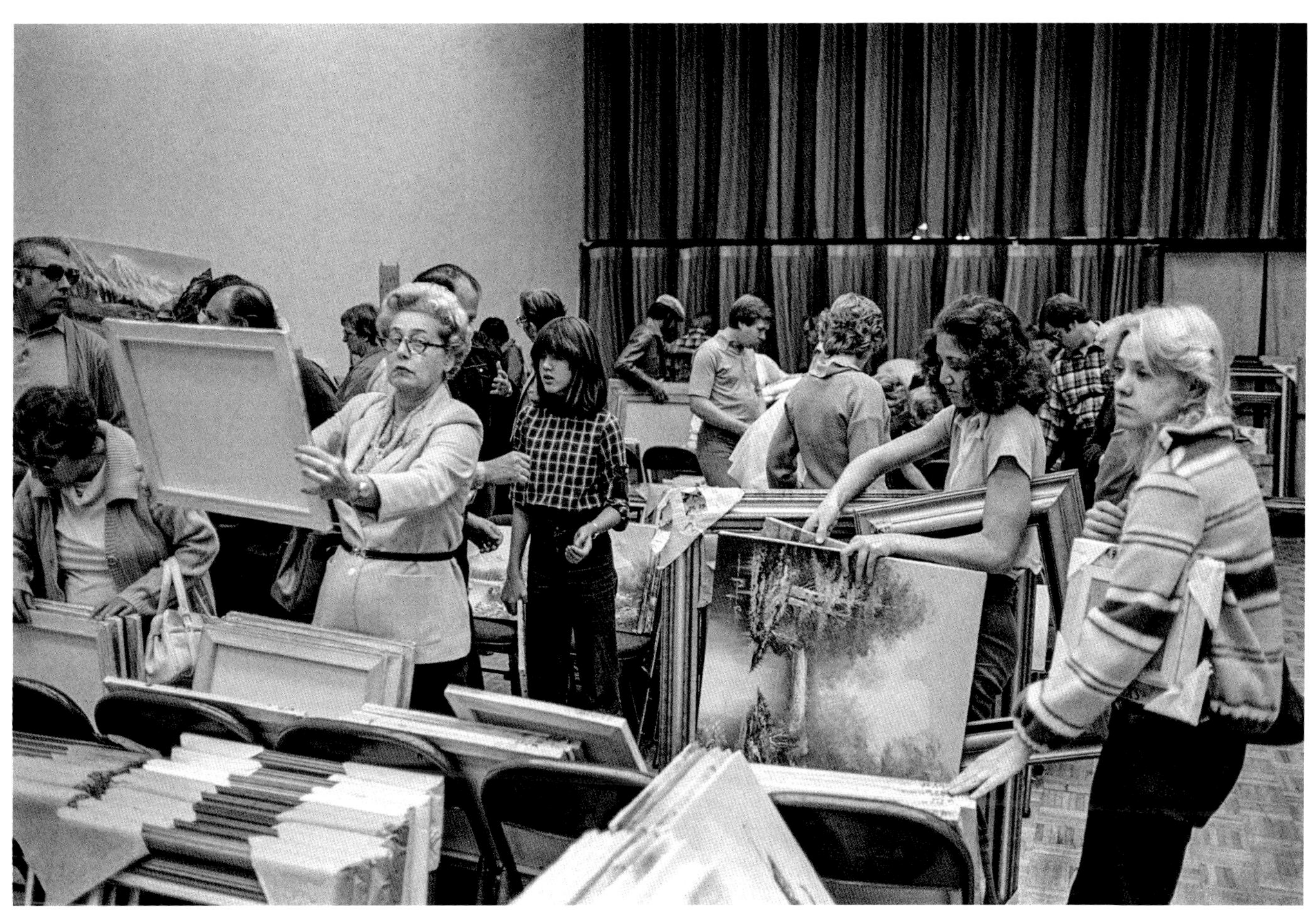

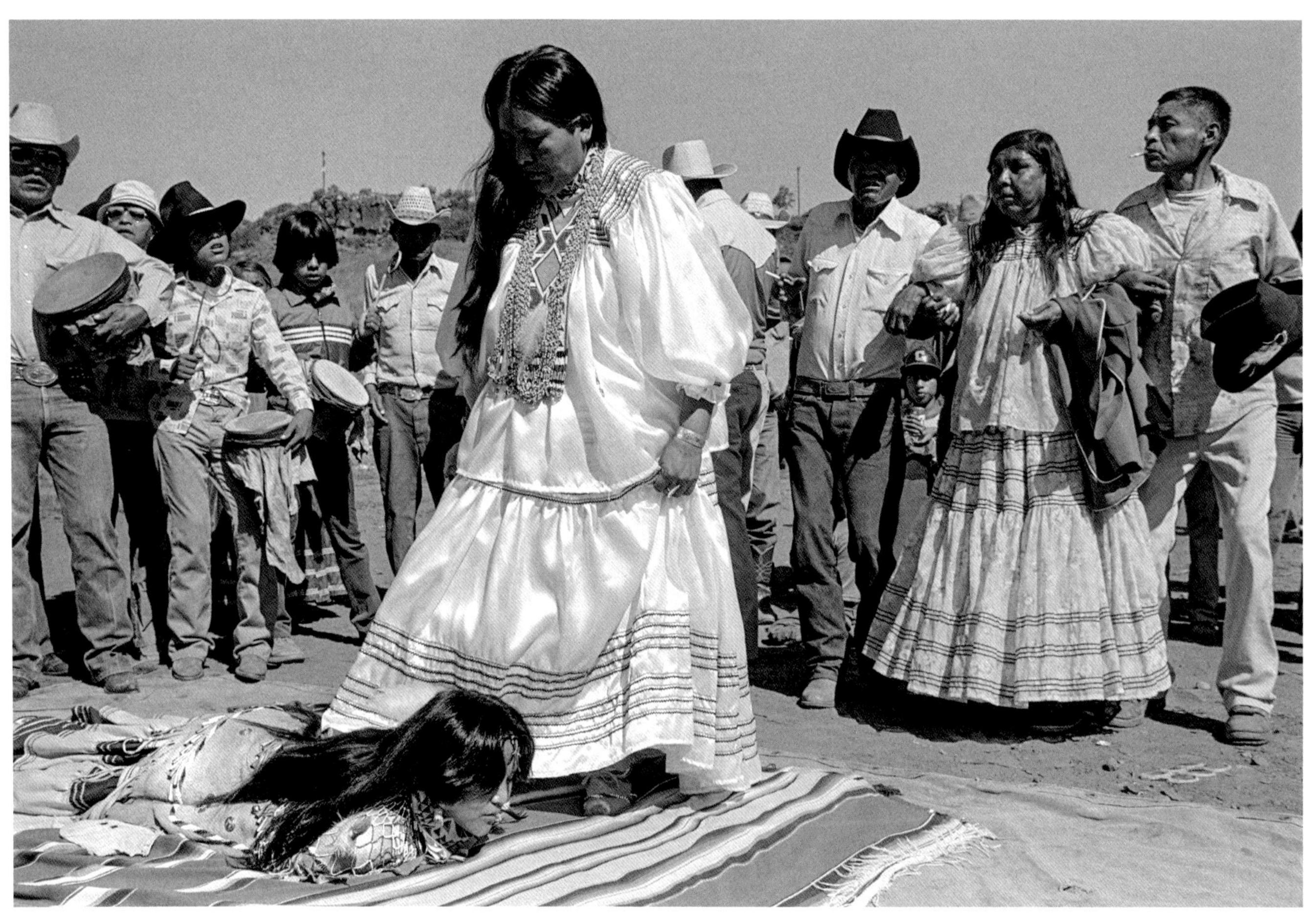

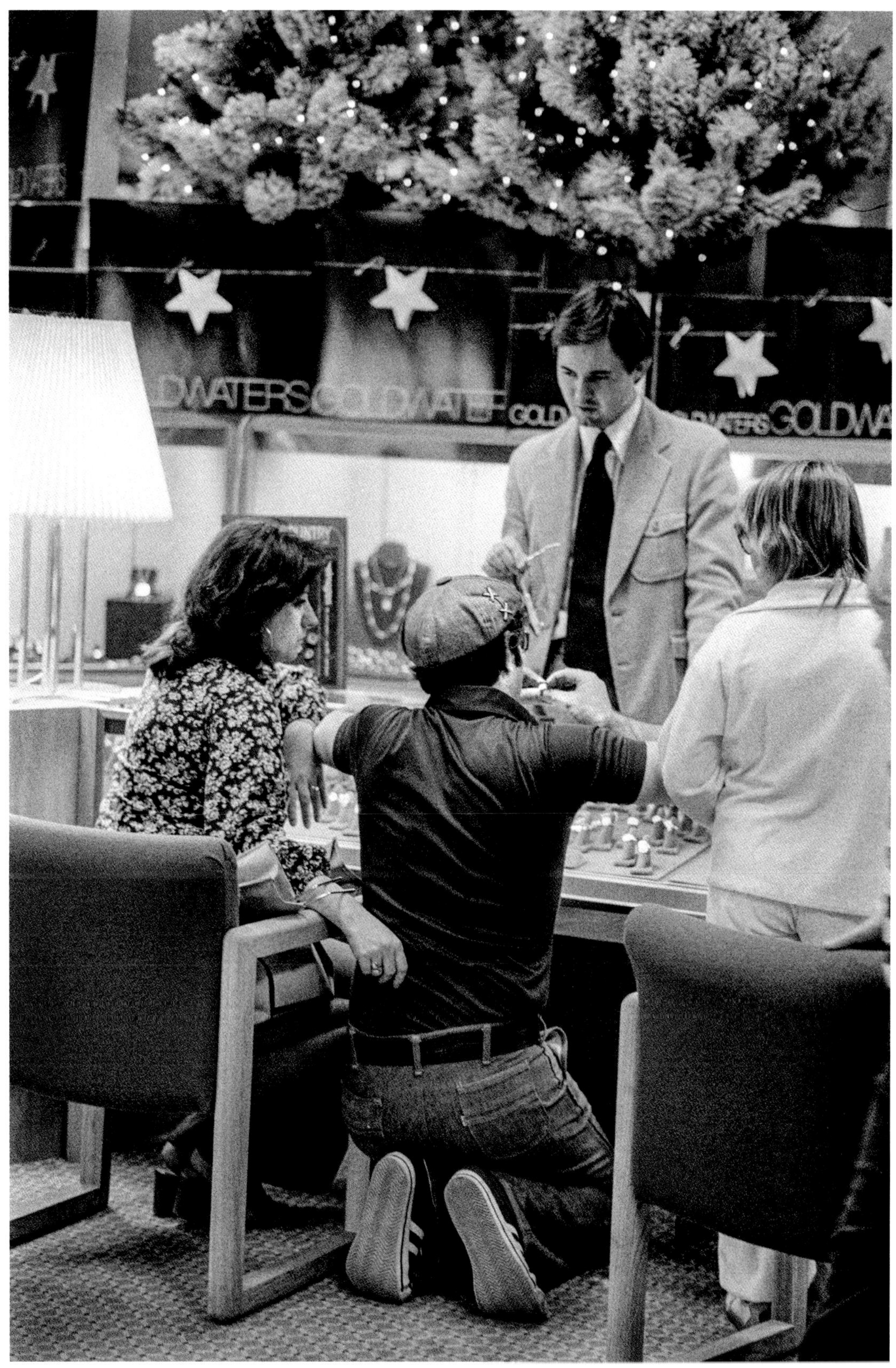

GOLDWATERS
GOLDWA

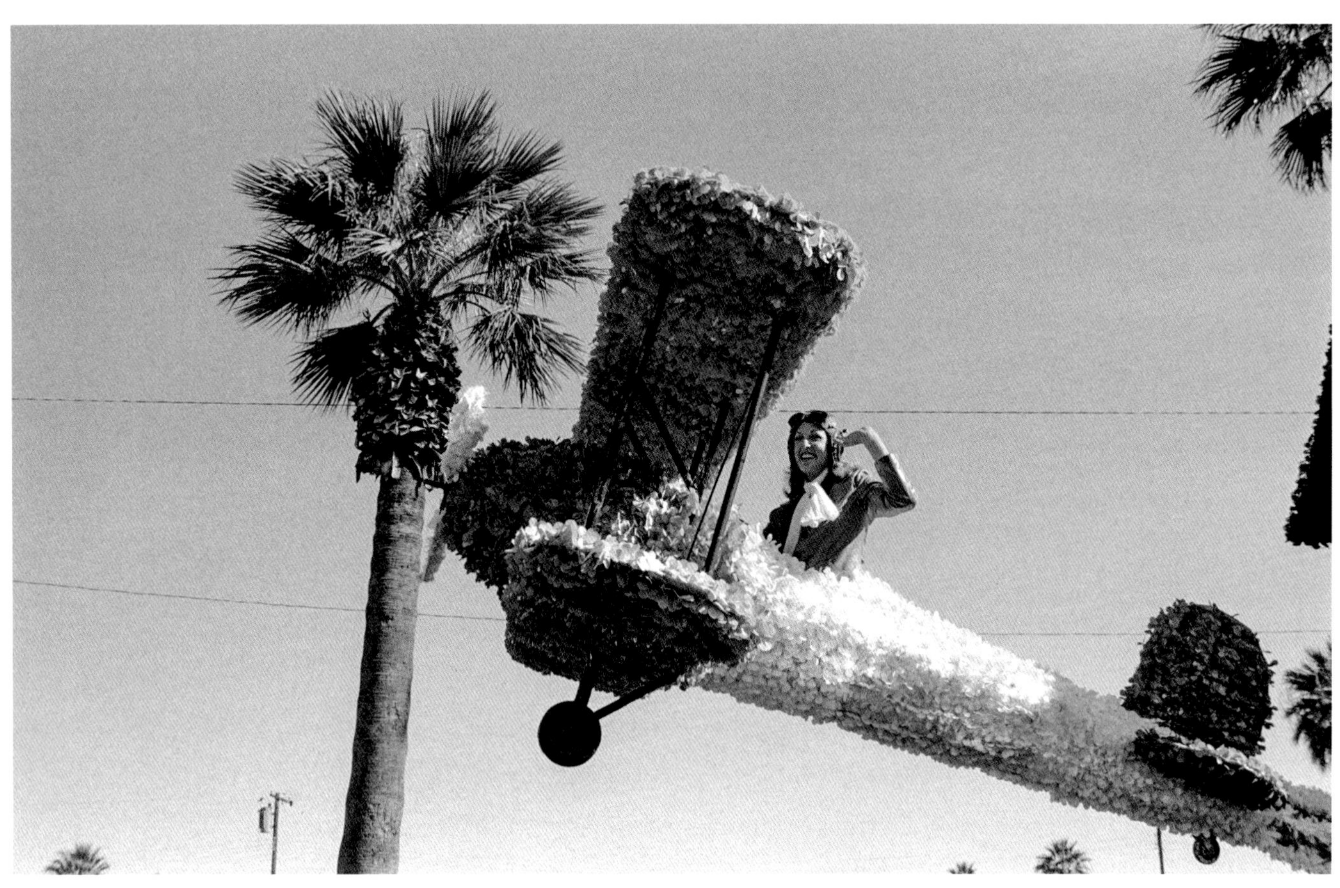

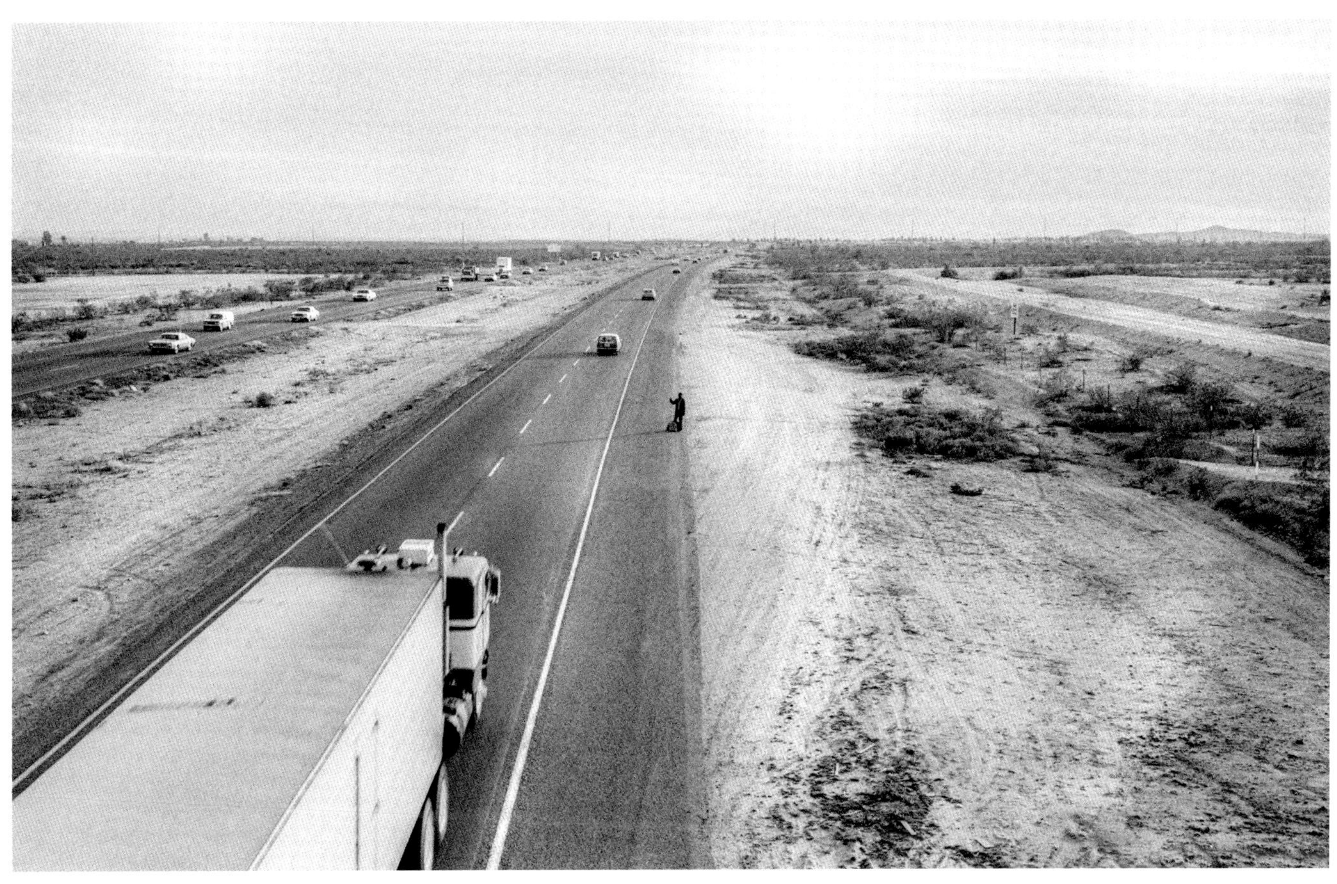

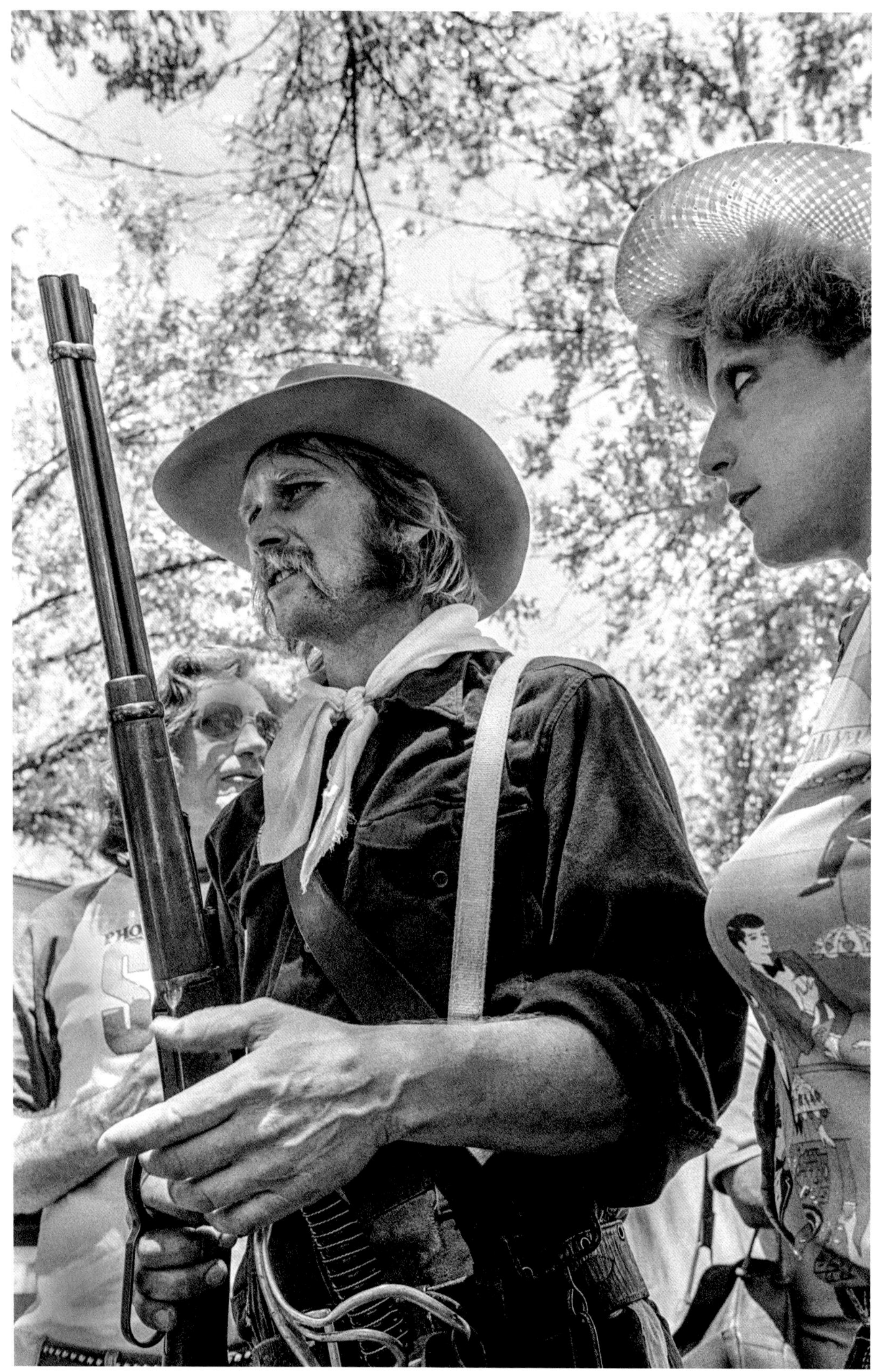

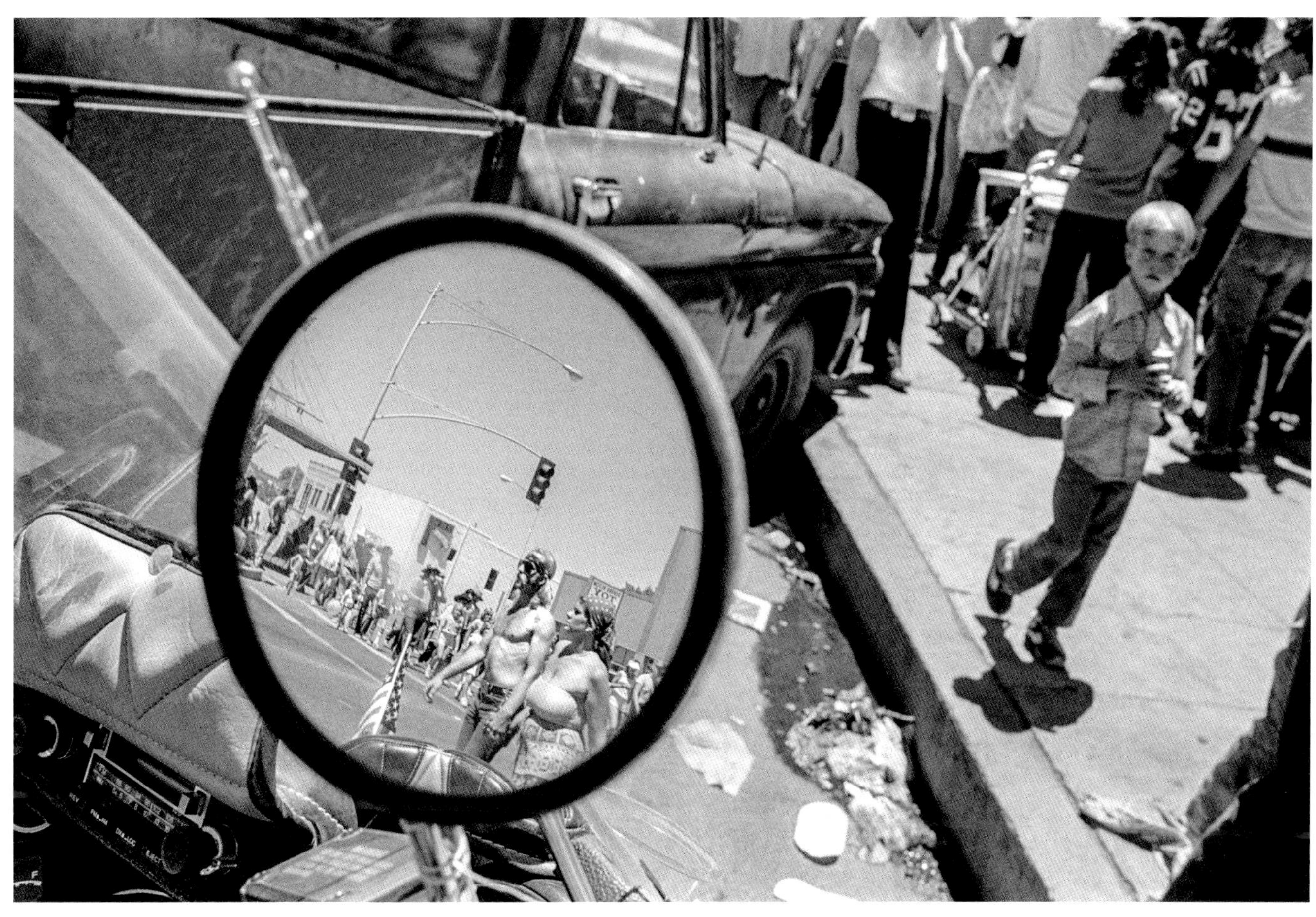

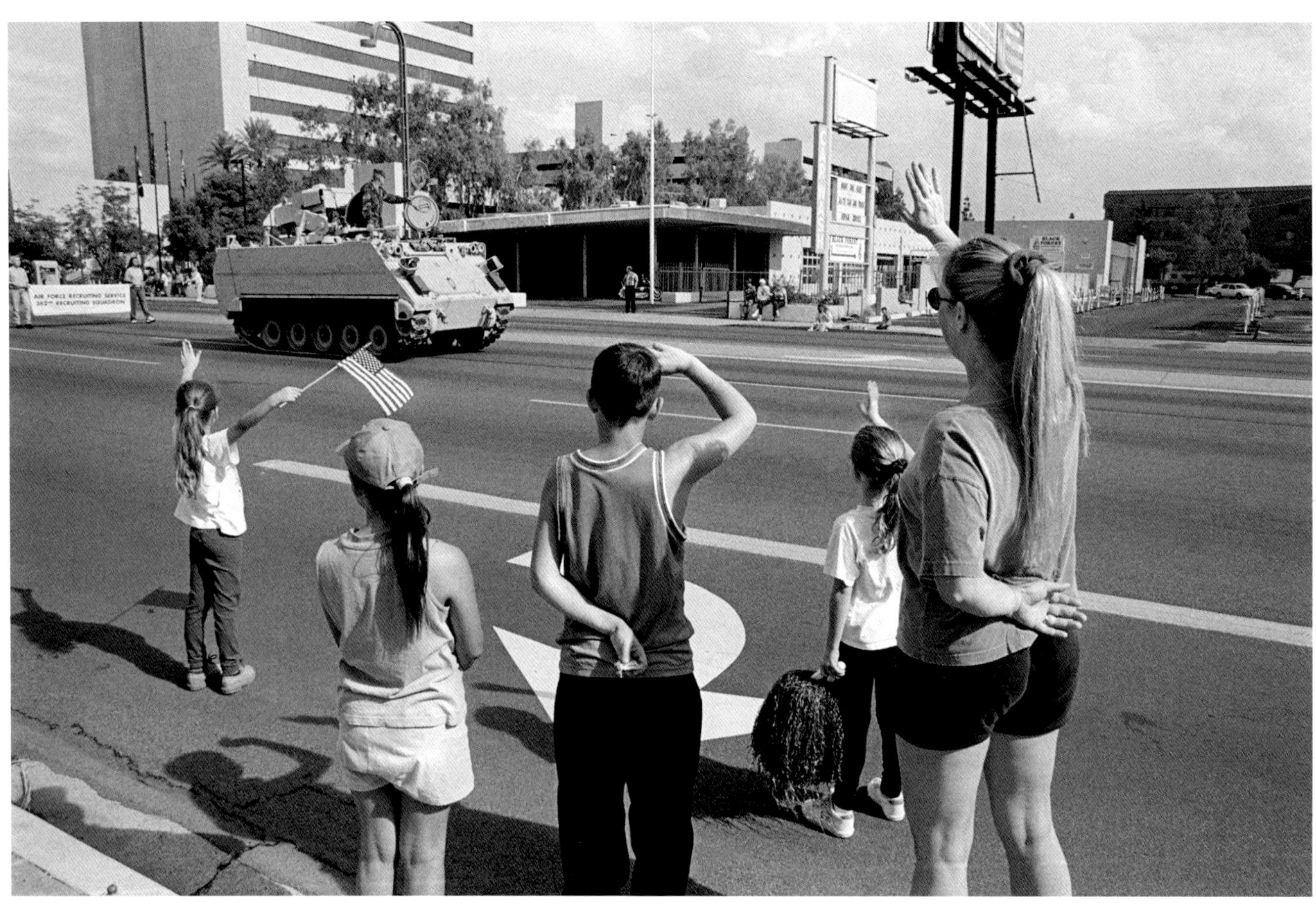

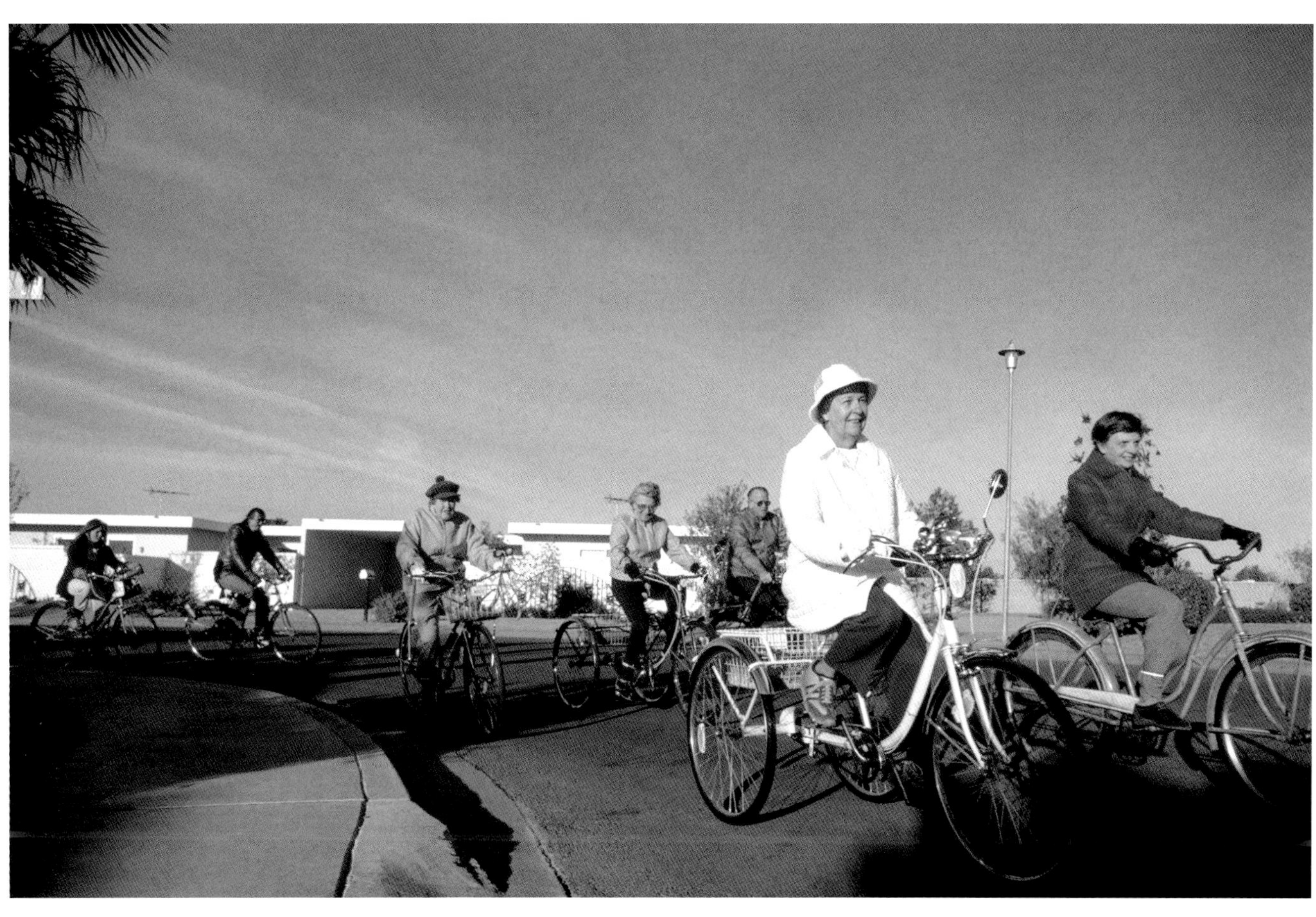

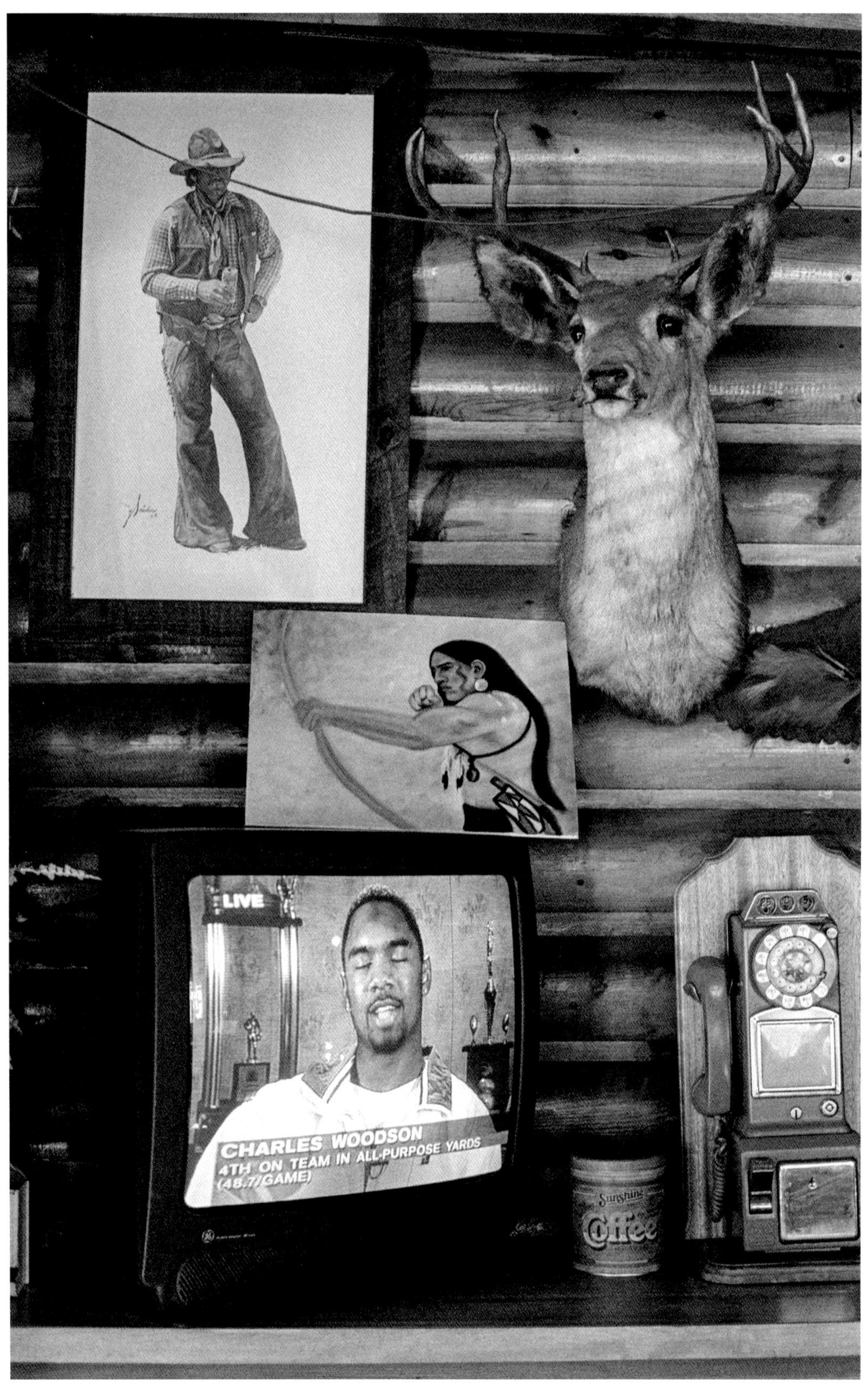
LIVE
CHARLES WOODSON
4TH ON TEAM IN ALL-PURPOSE YARDS
(48.7/GAME)
Sunshine
Coffee

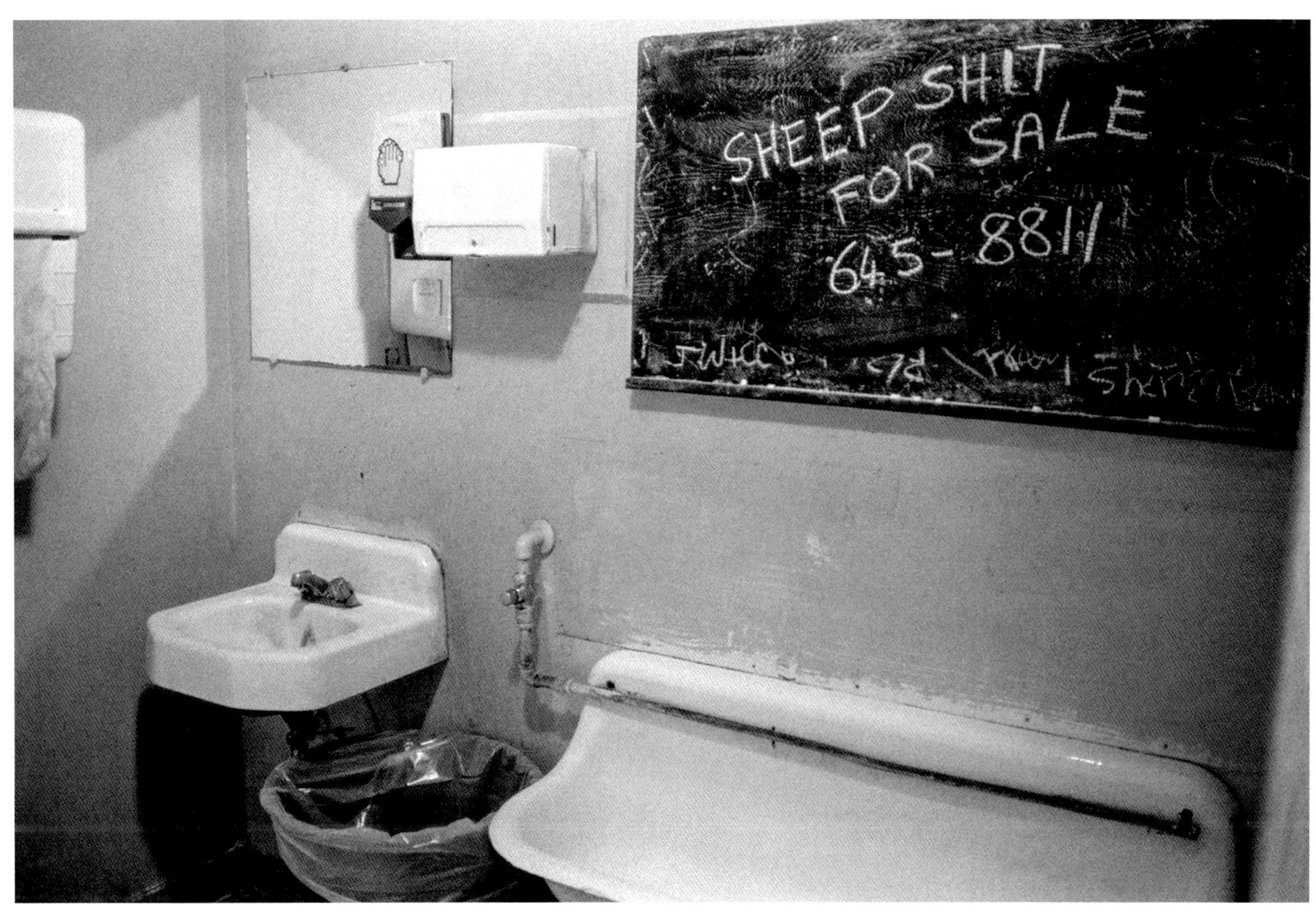

SHEEP SHIT
FOR SALE
645-8811

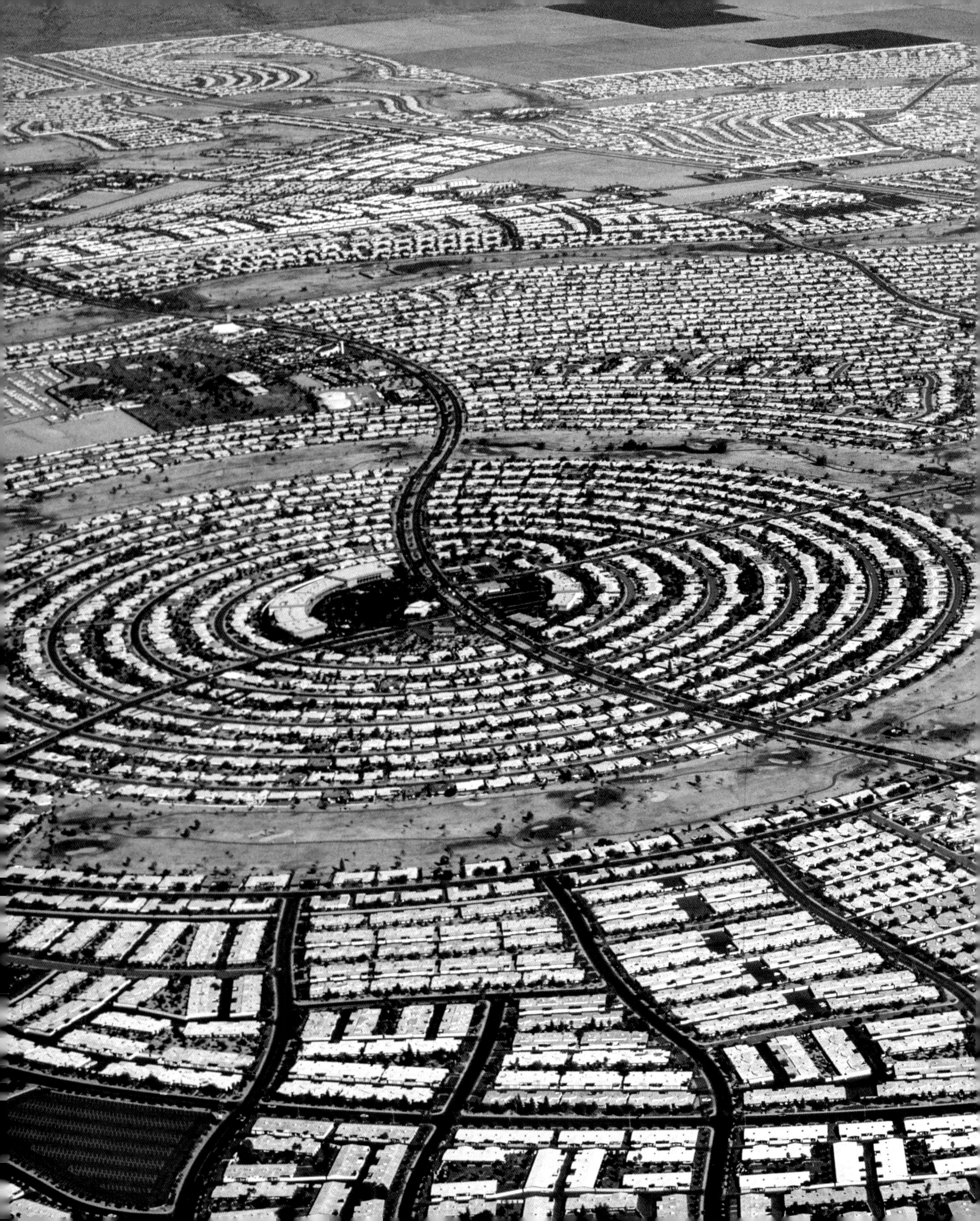

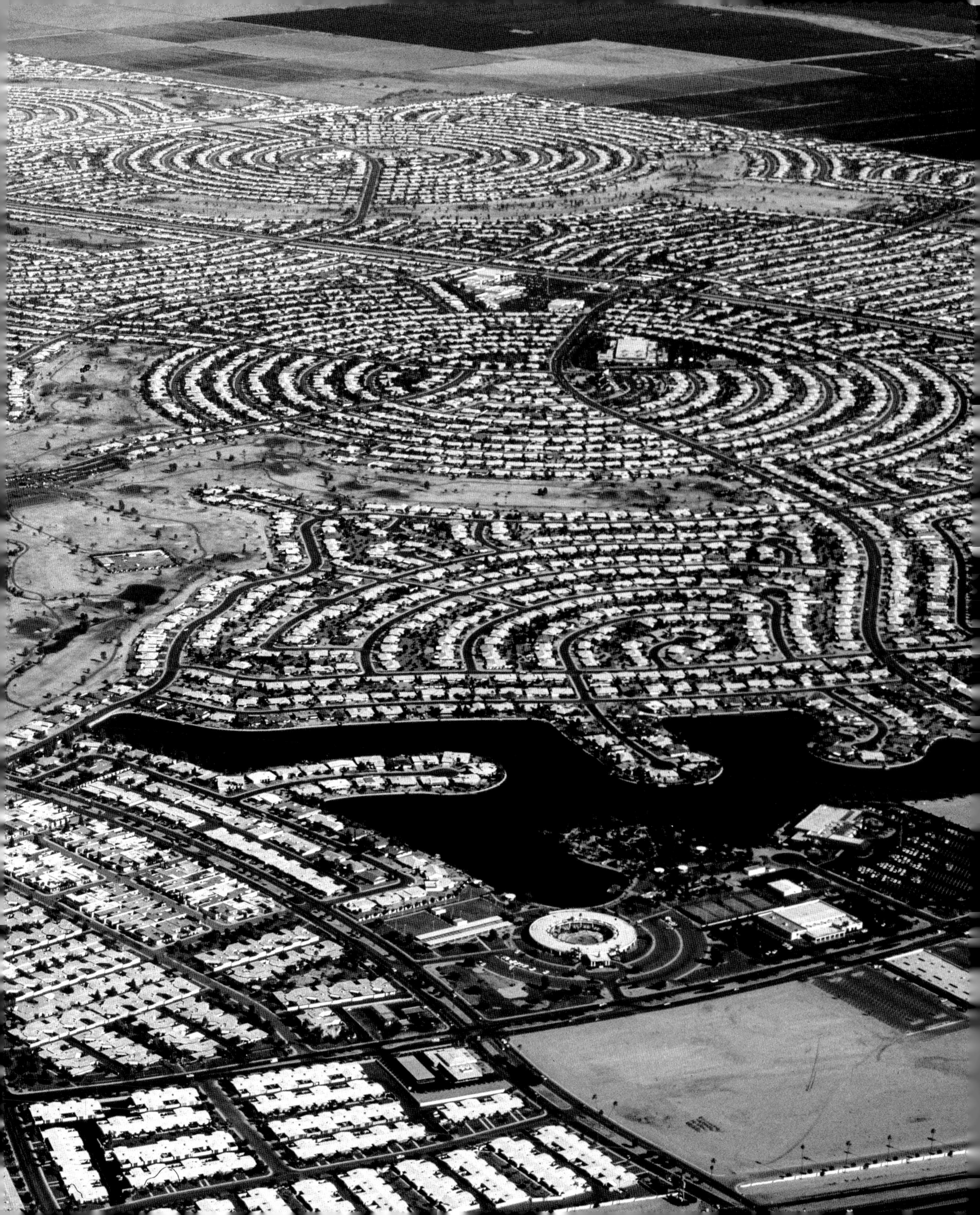

Captions

p.2 Montezuma Castle. 1978.

p.4 The desert between Phoenix and Tucson—the major area of potential housing expansion. 1979.

p.6 David Hurn, National Desert Botanical Garden inside a cactus house. Phoenix, 1980.

p.12-13 On the road from California to Arizona via Joshua Tree Forest. 1979.

p.14 Local motel. Tempe, 1978.

p.15 Photographer's studio. Tempe, 1978.

p.16 Phoenix is one of the fastest growing cities in the USA. Posters abound promoting the fact that it is a great place to live. 1979.

p.17 Building a new part of Phoenix. Despite being mainly desert, Arizona has more boats per head of population than virtually any other state. 1978.

p.18 Jesus on the high street. Inspiration, 1997.

p.19 Storage on the high street. Inspiration, 1997.

p.20 Front garden for ex-champion bowler. Sun City, 1992.

p.21 A householder goes for their afternoon stroll. Sun City, 1979.

p.22 Grandad and grandson fishing. Phoenix Park, 1980.

p.23 Father and daughter class of the roping competition during the rodeo. Mormon Lake, 1980.

p.24 Fraternity Dance, Arizona State University (ASU), Lambda Chi Alpha. Tempe, 1979.

p.25 Marcos de Niza High School Prom at the Hyatt Regency. 1980.

p.26 Conversation in the foyer of the Biltmore Hotel. Phoenix, 1979.

p.27 All Girls' rodeo evening at the Arizona State Fair. Phoenix, 1979.

p.28 Navajo jewellery for sale. Painted Desert, 1980.

p.29 Navajo rugs for sale. Painted Desert, 1980.

p.30 Indian pictographs. Montezuma Well, 1980.

p.31 Roadside art north of Phoenix on the road to Payson. 1994.

p.32 Sun City Ms Senior Pageant. The competition is not only about beauty but poise and talent. Held at the Sundome Center for the Performing Arts. 1997.

p.33 Miss Arizona, Hospitality Inn. Scottsdale, 1980.

p.34 Fountain Hills Parade. America has a long tradition of local parades, they are a way of showing off the local community activities and its commercial base. Fountain Hills has their parade just before Christmas—the Daughters of the American Revolution are always active. 1997.

p.35 Local Bike Club, Fountain Hills Parade. 1979.

p.36 Typical vegetation decoration on the outside of an apartment block. Lack of people due to the intense heat during the daylight hours. Mesa, 1979.

p.37 Industrial estate landscaping. Phoenix, 1978.

p.38-39 The main highway through the Painted Desert seems to have rather surreal road markings. 1980.

p.40 The round-up of the last wild horses in the desert of Arizona. Bullhead City, 1980.

p.41 Winter Range Cowboy Action Shooting. The National Old West Shooting Competition is the meeting place for enthusiasts of the Old West. Authenticity of the uniform, firearms, equipment and knowledge of the period is paramount. Phoenix, 1997.

p.42 Resident of Sun City at one of the wonderful clubs, in this case the Lapidary Jewelry Club. Sun City, 1979.

p.43 When there is entertainment in the outside arenas in Sun City the security is in the hands of the Sun City Posse, a part time volunteer force—no ex police allowed. They wear their Stetson hats and guns but no one can remember when one was last drawn in earnest. 1979.

p.44 Animal cemetery. Twin German Shepherds for burial. Tempe, 1979.

p.45 Shopping Mall. Phoenix, 1980.

p.46 A silicone breasst implant. Phoenix, 1980.

p.47 Preemie baby unit at St Joseph's Hospital. She has a head too large by half for her body. With little to flesh them out, her features are skull-tight and wizened. Her arms and legs are no thicker than her mother's fingers. Her ears have no cartilage. Not long ago she would have been a miscarried fetus, today she is a preemie baby. Although barely 2lb, she is destined to survive to be a normal child. Phoenix, 1980.

p.48 The three Icons: Lady Diana Princess of Wales, Elvis Presley and Marilyn Monroe. Baseline Phoenix, 1997.

p.49 Bookshop. Mesa, 2002.

p.50 Native American doll. 1997.

p.51 Backyard Barbie doll washing line is surreal. Mesa, 1992.

p.52 Republican State convention. Phoenix, 1980.

p.53 Republican State convention. Phoenix, 1980.

p.54 Driving east into the desert. There are frequently inventive signs suggesting wildlife in the area. Phoenix, 1980.

p.55 Tarantula racing by cowboys as a hobby. Apache Land, 1979.

p.56 Demolition Derby, Arizona State Fair. Phoenix, 1979.

p.57 Monster arm-wrestling at the Arizona State Fair. Phoenix, 1979.

p.58 A surreal pair guard a house at Halloween. Tempe, 1979.

p.59 Street scene, Halloween. Tempe, 1979.

p.60 Cheerleaders at Marcos de Niza High School football game. Tempe, 1979.

p.61 Football pre-match warm-up at Marcos de Niza High School. Tempe, 1979.

p.62 Gay Ball held in the Registry Resort in Phoenix. Tempe, 1979.

p.63 Dolly Parton look-alike competition. Phoenix, 1979.

p.64 Lloyd Bottimer aged 102, Veterans Day Parade. A celebration to honour the nation's veterans. Central Phoenix, 1997.

p.65 A winter desert mobile town. The 'Snow Birds'—RVs arrive from as far as Canada. Quartzsite, 1997.

p.66 Shopper's entertainment at Goldwaters, the major department store in Phoenix. 1979.

p.67 The central computer room at ASU. It is a joint facility for all students at the university. 1997.

p.68 Desert photography. Model Trish posing for photographer Kenda North. 1979.

p.69 ASU vs. Utah football game. A high school mass band and drum majors arrive for performance. Tempe, 1979.

p.70 *Penthouse* magazine Redneck shooting target in the Tonto Forest. 1994.

p.71 Cheeks, a Ladies Only club just outside the city limits of Phoenix. Male strippers are the main entertainment of the evening. 1980.

p.72 Prescott Frontier Days cowboy festival was the world's first rodeo and started in 1888. Wild horse riding and spectators dress up as though competitors. 1980.

p.73 Park 'n Swap. Phoenix, 1980.

p.74 The pet parlour. Quartzsite, 1997.

p.75 Annual Mutt Show open to all types of dogs. Phoenix, 1979.

p.76 Road intersection. Yuma, 2002.

p.77 Route 60 east of Phoenix. Electric pylons and Saguaro cactus peculiar to Arizona. 1997.

p.78 Mock-up of the gunfight at O.K. Corral. A great tourist attraction. Tombstone, 1980.

p.79 The studio where Wyatt Earp was photographed, now a tourist attraction. Tombstone is a historic Western city in Cochise County. It was one of the last wide-open frontier boomtowns in the American Old West. 1980.

p.80 Dud's Tavern, old stagecoach stop, 16 miles north of Douglas. 1980.

p.81 Hotel. Douglas, 1980.

p.82 Car window reflector to help keep the inside of a car cooler in the exceptional hot desert sun. 1980.